NAPOLEON'S CLOSET

GENDER AND CULTURE

GENDER AND CULTURE
A SERIES OF COLUMBIA UNIVERSITY PRESS

Nancy K. Miller and Victoria Rosner, Series Editors
Carolyn G. Heilbrun (1926–2003) and
Nancy K. Miller, Founding Editors

The #MeToo Effect: What Happens When We Believe Women, Leigh Gilmore
The Outside Thing: Modernist Lesbian Romance, Hannah Roche
An Empire of Touch: Women's Political Labor and the Fabrication of East Bengal, Poulomi Saha
My Brilliant Friends: Our Lives in Feminism, Nancy K. Miller
Critics, Coteries, and Pre-Raphaelite Celebrity, Wendy Graham
Tainted Witness: Why We Doubt What Women Say About Their Lives, Leigh Gilmore
"How Come Boys Get to Keep Their Noses?": Women and Jewish American Identity in Contemporary Graphic Memoirs, Tahneer Oksman
Extreme Domesticity: A View from the Margins, Susan Fraiman
The Global and the Intimate: Feminism in Our Time, edited by Geraldine Pratt and Victoria Rosner
Nomadic Theory: The Portable Rosi Braidotti, Rosi Braidotti
Unlikely Collaboration: Gertrude Stein, Bernard Faÿ, and the Vichy Dilemma, Barbara Will
Rites of Return: Diaspora Poetics and the Politics of Memory, edited by Marianne Hirsch and Nancy K. Miller
Nomadic Subjects: Embodiment and Sexual Difference in Contemporary Feminist Theory, second ed., Rosi Braidotti

For a complete list of books in this series, see the Columbia University Press website.

NAPOLEON'S CLOSET

The Emperor, the Priest, and the Men Who Invented Modern Fashion

MARGARET WALLER

Columbia University Press
New York

Columbia University Press
Publishers Since 1893
New York Chichester, West Sussex
cup.columbia.edu

Library of Congress Cataloging-in-Publication Data
Names: Waller, Margaret, 1954– author
Title: Napoleon's closet : the emperor, the priest, and the men who invented modern fashion / Margaret Waller.
Description: New York : Columbia University Press, [2026] | Series: Gender and culture | Includes bibliographical references and index.
Identifiers: LCCN 2025055085 (print) | LCCN 2025055086 (ebook) | ISBN 9780231164344 hardback | ISBN 9780231223331 trade paperback | ISBN 9780231224390 pdf | ISBN 9780231565882 ebook
Subjects: LCSH: Napoleon I, Emperor of the French, 1769–1821—Clothing | La Mésangère, Pierre de, 1761–1831—Clothing | Men's clothing—Social aspects—France—History—18th century | Men's clothing—Social aspects—France—History—19th century | Journal des dames et des modes | Fashion—France—Periodicals | Fashion—Religious aspects—Catholic Church | Masculinity—France—History | France—Social life and customs—1789–1815
Classification: LCC GT873 .W35 2026 (print) | LCC GT873 (ebook)
LC record available at https://lccn.loc.gov/2025055085
LC ebook record available at https://lccn.loc.gov/2025055086

Printed and bound by CPI Group (UK) Ltd, Croydon, CR0 4YY

Cover design: Milenda Nan Ok Lee

Cover images: Jacques-Louis David, *The Emperor Napoleon in His Study at the Tuileries* (1812) (National Gallery of Art); Jean-Auguste-Dominique Ingres, *Napoleon I on His Imperial Throne* (1806) (Musée de l'Armée, Paris, Wikimedia Commons); "Doctrinairian," M. l'abbé Thiron, *Album historique des costumes religieux depuis l'établissement du Christianisme jusqu'à nos jours* (Librairie générale, 1869), 167 (HathiTrust).

GPSR Authorized Representative: Easy Access System Europe, Mustamäe tee 50, 10621 Tallinn, Estonia, gpsr.requests@easproject.com

For my parents,
Without whom nothing

For Carol J. Ockman,
With whom everything

For Nancy K. Miller,
From the beginning

Men say they don't particularly care how they dress, and that it is little matter. I am bound to reply that I don't believe them and don't think that you do either.

—Oscar Wilde, on tour in Canada, 1882

CONTENTS

ACKNOWLEDGMENTS

MY DEDICATION to Carol—"with whom, everything"—seemed perfect very early on. What I did not know was that she is a brilliant editor. Her suggestions were essential to helping me finish *Napoleon's Closet*. For this and so much more, I thank her deeply.

My parents, Joan S. Waller and Robert A. Waller, have always loved me for who I am and supported what I do. There is no greater gift.

I am enormously grateful to three consummate professionals who believed in me and this project: Jennifer Crewe, associate provost and director of Columbia University Press; Victoria Rosner, series editor; and Nancy K. Miller, series editor and peerless model of feminist scholarship and mentoring.

I am indebted to historian Annemarie Kleinert's *Le "Journal des Dames et des Modes," ou la Conquête de l'Europe féminine* (1797–1839), the definitive study of La Mésangère and his famous fashion journal, as my scores of references to that book and her articles attest. Without her remarkable research, I could not have written this book.

The anonymous readers of this manuscript were generous with their praise and extremely helpful suggestions, and I am very grateful. For the pleasures of intellectual exchange and invaluable moral support, I thank Ellis Avery, Faith Beasley, Janet Beizer, Danielle Bobker, Ken Bowman, Ewa Lajer Burcharth, Ross Chambers, Pamela Cheek, Elizabeth Constable, Barbara Cooper, Denise Davidson, David Divita, Jill Dolan, Jennifer Freidlander, Pascale Froment, Rhonda K. Garelick, Michal Ginsburg, Dena Goodman, Darcy Grimaldo Grigsby, Katherine Hagedorn, Melanie Hawthorne, Carla Hesse, Lynn Hunt, Alice Jardine, Jennifer Jones, Gary Kates, Annemarie Kleinert, Sally Leabhart, Julie Liss, Sharon Marcus, Morag Martin, Mary McLeod, Virginie Pouzet-Duzer, Bryant T. Ragan, Jr., Erin Runions, Lawrence R. Schehr, Prageeta Sharma, Pamela Smith, Peter Starr, Valerie Steele, and Caroline Weber.

For all of the above plus enlightening and generous comments on drafts special thanks to Katharine A. Jensen, Peter L. Allen, Darcy Buerkle, Cecelia Cancellaro, Lisa Cody, Margaret Cohen, Elizabeth Colwill, Stephanie Ellis, Sima Godfrey, Chris Guzaitas, Jonathan Hall, Anne Higonnet, Paul Kafka, Rachel Kranz, Sheryl T. Kroen, Brian Martin, Jann Matlock, Cristanne Miller, David Powell, Arden Reed, Lewis Seifert, Hilary Schor, Naomi Schor, Susan Siegfried, Peter Starr, Helena Wall, and Kirsten Wasson.

To my colleagues in Nineteenth-Century French Studies, thank you for the excellent questions and advice and the joyful camaraderie.

For invitations to speak about *Napoleon's Closet* and related work, I thank Francine Goldenhar (Maison Française, NYU), Timothy Hampton (UC Berkeley), Katharine Jensen (Louisiana State University), Corinne Scheiner (Colorado College), Lawrence Shehr (University of Illinois—Champaign-Urbana), Peter Starr (University of Southern California), Andrea Tarnowski (Dartmouth College), Alexandra Wettlaufer (UT-Austin), Elizabeth Weed (Pembroke Center, Brown University), and Steven Winspur (UW-Madison). I am grateful to Susan Siegfried, Jann Matlock, and Denise Davidson for organizing "More than Fashion," a conference on *Journal des Dames et des Modes* at the University of Michigan. There, I had the privilege of meeting Annemarie Kleinert.

I would like to acknowledge Jacob Aplaca's advice, expertise in queer theory, and superb research on my behalf. My Pomona College research assistants—Jenna Archer, Anne Graybeal, Sarah Kerbeshian, Jessica Nakell Burroughs, Elise Nussbaum, Ngocthy Phan, Katie Stuart, Emma Vorenberg, Madeleine Wolf, and Jessica Whitlock—were vital to this project. For remarkably insightful and provocative readings of the manuscript, which pushed my arguments further, my immense gratitude to Rachel Tils. For years of illuminating observations, terrific feedback, great conversations, and expert editing, I owe a huge debt to Noah Pinkham. I could not have finished this manuscript without Hannah Lippard. Over the years and up to the very end, Hannah did so much, so well, and on so many fronts, which made this book far better.

Tamara K. Hanson and Carol Michelson grounded me when things got tough. They know how much they helped.

Information Technology Services at Pomona saved my life and this book many, many times.

Pomona College generously funded my research assistants as well as travel to conferences, Paris libraries, and other French sites. It also afforded me the opportunity to be part of the Faculty Success Program of the National Council for Faculty Diversity and Development, which I recommend highly. An early National Endowment for the Humanities summer grant helped launch my research. A fellowship from the Humanities Center at the University of California at Davis was an interdisciplinary tonic. An American Council of Learned Societies Grant gave me an entire year of uninterrupted thinking and writing as did a fellowship from the National Endowment for the Humanities. Two Borchard Foundation Scholar-in-Residency grants gave me the chance to spend months reading, writing, and revising in a château in France, surrounded by a moat.

An early version of parts of chapters 4 and 5 appeared in "The Emperor's New Clothes: Display, Cover-up and Exposure in Modern Masculinity," in *Entre hommes: French and Francophone Masculinities in Culture and Theory*, ed. Todd Reeser and Lewis Seifert (University of Delaware Press, 2008), 115–42. Some of the ideas in chapter 4 were first fleshed out in "Trouble in Argus City: Peacocking, Invisibility, and Masculinity," *Romanic Review* 107, no. 1–4 (2017): 25–46 and in "Disembodiment as a Masquerade: Fashion Journalists and Other 'Realist' Observers in Directory Paris," *Esprit Créateur* 37, no. 1 (Spring 1997): 44–54.

PREFACE

FATHER MCCRORY'S BELLY BUTTON

Clothes make the man.

—English proverb

The habit does not make the priest.

—French proverb

"WHAT IF I told you I don't have a belly button?" Father McCrory asked. Some of my classmates shifted in their seats. Silence.

His follow-up: "I'm a priest. Does that mean you should believe everything I say?"

It was 1967, and I was thirteen. Usually, I was quick to raise my hand, but this sounded like a trick question. Besides, I was more interested in what he was wearing.

With his classic good looks, Father McCrory resembled the photo of my father in high school or a Ken doll with black hair. That day, he was in his everyday priestly uniform, the modern one that had recently been approved by the Catholic Church: black shoes, black trousers, and a black shirt with a white tab inserted into its stand-up collar. I much preferred his old-fashioned priestly cassock, as in the picture taken of my First Communion class when I was seven. Fitted at the shoulders and chest, the long black robe featured small, cloth-covered black buttons marching in a tight row all the way up to the small square of pure white at his collar.

In those days, for most men in Urbana, Illinois, a black suit was for funerals or the occasional fancy party. Otherwise, they wore coats, jackets, shirts, sweaters, and shorts or trousers, usually dull in color, often ill-fitting, sometimes mismatched. I preferred Father McCrory's look: a sleek, tailored pillar of black cloth with arms, his only accessories a watch and a silver crucifix on a long chain. Despite the "dress," I found it very manly. The uniform also seemed to be a guarantee: He would always be a priest and stand for something greater than himself.

But Father McCrory kept interrupting my thoughts. He would not let the belly button question rest. Again, no one answered.

Impatient, I raised my hand and blurted out, "It's impossible! You *do* have a belly button. Everybody does."

Father McCrory ended up having to explain the point to us: Catholic doctrine stipulates that the Church is infallible, but priests are not. They are men. Father McCrory was too, but he was not louche.

I never bought the Church infallibility part of the lesson, but I did take Father McCrory's second point: A simple uniform, such as a cassock, can give the person who wears it and those who see him the impression that the habit *makes* him a priest, a man completely faithful to his vows. Similarly, military uniforms are supposed to convey the wearer's unwavering allegiance to the army. Yet that very same attire can also cloak all kinds of deviations from "normal," let alone the ideal. The same goes for gender differences. Humans are a complex lot.

■ ■ ■

Father McCrory's question about his belly button is far from the only reason I wrote this book, but it does encapsulate many of its throughlines: gender, clothing, power, and secrets.

I examine together for the first time the surprisingly parallel lives of two very different men from the lower provincial nobility who rose to the top: the emperor Napoleon and a defrocked priest turned celebrated fashion editor, Pierre Joseph Antoine La Mésangère. Although one took the military route and the other the clerical one, social norms of masculinity and the all-male or predominantly male institutions (army and Church) made them men, and the ways Napoleon and La Mésangère shaped the culture of clothing are the spine of this unconventional history of modern masculinity and male attire.

■ ■ ■

At this book's inception, I saw both Napoleon and La Mésangère as wholly "other." It did not take long for me to understand that this project chose me. A Catholic background, modest provincial origins, and an itch to be part of a larger world are just a few of the things we share. There is also the discomfiture of a social outsider whose appearance might, at any moment, reveal our imposture.

As a skinny, flat-chested White girl with straight black hair, my dream was to grow up to be Jacqueline Bouvier Kennedy. Despite our shared flaws, she had married a handsome man and become First Lady. However, with her French heritage, old East Coast money, and Parisian clothes, she was everything I was not. Studying French in junior high school was supposed to be my economy-class ticket away from cornfields and polyester dresses toward a cosmopolitan life. Surely, studying abroad in Paris would teach me how to tie scarves like French women do. During that first year in France, I feared that my American, Midwestern, and middle-class origins would give me away, and I was right, they often did and often still do.

I have never been able to pretend, as some, most often conventional men do, that I don't care about clothing. Following my mother's example, I'm a femme-y woman. I also use clothing and closeting as consciously feminine forms of play, display, and cover-up. Nevertheless, as a feminist, I am fully aware of the ways social norms of femininity continue to constrain the minds, time, values, and bodies of those who present as female with fraught consequences for our sense of self-worth, gender relations, income inequality, and the health of the planet.

Despite my gender-normative wardrobe, I have long felt like an outsider as well as an insider. During a marriage of almost three decades, my now ex-husband and my closest friends knew I also wanted and needed something else. Decades after Father McCrory left the priesthood to marry a woman, I met the woman who is the love of my life and left my marriage. Does that mean I came out of the closet? Yes. However, thanks to more than half a century of LGBTQ+ activism, I had a somewhat different impression: I *was* the closet. Rather than come out of it, I was simply deciding to leave the door open to share what had always been there: my queerness and plenty of light.[1] Today, when there are even more harrowing pressures to conform to heteronormative expectations, an insider-outsider perspective is even more urgent.[2] It enables us to see that many so-called timeless and universal "truths" are neither simple nor natural; they are historical, contingent, and often paradoxical. Often, what is usually seen as "straight" turns out to be queer—strange, odd, peculiar—and sometimes at odds with the very sexual and gender norms it is presumed to represent. My purpose in examining how my two subjects became very different kinds of men is to investigate the intricate, evolving cross-pollination of "normal" and "queer."

My first book, *The Male Malady: Fictions of Impotence in the French Romantic Novel*, examines *le mal du siècle* as a postrevolutionary crisis of masculinity in fiction from 1802 to 1834. In *Napoleon's Closet*, I focus on men and power but begin in the 1760s when my two protagonists were very young through the French Revolution of 1789 and their decades of success and final downfalls in the 1820s and 1830s. My investigations of the lives, wardrobes, and legacies of Bonaparte and La Mésangère owe a great deal to historians of this period in France—especially their work on schooling, the military, the clergy, the press, and, of course, the Revolution. My objects of study here are visual and textual, not literary: memoirs, fashion magazines, diocesan regulations about priests' dress, caricatures, fashion engravings, and celebrated paintings and portraits from the time. My analyses of these materials and the lives of my protagonists, informed by intersectional feminist and queer theory illuminate a decisive turning point more than two centuries ago when men of the elite chose, or were expected to conform to, new, heteronormative expectations that we now recognize as modern.

Why care about a time long gone? Despite the sudden breakdown in gendered dress codes during the political resistance and sexual revolution of the 1960s and after, many aspects of what it meant to be a "modern" man in the West two hundred years ago still pertain today. The protagonists in *Napoleon's Closet* are the precursors of the "men in black" of the last half of the nineteenth century, the "men in suits" of the twentieth, and the "normcore" millennials and Trump clones in the twenty-first. The cost of not following these expectations is high. As these examples demonstrate, conventional male attire enshrines certain cultural and usually heteronormative ideas about masculinity as if they were natural, which is far from the case. But as a result of these beliefs, anyone perceived as male who dares wear a dress risks social ostracism, violence, even death. Today, the backlash against individual rights, freedoms, and self-expression, not to mention political resistance, can feel like a juggernaut of oppression. But as this study shows, people can and do find ways to act up and fight back.

NAPOLEON'S CLOSET

INTRODUCTION

THE EMPEROR, THE PRIEST, AND THE CLOSET

NAPOLEON BONAPARTE (1769–1821), the Corsican upstart who crowned himself First Emperor of the French, tends to dominate whatever book he is in. *Napoleon's Closet* is the first to have him share equal time with one of his subjects and a highly unlikely one at that. Pierre Joseph Antoine Le Boux La Mésangère (1761–1831) was a boys' schoolteacher and ordained priest defrocked by the French Revolution of 1789. He reinvented himself as the editor of the most influential fashion magazine in Europe. After La Mésangère's death, an anonymous article in his *Journal des Dames et des Modes* [Ladies' Fashion Journal] extolled him as the Napoleon of the petticoat set, the "emperor" of fashion.[1]

Although a very odd pair, the world-famous hero/emperor/dictator and the mild-mannered-priest-turned-famous-fashion-editor are perfect for this genealogy of heteronormative male dress. My approach pushes back against the work of most biographers and historians who have written, always separately, about La Mésangère or Napoleon and have mostly taken their masculinity for granted. Masculinity is my central question. As Simone de Beauvoir famously wrote: "One is not born, but rather becomes, a woman."[2] No one is born a man either—let alone an emperor or a priest.

THE EMPEROR AND THE PRIEST

In many respects, Napoleon and La Mésangère could not be more dissimilar. The emperor married twice, had mistresses, and was a father. He may also have had sexual relations with other men, although such arguments are contested and speculative.[3] As for La Mésangère, following the priesthood was a common alternative to heteronormative life. Even after the Revolution annulled his vows of poverty and obedience, he never married and lived alone above his magazine's office. The two men wholly identified with their profession and appeared to live to work. However, the emperor's lavish splendor at his imperial court was the exact opposite of the fashion editor's look: a cornflower blue suit that had been out of fashion for decades and an old-style powdered wig.[4]

Given the quantum differences in Napoleon's and La Mésangère's social status, they never met. However, Napoleon was quite aware of the former priest's famous "women's" magazine, which his wife Josephine would have read, as did male and female members of his court and subscribers in France, England, and the continent. Given Napoleon's strict censorship of the press, it would have been hard for anyone, especially an editor like La Mésangère, *not* to know who Napoleon was and what he wanted.

Rather than focus solely on the man who became a legend as if he had always been exceptional and the priest/fashion editor as if he had always been anomalous, I also show how Napoleone di Buonaparte and Pierre La Mésangère were typical of their male peers. Studying their lives side by side reveals unexpected commonalities between them that make them *typical* of their peers as well. Both were sons of minor noblemen born in the far provinces, just eight years apart, La Mésangère in western France (1761) and Napoleon in Corsica (1769). Their class status meant that they were expected to wear *culottes* (knee breeches), which marked their superiority to girls of all classes as well as to peasants and other low-class boys in loose trousers made of cheap, rough cloth. Although our protagonists ranked far below the ultra-elite in Paris and the nobles at the court of Versailles, they enjoyed opportunities and privileges, most notably schooling, that were unimaginable for the rest of the male population. Against all odds, both provincial young men not only survived the French Revolution they also thrived because of it. For a decade, the political and cultural turmoil it caused laid waste to the past, but for Bonaparte, La Mésangère, and other lucky men and women, it also opened new opportunities. In light of Napoleon's and La Mésangère's somewhat humble beginnings, their success was meteoric albeit on vastly different scales.

How did these infants of the lower nobility born in the 1760s become schoolboys and then a cadet and a seminarian who turned out to become influential men—one a priest then a businessman, and the other an army officer then an emperor?

What roles did male-dominated institutions (schools, the army, the Church, the state, and the fashion press) along with breeches, uniforms, cassocks, civilian fashions, and court attire play in this process for them and for thousands of their social peers? How did they navigate not only the maelstrom of the French Revolution but also a long-term and profound evolution of ideas, values, and practices that dramatically altered upper-class men's clothing and ideas about gender roles?

THE GREAT MASCULINE RENUNCIATION

The sixty years between 1761 and 1831 in France, which is to say the lifetimes of Bonaparte and La Mésangère, happened to coincide with what is now usually called the Great Masculine Renunciation of fashion. It is still deeply embedded in Western culture, which makes it a trend that is now over three hundred years old. The term was invented and popularized beginning in 1930 with the publication of *The Psychology of Clothes* by John Carl Flügel (1884–1955), an experimental psychologist who was instrumental in disseminating the ideas of Sigmund Freud in Britain (1856–1939).

The Great Masculine Renunciation began not in France but in seventeenth- and eighteenth-century England, where the traditionally sumptuous and ornamented dress of upper-class males was increasingly seen as a sign of unseemly profligacy and effeminacy.[5] Saying no to past male flamboyance was supposed to be an indication of men's natural superiority to those who indulged in vain and immoral ostentation: women, first and foremost, but also any nonnormative man who didn't follow this rule. This included effete men and "exotic" savages, but also the French.[6]

Meanwhile, on the other side of the English Channel, Frenchmen of the higher classes mocked what they considered the typically parochial English notion that men of the upper echelons had to wear plain, austere clothing to divorce themselves from women's frivolity, or civilization would collapse. In the view of the French elite, the fine art of dressing *à la française*, which very much included men, constituted the quintessence of refinement the world over. However, by the 1760s when Bonaparte and La Mésangère were born, sober English norms for men had spread to other countries in Europe and colonized ones in the Americas. The popular writings of the French *philosophe* Jean-Jacques Rousseau (1712–1778), urging Man to turn away from civilization and back to "nature," gave the luster of high French seriousness to the "English" idea.[7] At the same time, the growing popularity of gender complementarity—the notion that one sex was naturally what the other was *not*—heightened men's reluctance to indulge in "feminine" preoccupation with their attire. It purported to value both genders "equally" but for the most part, simply reinforced gender binaries that were hierarchical, not egalitarian. In any case, the Great Masculine Renunciation was a relatively new gender paradigm in France. Eventually, caring about one's appearance would no longer be the defining project of both men and women of the upper classes. For men, it was to be a mere sideline; *la mode* was for the "weaker" sex—or at least that was the idea, as this study will show.

For the first decades of their lives, Bonaparte and La Mésangère were not immediately affected by this redefinition of upper-class manliness or femininity. In fact, I will argue, they were like generations of young men before them who were privileged enough to receive an education and become officers in the army or ordained in the Church. They were trained to believe an army officer uniform or a clerical cassock was a sign of their superiority to others. Even if these professions were more an obligation than a choice and although each may have required a personal renunciation of luxury, they were supposed to be an honor and a mark of male belonging. Technically, uniforms, whether military or clerical, are not fashions—although,

FIGURE 0.1 Scandal! The Old Regime meets the Directory. French etching, late 1790s. By Alexis Chataigier. "Ah! Quelle antiquité!!" "Oh! Quelle folie que la nouveauté!. . . . ." "Ah! How antiquated!!!" "Oh! Novelty is such folly!. . . . ."

Source: Gallica

as I show, they go in and out of style. But this project is not only a fashion history; it is also a cultural history of male attire. "Uniforming" certain classes of men was central to it.

For our protagonists and all of France, the most dramatic consequence and instantiation of the Great Masculine Renunciation of fashion came about when their lives and those of millions of others were sundered by the French Revolution from 1789–1799. Dress had always been political, but now it registered as such at a feverish pitch. Revolutionaries of various stripes legislated what could and could not be worn and by whom and favored what I call the Great *Political* Renunciation of fashion. The caricatural engraving (see figure 0.1) from 1797 shows a couple from the Old Regime on the right and a pair of counterrevolutionary royalists on the left who are scandalized by the other's costumes. "Ah! How antiquated!!!" The other pair replies: "Novelty is such folly!"

The clothing and accessories of the Old Regime pair represent the monarchical status quo before the French Revolution; they embody the twin privileges of high birth and wealth as a matter of showy extravagance. The silhouettes of their clothing (her tightly corseted and wide-skirted dress) as well as their wigs (hers piled high and ornamented; his a tall toupee and a "club of hair behind, . . . garnished with a large black satin wig-bag trimmed with bows") make their gender unmistakable.[8] All the other aspects of their aristocratic garb, however, are ones we now associate almost exclusively with women and femininity: makeup, beauty marks, silks and satins, lace, bows, flounces, passementerie, and intricate and colorful embroidery.

By comparison, what the counterrevolutionary royalists on the left wear, about a decade after the Revolution, is so simple, it looks streamlined. The woman's garb is decidedly less fussy than what her Old Regime female counterpart is wearing, but fashion historians rarely monumentalize this period as the Great Feminine Renunciation of fashion. Even today, what gets more attention is her male companion. He is depicted as an *Incroyable* [Incredible One]—a mocking term for male royalists who protested the Revolution and its values with their outlandish dress, stripped of the usual elite luxury and frills. This is what makes him seem more modern than his Old Regime counterpart.

Today, the details of his attire make him look almost contemporary: large hoop earrings, an extravagant ascot, and gathered ribbons at the bottom hem of his *culotte*. Although this male type would not apparently dream of wearing the frippery of the Old Regime, it was not, as we might say, because he was afraid of his feminine side. This depiction of the figure makes the whole look come off as confidently swashbuckling. The fact that his walking stick was a cudgel is key to this effect. *Incroyables* used to threaten or even beat up their "enemies"—presumably republicans dressed to meet the new rules of the Great Political and Male Renunciation of fashion.[9]

■ ■ ■

The "Great Masculine Renunciation" has been evoked so often by fashion historians that it has come to seem a truth universally acknowledged. But in the past thirty years, Flügel's claims, quite rightly, have been reexamined. Most importantly, a few recent critics argue, as I do, that many previous commentators have not understood the sexual, racial, and class politics of upper-class men's more sober look. In effect, the Great Masculine Renunciation shored up the supposedly inherent moral superiority of the White male elite to women in general and to men who were not "civilized" or "manly" enough to adopt more circumspect and heteronormative attire, comportment, and behavior.[10]

Tracking the Great Masculine Renunciation through the lives and wardrobes of our two "emperors" reveals this phenomenon to be far more varied and nuanced than the capitalized words "Great," "Masculine," and "Renunciation" imply. Nevertheless, I continue to use the term Flügel coined because of the powerful insights of its psychoanalytic roots.[11] Rather than a single act or feeling, *renunciation*, in psychoanalytic terms, describes what happens when human instincts including narcissism and exhibitionism, are deemed socially unacceptable. Instead of simply disappearing, they may take other psychic forms: denial, projection, displacement, and sublimation. My aim in insisting on the complexities of this process is to deepen and widen its meaning by giving due attention to other related psychological patterns and behaviors—chief among them homophobia and misogyny.[12] While these are themselves labile psychological states, fear of homosexuality and "hatred of, aversion to, or prejudice against women" often erupt in harsh, hateful, and sometimes violent moral condemnation, which is to say a "renunciation" in the everyday meaning of the word as well. I insist on homophobia and misogyny because they often get lost in comments on Flügel but are, to my mind and in this analysis essential to understanding the multivalent gender and sexual politics of the Great Masculine Renunciation.

I take another approach that does even more, I believe, to queer the Great Masculine Renunciation. *Closeting* usually refers to safe spaces, literal and psychological, that serve people who are exceptions to gender and sexual norms. But I find the expression also aptly describes what normative conventions do by definition: Through the force of repetition, reinforcement, and disincentives, they make what is cultural seem natural. It is, we might say, an everyday form of closeting. Similarly, instead of focusing only on the damage that men's renunciation of fashion can have on them and others, I also look at its compensations. For the six decades under discussion here, the period from 1761 to 1831, schools, the army, the Church, the Bourbon monarchy, the French Revolution, the Directory, the Consulate, Napoleon's empire, the Restoration, and the July Monarchy imposed restrictions on individual liberties, creativity, and self-expression as forms of resistance. But the fact that this attire was required offered a partial refuge from psychosocial demands. For Napoleon Bonaparte and Pierre La Mésangère who were not to the manor born and others like them, this cover-up had other advantages too. Requiring boys and men of the upper echelons to wear school uniforms, clergymen's cassocks, military attire, and court dress made them look like each other as if they all measured up equally to gender, sexual, regional, class, professional, and other expectations. Wearing regulation attire helped conceal their disadvantages vis-à-vis their social superiors, which partially assuaged psychological anxieties about fitting in. In addition, uniforms helped such boys and men "pass" as what they were supposed to be, although sometimes only for observers who didn't know enough to spot the masquerade.

CHURCH RULES

Most books about fashion and male clothing during the three decades before and after the French Revolution of 1789 do not have much to say about priests. It is as if once they were ordained and in cassocks, they were no longer men, and neither they nor anyone else cared about their appearance.[13] This is false on many counts as this study will demonstrate. The assumption that a single social identity trumps all others also runs contrary to the syncretic approach I have taken: to see the boy in the emperor, the man in the priest, the seminarian in the fashion editor.

Priests and the Church are central players in the story of masculinity in France, as they were in other Catholic countries during this period. First, they were, quite simply, ubiquitous. Second, for the small percent of boys who received any schooling, their teachers were almost always clergymen. This made men of the cloth often boys' first important male authority figures outside their family and the local church—men with whom to identify or disidentify, or some of both.[14]

Folding the Church into my argument provides an important perspective on renunciation. Although priestly attire is usually understood in our day as an obligatory spiritual renunciation of fashion, vanity, and materialism, the history of the early Church suggests the opposite. In the early centuries, priests were under no obligation to renounce worldly goods. Nor were they required to refrain from wearing certain articles of clothing. In fact, there were no regulations per se—only general principles. A man of God was to wear modest, which was to say less revealing, less luxurious, and less brightly colored versions of the robes worn by the upper classes. In the beginning, the colors considered appropriate for priests were not black or even brown, as is common today, but rather subdued shades of colors such as red, violet, green, and blue.[15]

Beginning in the fifteenth century, however, quite a few rank-and-file priests of means began to dress up their relatively plain, usually dark robes with the ribbons, lace, and bows that were the height of style for their secular peers. Some even replaced traditional priestly robes with a *justaucorps* (a knee-length fitted coat and knee-length breeches), a favorite of men in the upper classes.[16] Instead of jumping at the chance to discipline wayward clergymen, it took over a century for the Church hierarchy to begin to discipline the liberties that were being taken. Finally, goaded by the Protestant Reformation's denunciation of "degenerate" priests in the sixteenth century, the councils of Catholic bishops began to write regulations to prevent freedom of dress. Still, there was resistance, and further revisions of the rules had to be made. Having put an entire bureaucratic process in place to monitor clerical attire, the Catholic bishops were eventually able to quash ostentatious accessories and other kinds of sartorial display. I call this period from the sixteenth to the eighteenth century the Great *Religious* Renunciation.

Thus, in 1784, when La Mésangère, newly ordained at age twenty-three, was vested in the ankle-length cassock and white collar of the Fathers of Christian Doctrine, the battles to make the modest, dark cassock the distinctive and only priestly uniform were long over. Novitiates and priests generally accepted the top-down imposition of those dark, simple robes in part perhaps because they were by then allowed to wear silk or cotton stockings and, most luxurious and costly of all, a powdered wig, which had long been prohibited. In these ways, the new clerical attire was an institutional forerunner of the more diffuse and "voluntary" Great Masculine Renunciation, a mindset that had been rising in popularity in France around the same time that priests had finally shouldered their forced religious renunciation.

While Church officials forbade lavish attire, *la mode*, and other vanities for low-level priests, the ecclesiastical "one percent" (with the exception of the pope) faced no such restrictions. At ceremonial occasions, bishops, archbishops, and cardinals were permitted, but also obliged, to wear their centuries-old venerable status symbols: luxurious fabrics, bright colors, highly ornamented vestments, stunning jewels, and other such appurtenances. These included the dazzling and costly silver miters the bishops carried and the bright scarlet robe, cape, and skull cap of the cardinals. The one person whose wardrobe, even during the most ceremonious occasions, had to be understated was the pope. He was required to practice his own version of renunciation by wearing pure white robes albeit in elegant and rich fabrics. Frills, sumptuousness, and flamboyance were expected, admired, and even required. Although anticlerical tracts took these as signs of corruption, feminization, or suspect sexual proclivities, for the faithful, it was a fact of life. The Church continues to maintain this distinctly bifurcated hierarchy today.

THE CLOSET

My title, *Napoleon's Closet*, is willfully anachronistic. The French word for *closet* (*un placard*) did not appear in the official dictionary of the Académie Française until 1832/1833, the very end of the period studied here.[17] Moreover, in that dictionary entry, *placard* refers to a cupboard—not a small room for storing clothes and other personal items. In Bonaparte and La Mésangère's lifetime, there were many ways to store clothes, but *un placard* was not one of them. The well-to-do had servants who would hang them in stand-alone *armoires* or *garde-robes* (wardrobes) or fold them in dressers with compartmentalized drawers called *commodes*, *buffets*, or *cabinets*.[18] The lower classes had to content themselves with old-fashioned chests, trunks, or simply pegs on the wall. Nor did *un placard* imply hiding nonnormative sexuality as it does now.

A different term from the period does convey the contemporary meanings of the words *closet* and *placard*. The very wealthy had furnished rooms called *cabinets de toilette* for socializing with intimates and getting dressed, and, sometimes, hiding secrets; in that sense, they had "closets."[19] Such a room plays a pivotal role in Beaumarchais's wildly successful play *The Marriage of Figaro* (1784). In act 2, Chérubin, a preadolescent boy, lets himself be dressed up as a girl by the countess with whom he is besotted. The idea is to trick the count, a jealous husband and notorious womanizer, into seducing "her," thereby exposing his nefarious ways. When the count barges in on the scene, Chérubin, panicked, darts into the *cabinet de toilette* adjoining the countess's bedchamber, locking the door. The count storms out to get something to break down the door and find out who his wife is hiding from him, which gives Chérubin the chance to escape.[20] In this and other such scenes, both fictional and real, a *cabinet de toilette* combined both current meanings of the English word *closet*: It had to do with clothing and it could conceal someone and secrets of a sexual kind.

In making this analogy, I am not suggesting that during this period there was a medicalized or psychologized concept of sexual identity—homo, hetero, bi, queer, trans, or other—as we think of it now.[21] Similarly, today's metaphorical expressions about being in or coming out of the closet—*être dans le placard* or *sortir du placard* would not appear for two centuries after Napoleon and La Mésangère's deaths.

Nevertheless, nonnormative sexuality was far from unknown during the period studied here. Aware of the condemnation of sodomy from the pulpit and the threat of fines, imprisonment, and public execution, most men and women closeted their same-sex desires or resistance to gender norms. On the other hand, when such men and women were members of the elite, they were often not just tolerated but envied and imitated.

During the Renaissance, in some Italian cities, "sodomitical subcultures or networks" flourished and, in France, King Henri III had his coterie of male favorites, *les mignons*. In the seventeenth century, Philippe d'Orléans, the younger brother of Louis XIV, was "an enthusiastic cross-dresser."[22] By the early eighteenth century, in large European cities such as London, Paris, and Amsterdam, "the first 'gay' subcultures developed."[23] More and more men, and some women, dressed to flout social mores publicly.[24] As historian Randolph Trumbach writes, "a minority of adult men whose sexual desires were directed exclusively toward adult and adolescent males . . . could be identified by what seemed to their contemporaries to be effeminate behavior in speech, movement, and dress."[25] For the police in Paris in the 1790s, according to historian Peter McNeil, there were telltale signs that "pederasts" had a preference for shoelaces rather than buckles and favored attire with "colorful and clashing components," perhaps as a way to recognize each other.[26]

Sartorial performance and performativity have been essential to the history and culture of homosexuality and, for centuries, to fashion itself.[27] But this book also makes queer use of queer analytical tools: To study Bonaparte, La Mésangère, and others in their time who embodied, followed, and enforced gender norms.[28] Doing so reveals normative masculinity's strictures but also its feints, dissects its internal contradictions but also detects its secret pleasures. Instead of assuming that "normal" and queer are opposites, I examine the ways they are co-constituted and explore the porous boundaries they share. Following Eve Sedgwick, this work aims to counter "culturally central, apparently monolithic constructions" like gender, heterosexual identity, and desire as self-evident and natural by rendering them "newly accessible to analysis and interrogation."[29]

Let me be clear. I do not seek to *out* any of the historical figures who appear here by certifying them queer *avant la lettre*; nor do I want to defend any of them as properly cisgender and hetero.[30] On the contrary, as Carla Freccero states in *Queer, Early, Modern*, I am interested in limiting my use of *queer* "as an entity, an identity, a thing, and instead allow it to continue its outlaw work as a verb and sometimes an adjective."[31]

Like other scholars of feminist and queer studies, I see gender and sexuality as evolving, precarious processes that require constant iteration and internal and external surveillance. As Judith Butler writes, gender is "an assignment whose addressee never quite inhabits the ideal s/he is compelled to approximate." While "this approximation" may seem liberatory, it "is not necessarily subversive."[32] I use this insight to examine the clothing that Bonaparte and La Mésangère were made to wear to make them legible as boys and men of their class; the clothes they chose for themselves the better to fit in and/or rule; the attire they demanded or encouraged others to wear; and the nonconformist clothes they made their signature attire.

A WORD ABOUT SOURCES

Annemarie Kleinert's encyclopedic tome and many articles on La Mésangère's life, times, and magazine offer a trove of excellent, well-researched information, and I quote her throughout.

In the absence of an autobiography by La Mésangère and access to his correspondence, I explore a memoir by his contemporary, François-Yves Besnard (1752–1842). Although the two men did not know each other, they both grew up in the Angers region (Besnard was just nine years older), became priests, and were keenly interested in clothing. Besnard's recollections do not of course tell us what all provincial boys and priests felt—least of all La Mésangère. But his reactions to other people's attire (including his clerical teacher's silk stockings), to his own clerical dress, and to a handsome young seminarian suspected of being a *mystiqueur* (a priest's pet) open windows into the phenomenology and social psychology of dress and the ways homophobia could get in the way of male friendship and intimacy during this period.[33]

As for Napoleon, thousands upon thousands of books were written about him during his lifetime and over the course of the two hundred years since his death. The challenge is to discern which sources to use and with what degree of skepticism.[34] I have consulted and cite many biographies of Napoleon, but I quote most frequently from Patrice Gueniffey's *Bonaparte*, especially with respect to Bonaparte's formative years.[35] Widely praised for its first-rate research and narrative fluidity, some have taken issue with its "Great Man" approach and his partiality for his subject. I have selected what seem to be the best examples of well-documented even-handedness in his work.

The most revealing sources for this study have been those that uncover rich primary sources but also express deep biases, common at the time of their writing regarding non-heteronormative attitudes and behavior. Thus, for Bonaparte's schooling in

Brienne and at the Royal Military School in Paris, I turn to chapters from a well-known but famously subjective and impressionistic book, *La Jeunesse de Napoléon* [Napoleon's Youth], by a late nineteenth-century historian, Arthur Chuquet (1853–1925). I pull from his extensive research in the archives about boys' sexual behavior at the military school at Brienne and the Ecole Royale Militaire. However, I also analyze the myths and prejudices in his account. Chuquet's prose sometimes turns theatrical, as when he presents invented dialogue between Bonaparte and a cadet whom he chastises as factual, I treat these passages as a secondary source.

Chuquet's remarks are a classic example of one of the hybrid psychological forms that homophobia often takes: a fierce renunciation of homosexuality and an intense fascination with it. Chuquet adds to this standard mix a dramatic and transparent attempt to "protect" Bonaparte from any hint that the boy might have been curious about alternatives to the straight and narrow. Similarly, appraisals of the aging La Mésangère and mockery of his reportedly antediluvian clothing and habits by the journalist Jules Janin (1804–1874) are exaggerated and vicious. As such, they reveal a great deal about the prejudices with respect to class, taste, and social proprieties that motor Janin's acidic sarcasm, which he presumes his fashionable readers share.

■ ■ ■

Focusing on conspicuously different protagonists who share unexpected communalities, this book proposes to widen the scope of masculinity studies of heteronormative male attire. Pressing on Flügel's concept of the Great Masculine Renunciation, I deepen and expand its psychoanalytical meanings, insist on its connections to homophobia and misogyny, and identify the strong parallels it shares with the history of priestly and revolutionary attire. I also point to the surprising opportunities that "uniform" appearance gave some male outsiders to make their way up the social ladder while hiding in plain sight.

Chapter One

BOYS, *CULOTTES*, AND CASSOCKS

HOW COULD you tell a boy from a girl in eighteenth-century France? For the first several years of their lives, you couldn't—at least not by the color or types of clothes they wore.[1] As mewling newborns and fidgety infants in 1761 France and 1769 Corsica, respectively, Pierre Joseph Antoine de La Mésangère and Napoleone di Buonaparte were wrapped in swaddling, just like their sisters.[2] Boys and girls continued to look alike for the next two to seven years: They wore their hair long and were dressed in "long, loose gown[s] open down the front."[3] When, as early as age seven, sons of the well-off were readied to "leave the care of [women] to go to school" and those in more straitened circumstances were considered old enough "to enter the adult world," the idea of gender difference as a natural dichotomy in attire took effect.[4] Girls were forbidden from showing their legs; boys *had* to show theirs.[5] The latter would shun the long dresses of their childhood—which girls were never allowed to outgrow—in favor of a shirt, vest or jacket, and trousers.[6]

Clothing in mid- to late eighteenth-century France was not determined by gender alone and, as we shall see, there were many exceptions. Sometimes, one's choices indicated resistance to heteronormative expectations. In other cases, cultural norms themselves fostered nonnormative behaviors. Priests continued wearing "dresses" for centuries. French military officers added "often flamboyant" frills to their uniforms. Meanwhile, boys' class status and anticipated profession (or lack thereof) were paramount.

GOT BREECHES?

Pierre La Mésangère, son of a local magistrate and noble of the robe living in rural western France, and Napoleone di Buonaparte, son of a minor nobleman in rugged Corsica, were not well-off compared to the sons of courtiers, extravagantly well-heeled denizens of Parisian high society, or even the wealthy bourgeoisie. Yet, as members of the lower nobility, they were far more privileged than at least 95 percent of the population who were neither nobles nor clerics: from wealthy bourgeois down to commoners, farmers, and peasants, many of whom were barely scraping by. What sealed that distinction was one important and prestigious item of clothing that they shared with boys in the highest elite: the *culotte*. These short pants or knee breeches covered the waist, buttocks, pelvic area, and legs down to the knees or just below them. In theory, wearing them ensured that boys of the upper crust would be treated with due deference.

For the most affluent, a *culotte* was made of fine satin, brocade, or velvet in an array of colors. At the knees, expensive steel buckles or even costlier silver ones cinched the fabric, below which one wore silk stockings. Steel or silver buckles on leather shoes completed the outfit. Napoleon and others for whom money was far scarcer would have had to make do with cheaper fabrics—hemp, linen, or cotton—and their shoe buckles were never silver. Some would also have had to forego the frock coat that usually accompanied a *culotte*. Much further down in the social order, few members of the Third Estate owned any form of tailored garments. They wore blousons, loose jackets, and long, often ill-fitting, and decidedly unfashionable full-length trousers. These were usually dull brown—the cheapest dye available.[7] Not only did these boys and men lack the means for dressing above their station they faced sharp social disapproval for trying.

Wearing any kind of leg coverings, from the fitted, short *culotte* to long, loose trousers, presumably "made" the boy or man.[8] However, clothing could also lie. This was particularly true when, over the course of the eighteenth century, would-be elite boys and men increasingly wore *culottes*. Some even had enough money and cultural capital to pass. Yet pretending to look the part could also be cause for anxiety: Will I be found out? Shoddy workmanship, inexpert or inadequate laundering could quickly expose one's relative poverty and laughable pretentions. While wearing pants *en matelot*, styled like those of sailors, could mean enjoying less constraining clothing without fear of scandal, it would also indicate a boy's lower status.[9]

Even those in the prestigious *culotte* and stockings were not entirely safe from belittlement. Such garments covered the lower body, but they also revealed the shape of what lay beneath: waist, buttocks, thighs, pelvis, knees, calves, and ankles. If one's body was misshapen, pudgy, or puny, wearing the upper-class male "uniform" would be a daily mortification. Some boys and men used corsets to rein in extra flesh or padding to give the curve of the calves more prominence.[10] In these ways, elite dress for boys and men constituted high-class cover as well as obligatory display and potential exposure.

Napoleon's and Pierre's notions about how attire signaled class would have been closely tied to their parents' status, wealth, aspirations, and values. As it happens, the two boys' fathers represented starkly different versions of low noble/bourgeois masculinity in the provinces in eighteenth-century France. While Carlo Mario di Buonaparte delighted in elegant and expensive ostentation according to which masculinity was a matter of aesthetic self-presentation, Pierre-Joseph Le Boux Sieur de La Mésangère, who had given most of his names to his son as if creating his own double, appears to have believed that relative modesty and austerity signaled a moral superiority true to his provincial Catholic roots. Despite these divergences, both fathers would have given their sons mixed and contradictory messages about what clothing could hide and show.

LIKE FATHER, LIKE SON?

Ajaccio, the capital and biggest city in Corsica, where Napoleon's father Carlo di Buonaparte (1746–1785) was born and lived with his family on the southwestern coast, was the island's pride. However, for those in the lofty one percent preening in Parisian salons or vying for the king's favor at court, Ajaccio, like Corsica itself, was the boondocks, a remote place believed to be full of dirty peasants. French troops defeated Pasquale Paoli (1725–1807) and his fierce Corsican followers in early May 1769, just a few months before the birth of Carlo's second son on August 15. This made the infant officially French as well as Corsican.

Many on the island scorned and resented the colonial aggressors, and Carlo, given his patriotic sympathies and pride, might have been one of them. Nevertheless, this land-rich, cash-poor, fourth-generation minor nobleman was smitten with all things French, including the monarchy and the latest luxuries and fashions. He reveled in purchasing elegant, French-styled attire that he could not afford. One historian of the family writes that Carlo's account book "suggests a costly and colorful wardrobe: suits in black silk and velvet, in satin, in blue material with braiding, in yellow, and a complete outfit in bronze-colored cloth." We also know that "he sometimes dressed up in a cerise jacket with puce breeches" and wore a wig, which was de rigueur at the time for men of the upper echelons.[11] In the eighteenth century, clothes in fine fabrics and rich colors were par for the course for men of means with the status, wealth, or (in Carlo's case) cheek to pull it off.

FIGURE 1.1 Presumed portrait of Carlo Maria Buonaparte in aristocratic finery, attributed to Anton Raphael Mengs, ca. 1766–1779.
Source: Copyright ArtRes

In 1777, when Napoleon was seven, by finagling with the powers that be Carlo finally saw some of his ambitions realized. He would be Corsica's representative to the French court of Louis XVI, a post that came with some supplementary income for finery.[12] During his years at Versailles, in his thirties and forties, Carlo may have looked like the man depicted in figure 1.1, which is the only extant portrait presumed to be of him. It shows a clean-shaven, middle-aged man of light complexion and florid cheeks (perhaps rouged, common at the time), decked out in a fine curled and powdered wig pulled into a ponytail and a lustrous pastel blueish-gray silk, or satin, frock coat trimmed with generous gold embroidery, a delicate lace cravat, and cuffs.[13] Although only a three-quarter image, the painting leaves no doubt that, below the waist, Carlo wears an equally noble *culotte.* The fitted frock coat, black hat tucked under one arm, jeweled pinkie ring, and even the style and shape of the wig, tied with a black ribbon, clearly indicate his gender and his upper-class status. At Versailles, failure to get all the details right would be reason enough for mockery or ostracism. A courtier's position depended on the will of the king and the acceptance of one's peers—both precarious. Any slip in sartorial protocol would have confirmed that Carlo barely occupied the court's unfashionable fringes.

According to published comments allegedly made by his mother, Maria Letizia Buonaparte (1750–1836), the young Napoleon fell quite far from this branch of his father's tree. She describes him at age eight as a boy with no time for pretention, let alone propriety, who cared not at all about how he looked. After a day hidden away reading, Napoleon would walk around the streets of Ajaccio "without having made himself presentable and without even bothering to pull up his stockings."[14] This comment reinforces the idea, still current, that Napoleon was a modern man's man, naturally uninterested in supposedly vain, feminine concerns even as a youth—despite his later, absolute dependence on these preoccupations as a means of rule when he became emperor.

Meanwhile, six hundred miles from the island of Corsica, the young Pierre La Mésangère grew up in a rural village among the fields and sheep pastures of western France, about twenty-four miles from the provincial capital of Angers. Compared to the titles, wealth, and holdings of those in the highest social circles in the region, his family had almost nothing—not even the distant connection to the royal court that Carlo Buonaparte parlayed for himself.[15] Nevertheless, his father, Pierre-Joseph Le Boux Sieur de la Mésangère, was a minor member of the *noblesse de robe* married to a bourgeoise and the owner of a very modest country château called "La Motte." Like Carlo Buonaparte, La Mésangère's father was lord over his tenants. They paid him to live on his land, farm it, or use it for grazing sheep. But there the similarities appear to end.

Sieur La Mésangère's bywords, like those of most of his provincial peers, seem to have been piety, morality, austerity, and frugality—the opposite of Carlo's. La Mésangère's father found elaborate and expensive lifestyles and fashions to be inimical to traditional Catholic values of modesty and self-denial. However, to the faithful, priests' use of finer chasubles for the celebration of Mass along with the bright and ornamented attire of Church prelates would have been clear and well-justified exceptions.

On the other hand, as a condition of their higher status, La Mésangère, his wife, and men and women of their class were obliged to care about what they wore and how they looked. La Mésangère *père*'s social status would also have meant following unwritten but no less prescriptive social codes. He and his peers were expected to display their relative wealth and status by powdering their hair at the very least or, better, wearing a wig. Exorbitantly expensive not only to buy but to maintain, a *perruque* was one of the most common public signs of social superiority.

Given how showy wigs were, we might expect them to be a female vanity to which husbands only reluctantly acceded. But this was long before the Great Masculine Renunciation swept France. In fact, as Pierre's contemporary and fellow Angevin, François-Yves Besnard (1752–1842), writes about his own country upbringing, to be seen as respectable, neither sex left the house "unless they had had their hair or wigs curled and powdered."[16] Furthermore, it was men, not their wives or daughters, who tended to have their own *cabinet de toilette*, a true and truly expensive luxury. For the daily and always messy ritual of dressing and powdering the wig, boys were hired to come to the house and do that job in a small closet-like room or recessed space.[17] Insofar as separate rooms were far from common at the time, assigning even a small room for ministering to wig did what the modern closet, literal and figurative, does today. On the one hand, it concealed what one had and did in there. On the other hand, the very fact of having such a room indicated the wig's importance to the owner's sense of self and the way he or she wanted others to consider them.

In the mid- and late eighteenth century, social class was considered part of God's foreordained order, and so were the differences in attire that went along with it. Besnard writes, "You could identify a person's social standing and profession at a glance. . . . The shop boy did not dress like his master; nor did the shopkeeper dress like the cloth merchant, the metalworker or the jeweler, and even less like the bourgeois who did not have to work for a living at all and simply lived off his income."[18] Being toward the top of the pecking order in effect required displaying a certain degree of luxury and up-to-date dress. In the Angers region, one might frown on those who wore the latest fashions from Paris as snobbish and morally dubious. However, slumming, by wearing, for example, the brown cloth of commoners rather than fabric dyed in light colors, white, yellow, or red, could look like false modesty.[19]

For certain professions, ceremonial occasions, or events such as masked or costume balls, anachronistic clothing was required. Yet going about one's daily business in Renaissance-era slit sleeves, for example, would have been considered folly. Social convention also demanded that La Mésangère *père* and the other members of his family indulge in a certain degree of acquisitiveness. One historian estimates that nobles in the region owned ten times the number of clothes of master artisans.[20] As a result, in the second half of the eighteenth century, for "nobles living in Angers and other large cities in the kingdom, clothing is an element of social distinction. They use luxurious fabrics—hot in winter, light in summer, like silk, satin, woolens, twill."[21]

In all these ways, those who could afford luxuries but refused to indulge in them to excess were performing socially legible luxury in proper moderation. Thus, for Pierre's father, wearing plain trousers rather than a *culotte* would not have done at all. If he abjured silver in favor of steel buckles for his shoes, the vast majority of the impoverished Third Estate, for whom steel was an unimaginable expense, would not necessarily have registered this "renunciation" of finery.[22] Like clerical modesty, the provincial version constituted a paradox: Renunciation was a given, but it had to be exhibited in very particular ways. For those with a profession, like La Mésangère's father, who wore a robe and a wig, this double injunction both limited and freed them.

BEWIGGED AND BEROBED

As early as 1550, judges and lawyers had been obliged to wear long black robes.[23] In this gown and his curled and powdered judge's wig, *sieur* La Mésangère would have enjoyed the ancient social prestige of his costume. It clearly marked him as a man of power and high social standing in the small town of Pontigné and the rural area nearby.[24] Whatever his personal thrill arriving at court or walking through town in this garb, no one could accuse him of vanity: Wearing this official attire was his duty. Although the costume marked him as superior to most of those in his immediate environment, it also identified him as belonging to the lower ranks of the provincial *noblesse de robe*. The jurists at the Parliament of Paris, by contrast, wore vivid scarlet gowns.[25] Like other uniforms, *sieur* La Mésangère's robes severely limited his options for exercising his personal style, let alone dressing for comfort. During the dog days of summer, the ankle-length judicial gown and heavy, scratchy wig may well have been a private purgatory. Yet going to court without either was out of the question: Clothes made the man. Without them, he was not and could not be a judge of others.

By the time *sieur* La Mésangère's son, Pierre, and Carlo di Buonaparte's son, Napoleon, were growing up, wigs were no longer *just f*or wealthy laymen and women. Priests, even teaching priests who, by then, had a bit more leeway in their wardrobe, were not interested in taking up the lace, jewels, cufflinks, buttons, or short cassocks that the Church began banning in the sixteenth century. They assented to the sober, long black cassock that was to signal their repudiation of vanity and affluence. Times had changed so much that religious orders' periodic statements about clerical dress during this period were no longer proscriptive or even prescriptive but descriptive—factual records of what members of the teaching clergy were wearing.

However, wigs, which were costly and conspicuous and had been outlawed a century earlier, were the clear exception to the "rule" of renunciation. Thus, religious orders that had outlawed *perruques* a century earlier were turning a blind eye when teaching clergy wore them if, that is, those men of the cloth followed the golden, if slippery, rule of moderation. A teacher's *faux* crowning glory was supposed to be long, but not too long, curled but not too curled.[26] This relative but vague leniency put teaching priests in an enviable but potentially compromising situation: What constituted "too much" was sometimes guess work.

In his memoir, Besnard, who grew up near Angers, remembers his delight that his family had pledged him early on to the Church. At age twelve, he writes, his hair was tonsured (cut long on the sides but close at the top as if he were balding). He could and did wear a *culotte*, but he was allowed to wear with it a knee-length version of the ecclesiastical cassock. Although many of the thousands of other boys in his position might have been resentful or ashamed of these telltale signs of family poverty, Besnard avows that his hybrid existence, which made him a "half-secular, half-clerical" creature, was a thrill.[27] His attire garnered him and his peers a "fair amount of respect" and "a lot of curious and admiring looks from both sexes." He adds that these "never failed to flatter me."[28] For Besnard, his clerical attire was a mark of superiority, not inferiority, and a boon to his pride.

Given Besnard's awareness of the pleasure he derived from his distinctive haircut and clerical garb, it is no surprise that his memoirs reveal his keen observations of one of his teacher's fashionable differences from the traditional clerical norm. At the Oratorian middle school, which La Mésangère would attend soon after, Besnard reports that Father Limonas cared a great deal about how he looked and what others thought of him.[29] Limonas left his cassock partly open to "display his shapely legs," which were "always sheathed . . . in silk stockings"—a suggestion that the priest was vain and possibly profligate since such stockings were "still quite uncommon in Angers." Yet his teacher Limonas's self-display and attention to his wardrobe clearly enthralled Besnard as a schoolboy.[30] Limonas, he writes, was "attractive [and] meticulously elegant in his clothing." He "always showed up in class in his well-groomed, curled, and powdered wig." Besnard also pronounces him "the most likeable and interesting of all the tutors and teachers [he] had ever had."[31] These admiring comments, in addition to Besnard's praise for Limonas's "ease, grace, mellifluous voice, wit, and talent for banter," may suggest a schoolboy crush fondly remembered. However, Besnard adds a rather cheeky assessment of Limonas's physical assets: a handsome body but a "rather ugly face."[32]

Unlike some of their schoolteachers, boys who went away to school enjoyed not even the slightest leeway in their uniform attire. This was presumably to protect these boys of the elite from accusations of a suspect, effeminate attention to their looks. Whether the middle school education in question was civilian, as for Pierre La Mésangère, or military, as for Napoleon, the disciplinarians were men of the Church. Their job was to mold their charges by micromanaging their behavior, attitudes, and attire—a process one might call male "uniforming."

Removed from the mixed-gender environments of their childhoods and from their families, boys entered male-only institutions and accommodations where upper-class masculinity was drilled into them as a matter of conformity and homogeneity. There, girls and women were supposed to be out of sight and out of mind, not only for the pupils but also for the men who educated them.[33] Even during their six-week yearly vacation, the boys had to stay at school, where the only girls or women to be found might be nurses in the infirmary, maids, or kitchen help. In effect, unless they were family members on an occasional visit, females were personae non gratae.[34] The absence of the female sex was essential to the school's mission of creating masculine, military-identified, would-be men.

Those boys who became officers or joined secular professions were expected to marry and have children. Yet nothing in their six years of same-sex confinement would have prepared them for the most basic interactions with the opposite sex. In theory, contact among and between boys and teachers was also out of bounds. However, years of studying, exercising, eating, and sleeping alongside dozens and dozens of their peers in close quarters sometimes had the opposite effect.

BOYS' TOWNS

For Napoleon, the challenging transition from home life with his family to boarding school was intensified by the fact that he had to emigrate to do so. In 1779, Carlo Buonaparte's social and political ambitions gave Napoleon, age eight, and his brother Joseph, age nine, only one option: moving over a hundred miles from Corsica to France to live among the French, whom Napoleon considered a hostile occupying force in his homeland. In midwinter, after a lengthy boat ride and days of travel over land, the boys arrived in the small town of Autun, in provincial Burgundy, to be tutored in speaking, reading, and writing French. Without these skills, they would have no chance of making good.

Although it was usually firstborn sons who were expected to attend military school, Napoleon was considered a better prospect than Joseph. As an impoverished nobleman, Carlo was able to secure a royal scholarship for his second born, which gave him the right and the financial wherewithal to attend a military prep school. Brienne, the one chosen for him, was a feeder school for the prestigious military academy in Paris, but for the young Napoleon, the location was just another small French town even farther from Corsica than Autun, not to mention colder and more landlocked.

As for previous generations of French noblemen, military school was Napoleon's first experience of full-scale male and masculinist state indoctrination. To instill the values and norms of elite masculinity, boys' family ties and provincial roots were effectively severed for six years without a break. Making young boys into the right kind of little men entailed hardship, regimentation, and what amounted to enforced incarceration. Yet in these places, many putatively heteronormative boys engaged in homosexual liaisons, and some of the boys of the higher classes who were dressed in impeccable uniforms were treated like servants.

Before arriving at Brienne, Napoleon, like other cadets, was sent detailed instructions about the expensive military wardrobe he needed to assemble, the cost of which would not be covered by his fellowship. Cadets "wore a blue cloth coat with red facings, lapels, and collar, with white buttons featuring the school crest, and, depending on the circumstances, a blue or black culotte."[35] The *culotte* made it clear that these sons of noblemen still had legs, as was their right. The uniform also left no doubt that the students would be trained to act and to think of themselves not as individuals but as boys who would serve as look-alike cogs in France's all-male military machine.

Regulation garb was essential because it was a rare and important equalizer among different ranks of the elite. More than half of the 110 boys at Brienne came from the highest and wealthiest echelons of the aristocracy. For them, military school meant renouncing, for more than half a decade, the rich fabrics, fine wigs, and expensive accessories in which they might have strutted about in the civilian world. However, for Napoleon and the fifty or so other pupils who received a royal fellowship, the school's clear dos and don'ts about attire would have had one very important benefit. They forestalled a great deal of anxiety-producing guesswork about what to wear.[36] In this sense, for the fellowship boys, Brienne was a safe harbor—a place where merit *might* win out over rank. On the other hand, at a time when uniforms were made by hand or obtained through used-clothing vendors, all uniforms were not in fact alike. Any number of particularities could give away a cadet's family income or lack thereof, a reminder, as if anyone needed one, that the uniform offered only an illusion of equity.

At Brienne, the boys were subject to strict regulations and regular privations. The dormitory rooms "were six-feet square, and the only furnishings were a trestle bed, a water pitcher, and a wash basin."[37] The boys were locked in and Minims who stayed up all night patrolling the halls made sure that they would not get out.[38] Brienne's pupils were also expected to attend daily Mass and prayer, weekly sermons, and monthly confession—a heavier dose of mandatory Catholicism than most of the boys would have known at home.[39] In many ways, then, Napoleon and his young peers were learning to become men by leading not just paramilitary but also para-monkish lives. These two modes were, in some ways, opposite versions of masculinity. Nevertheless, they overlapped in ways that made them mutually reinforcing.

That the state's future military officers got their early education from priests may strike modern readers as improbable. Certainly, the fact that the Minim friars, part of the Benedictine order, were poor and poorly educated did not make them ideal teachers and supervisors. On the other hand, the courses they taught were standard for boys in middle school: French, Latin, German, history, geography, and math. Drawing, music, dance, and fencing were taught by secular men hired for the purpose. Although priests and friars in French *collèges* [middle schools] and universities were "generally administered or staffed by the Church, they were overseen, financed, and supported by government authorities, often accounting for 10 percent of municipal expenses."[40] Although the Church and monarchy were often in competition and at loggerheads, in this realm, they buttressed one other. The friars and clergyman who trained young boys in military schools taught them to obey God, king, and army, though not necessarily in that order.

The type of garb the Minim friars wore at Brienne—black, ankle-length, long-sleeved tunics made of coarse material—had been monks' dress for so many centuries that their attire might have seemed to have been consecrated by Christ himself. In fact, this was far from the case.[41] The only decorative element was a thin, tasseled black cord knotted four times at the waist, each knot a reminder of the vows of renunciation expected of them: chastity, poverty, obedience, and abstinence from meat and dairy. By contrast, their pupils' *culottes* indicated that their all-male institution was basic training in masculinity for a future in which they were expected to reproduce and rule over women and the lower classes.

During the cadets' formative years, the Minims' job was to indoctrinate them in religious, national, gender, class, military, and sexual norms. In the best of circumstances, the boys, who had presumably already been steeped in many of these beliefs, would become even more invested in the system, which simultaneously held them above others while keeping them in line. The more the cadets internalized these "shoulds" and monitored their peers for compliance, the better they would serve as pawns for the status quo.

The Minims, however, were not very good at any of this. They were known for mediocre teaching, ineffectual leadership, and lax discipline.[42] On the other hand, they do not seem to have spared the rod when it came to Napoleon's noncompliance. He appears to have been one of the boys at Brienne least inclined to buckle down despite corporal punishments. He got three days' detention for singing outside the new principal's window at night. For disobeying the regents, he was thrashed with a stick. For a "slight infraction," his punishment required him to replace his uniform with "a monk's coat and coarse pants rather than the upper-class *culotte*, and rustic, shapeless shoes." In that embarrassing outfit, he was made "to dine on his knees in front of the refectory door." As a result of his public humiliation, Napoleon is said to have suffered "a violent attack of nerves and vomited all that he had eaten."[43]

Despite these examples of his delinquency, Napoleon appears to have taken to heart many hardcore manly values of austerity and control. This, ironically, made *him*, not the Minim friars, the resident disciplinarian. School reports describe him as "domineering, imperious, and stubborn."[44] He is said to have picked fights, promised Corsican liberation, and threatened Corsican revenge. This made Napoleon at once a standard-bearer for righteous masculinity and a rebel against the rules that constrained him.

STANDARDS AND DEVIATIONS

Foreigners at the Brienne school were probably mocked for their differences from French norms. Biographers usually intimate, however, that Napoleon, who was technically French, may have been bullied the most.[45] The other boys generally considered the penurious, antisocial, unprepossessing, and undersized young Corsican patriot with the funny Italian name and even funnier accent "bizarre and ridiculous"—an inferior, conquered subject.[46] However, some of the best-known and oft-told tales about Napoleon as a misfit now appear to have been based on counterfeit letters and pamphlets of dubious legitimacy.[47]

Nevertheless, the one authenticated letter written by Napoleon from Brienne reveals his own self-important, judgmental attitude regarding strict military standards of masculinity. In 1784, appalled to learn that his older brother Joseph was quitting his ecclesiastical studies to undergo his own military training at Brienne, Napoleon wrote to his uncle to protest. Every comment couched as a compliment about Joseph also implied that he was just not man enough to be in the military. "Yes, my dear brother would be a good officer in the barracks. He is good-looking and lighthearted, which makes him adept at frivolous compliments. His talents will be great assets in society but not in combat."[48] In sum, Joseph is everything Napoleon prides himself on *not* being: sickly, lazy, superficial, and a profligate pretty boy. The only rightful place for Joseph, he concludes, was the Church. Napoleon's standards of military masculinity were so far above those of his peers and the friars that the other cadets are said to have nicknamed him "the Spartan."[49]

As such, Napoleon had even more austere values than many of the Minim friars who were his teachers. Some famously flouted not only the order's rules but also their vows of chastity.[50] While the vice-principal, Louis-Sébastien Berton, was reputed to have garnered a great deal of respect, Jean-Baptiste Berton, the principal and Louis-Sébastien's brother, had a far sketchier reputation. A former army grenadier-turned-friar, he was rumored to have had a long-standing affair with a Madame de Pernon. This, at any rate, is how the famous multivolume biography, *La Jeunesse de Napoléon* [Napoleon's Youth]

(1887–1889) by Arthur Chuquet (1853–1925) represents Napoleon's clerical teachers at Brienne.

Chuquet's work has long been a favorite source from which biographers continue to draw. However, Chuquet's pronounced bias—especially with respect to close, "improper" relations among the cadets and purported trespasses of men of the cloth—make his comments particularly apt here. His late nineteenth-century work is typical of a long tradition of anticlerical muckraking in France that primarily targets sexual hypocrisies and misdeeds. Chuquet alleges that the friars were not scandalized when a "plump, fresh, and pretty" girl in the infirmary was impregnated by a "strong and vigorous" twenty-year-old, sergeant major Des Roys. She was sent away; he was not punished. The head nurse treated the matter as negligible. "The rumor went around that what had ruined poor Nanette had often happened to [the head nurse] with Father X***" when she was younger. Although Nanette was doomed to her fate, the head nurse and the priest "were luckier or more prudent."[51] Chuquet writes that the principal at Brienne was also deemed "harmful for many young men whom he attracted to his quarters and entertained"—a likely allusion to pederasty.[52]

Chuquet makes similar charges of permissiveness against the military brass but fixates almost exclusively on male homosexuality not brothels or extramarital affairs. He quotes a short anonymous text, purported to be a bona fide memoir by a cadet who had attended the military *collège* at Tournon, also run by clerics. It indicates that there were pleasures to be had, and these did not have to involve girls or women. "Despite all the surveillance and precautions taken by the superiors," cadets would find a way to enjoy the "vile pleasures" of mutual masturbation "under the study and game tables."[53] Even "the best behaved" took part. The former cadet, however, claims that he was so afraid that masturbation of any kind would lead to madness and death that he resisted all overtures made by *les indécents*. When the Ecole Militaire in Paris was shut down, the same young man was transferred to Brienne (not the *collège* that Bonaparte attended, which was for younger students), where he spent more than three years, from 1788 to 1792. There, the anonymous author reports, the kinds of vices that also went on at Tournon were even more pronounced, and the "indecent ones" who practiced it had a different nickname: "nymphs."[54]

One might suppose that around this same time, from age sixteen to twenty-two, Pierre, attending the Oratorian seminary in Angers, was getting the opposite kind of school experience. To read the memoirs of Besnard, who attended a comparable seminary, run by another teaching sect, the Sulpicians, also in Angers a few years before, is to see that the dangers, temptations, and frustrations there were very similar even if the young men's plain, dark cassocks were supposed to ensure that they were not like the scandalous cadets in military schools.[55]

INSIDERS, OUTSIDERS, TEACHERS' PETS

Like cadets' uniforms, seminarians' robes hid the young men's diverse and sometimes humble origins by associating them individually and collectively with the all-powerful Church. For the large number of anticlerical skeptics in the second half of the eighteenth century, this attire made them easy targets of derision and suspicion. The young Besnard and La Mésangère, distinctive in their clerical attire, would have seen and felt some of this.[56] On seminarians' outings to the country house owned by his teaching order, Besnard writes, "the whole pension was frequently greeted by groups of street urchins who seemed to wait for the time we walked by to greet us with deafening cries of 'Caw! Caw!'"[57] Tarred by the same black brush, the cluster of clerics was supposed to feel as trivial, unappealing, and maleficent as a flock of crows. If the urchins in question were in a fighting mood and those black "birds," the seminarians, attempted flight, they would have been hampered by their long cassocks. These robes not only associated the seminarians with the priesthood, they also restricted their movements, making them potential targets. Clearly anxious to set themselves apart from those who refused to be "real" men, the boys may also have been imagining or intimating specific temptations of the flesh: when boys in "dresses" frequented boys and other men in like attire. If so, they would not have been the only ones.

Fifteen years before Napoleon entered Brienne, the Enlightenment philosopher François Marie Arouet de Voltaire (1694–1778) published "A So-Called Socratic Love." For him, the "unnatural" desires between boys and men have one simple cause and an equally simple remedy. They were the result of the constraints of same-sex institutions (schools, the army, and religious orders) that frustrate boys' "natural," aggressive *heterosexuality*. This makes boys "turn to beautiful boys who resemble girls" and leads to teachers' "abuse of youngsters of rank" and to the boys' indulgence in "nocturnal entertainments and orgies." However, Voltaire opines, when those boys' "resemblance [to girls] vanishes, the misapprehension stops." In other words, celibacy is unnatural, but the homosexual aberrations it leads to are inconsequential because boys naturally return to heterosexuality.[58]

Seminaries in eighteenth-century France established rules and practices to break up and, ideally, forestall entirely not only homosexual attraction but any kind of close relationships among young men including ones based on regional or national politics, social or intellectual affinities, and even simple friendship. The fear was that these might devolve into "small leagues and cabals," that "would wreak havoc" on the institution.[59] The superior would therefore personally assign partners "for games, conversations, or walks" to ensure that no casual fraternization or special relationships (*liaisons particulières*) would get in the way of a novitiate's spiritual calling. Rules prohibited the seminarians from entering their peers' sleeping quarters or "disrespect[ing] silence and solitude."[60]

There is no record that Pierre La Mésangère experienced close encounters of this kind. However, in Besnard's recollections of the Sulpician seminary in Angers, as at Napoleon's school in Brienne, a certain amount of deviance was the warp and woof of normal behavior. While Besnard's account of his teacher, Father Limonas, with his silk stockings and attractive legs but an ugly face, was clear-eyed and somewhat impertinent, his recollection of other relations at the seminary consists of equal parts indignation, titillation, and guilt.

Besnard's complaints begin with his first contact with the Father Superior. In their obligatory, private meeting, he writes, the priest stood "chest to chest" with him, digging painfully into his chest, coercing him through physical proximity and emotional intimidation to reveal all his "defects and vices."[61] Rather than object to laying open his innermost self to the highest authority at the school—a practice not dissimilar to Catholic confession—Besnard grouses that he should have been told about this physical, spiritual, and emotional hazing, so that he could have impressed his superior instead of botching this first meeting.[62] Even if it meant enduring an encounter that was too close for comfort, for Besnard, and in theory for the seminary as a whole, conformity and obedience counted above all else.

For Besnard, so did fairness. He was affronted by the blatant favoritism at the seminary, which completely belied the egalitarianism that the uniform robe for seminarians seemed to represent. He writes, "Most of the Sulpician priests selected one or two pupils to whom they had taken a liking, devoting special attention to them and offering them special favors."[63] Not only did such practices exclude him personally, but also they seemed too intimate to be above suspicion. He and the other seminarians, he charges, knew that the select few were in the rooms of the headmasters "at every hour of the day." In public, "the boys did not leave their side at recess, not to mention during the holidays in the countryside."[64]

Despite their great show of religious devotion, he and the other students considered them "spies and tattle-tales" and dubbed them "*mystiqueurs* and *mignons*."[65] Both monikers put the onus of favoritism on the young men, not the priests, who engaged in this behavior. Like *les mignons*, the term used in the sixteenth century for the clique of provincials from the lesser nobility who enjoyed "tender, passionate, erotic" relationships with Henri III (1551–1589), the word *mystiqueurs* thus denoted insider groups whose goings-on were supposed to be discreet, even secret, but were widely known or at least suspected.[66] Once again, Besnard's resentment of his *mystiqueurs* or *mignons* peers appears to stem less from his moral objections than a feeling of indignation: Fellow seminarians whom he considered deviants received far more attention and favors than those, like himself, who followed both the letter and the spirit of seminary rules. In this topsy-turvy world, the seminarians on the straight and narrow were cast in the role of outsiders looking on with consternation and envy at a form of belonging from which they were excluded.

Besnard admits that he felt a hankering for human connection as well as the stirrings of desire for one of those priest's "pets." He describes a young seminarian named Bouchard, who had, "in addition to the prettiest face in the world, the most beautiful eyes that held a remarkable look of languorous sweetness." Besnard hastens to add that Bouchard was the initiator. "Although talking was forbidden, [Bouchard] never passed me without saying a few honeyed words"[67] and "seemed to want to have special relations (*des liaisons particulières*) with me."[68]

Besnard hurries past the question of his own temptation to forestall any questions about his innocence: "The reservations I had, due to the fact that he was a *mystiqueur*, were so strong that I dismissed his overtures out of hand."[69] In this way, Besnard's tale resembles that of the anonymous cadet who spent time at both Tournon and Brienne for misbehavior: "*they* were at fault, not I."

Whether the boys of the upper classes in military schools and in the seminary were the objects or subjects of these kinds of desires and conscious or unconscious of their gravitational pull, many appear *not* to have succumbed to temptation. Others, such as the *mystiqueurs*, embraced or, like Besnard, were intrigued by the chance to have more intimate relations than were allowed. In all these cases, these young men were being made in the image of acceptable masculinity, which is to say a tangled web of more-or-less-explicit yearning and denial. In this way, the conventional and even righteous includes within it what supposedly exceeds and negates it.

■ ■ ■

After finishing at Brienne and the seminary respectively, Napoleon and Father La Mésangère would continue to experience these kinds of personal and institutional contradictions. From this point on, however, they would be doing so in places that offered far more prestige, material comfort, and luxury than they had ever known.

In October 1784, at age fifteen, Napoleon left Brienne in southwestern France for the new and highly selective Ecole

Royale Militaire [Royal Military Academy] whose majestic dome dominated the Paris skyline. Just two years later, the twenty-five-year-old La Mésangère, ordained as a Father of Christian Doctrine, also got a plum assignment: teaching literature and rhetoric at the former royal *collège* in the small town of La Flèche. In some ways, life at the royal military school and the royal middle school would be more of the same: Uniforms, routines, and a same-sex environment reinforced social and institutional norms while sometimes fostering deviations from gender and sexual standards.

However, at this point, far more was at stake: nothing less than our protagonists' future professions and livelihoods. This was going to be doubly tricky for the new Father La Mésangère. He would be obliged not only to mold himself according to rules set in place by his religious order but also to enforce his young charges' conformity to them. Living in elite surroundings changed both young men's ideas about how and whether they, or others, might be found wanting: desiring something or someone, or being perceived as lacking.

Chapter Two

BOYS TO MEN: TRAINING AND CLOTHING THE ELITE

IN 1786, Father La Mésangère, newly ordained, moved to La Flèche. With just 5,000 residents and paltry amenities, the town was a *big* step up from Pontigné, but that was not saying much.[1] Fifteen years later, around 1801, Charles Boucher (1742–1812), a surgeon in La Flèche, boasts in his memoirs that the townspeople were modest provincials for whom the latest fashions meant little. "Luxury was unknown . . . the wives and daughters of the highest-ranked townsmen (*les premiers bourgeois*) were less elegantly dressed than today's chambermaids. For a long time, there was only one female hairdresser. There were no women's dress merchants until 1770. The bourgeois generally had only one outfit of fine fabric for Sundays and wore very common materials all the other days of the week."[2]

Yet Father La Mésangère would not be living in town. He was headed for its crown jewel, the former Royal School founded by Henri IV in 1604. Just off the tiny main square, secluded behind heavy, carriage-height wooden doors and even taller masonry walls, the school was near the king's impressive summer château. For two centuries, it had enjoyed an illustrious reputation under the Jesuits. However, when Louis XV expelled the religious order from France, it became a military academy for boys, which soon fell on hard times. Twenty years before Father La Mésangère arrived, Louis XVI (1754–1793) had selected the Fathers of Christian Doctrine (the Doctrinarians) to run a nonmilitary boys' *collège* [middle school] there.[3] Thanks to the king's generosity and the considerable income from the properties that Henri IV had bestowed on the school, the faculty-student ratio was an unprecedented one to nine. Salaries were the envy of other teachers, even those who taught at the universities in the provincial capital, Angers.[4]

Once the Doctrinarians restored the school and grounds, which had fallen into disrepair, the campus was once again hailed for its four, large rectangular courtyards lined on all sides with elegant, multistory buildings.[5] Behind them lay manicured gardens, "groves, rows of trees, ornamental ponds, and fountains that spurted up eliciting cries of admiration even from visitors who had been there before."[6] They marveled at the refurbished buildings, including the "grand library [and] the auditorium adorned with magnificent paintings."[7]

Unlike Napoleon's para-monkish school in Brienne, Father La Mésangère's Oratorian seminary in Angers, and most others, the Doctrinarian school at La Flèche was a place of relative luxury. Three hundred and twenty pupils, two-thirds of the student body, were wealthy enough to pay a pricey seven hundred livres for room and board, twice the cost of the Oratorian school in Angers.[8] These boarders had servants, and male domestics made their beds. The living conditions for about fifty less well-off gentlemen's sons who received royal fellowships were far more modest. Boys who had neither a noble pedigree nor family wealth were not allowed to board at the school. Nonetheless, tuition was free, so if such students could afford a cheap rooming house or live even more economically at home, they could receive a fine education and the professional opportunities in the Church or the magistracy that might follow.[9]

The resulting range of social classes in the student body indicated a rather progressive attitude for the time. The Collège des Doctrinaires nevertheless required that the boys' relative social rank show—not only in their distinctly different living situations but also in their clothing. Wealthy and noble boarders could not have slummed it even if they had wanted to. They were required to pack combs, brushes, powder, and a mirror for their wigs. The wig-dresser came every morning "to take care of these [young] gentlemen, 'arrange' them, 'curl' them, and provide them with powder and pomade." As one prominent historian of the Doctrinarians quips: hardly "a Spartan education!"[10] Boarders' uniforms (see figure 2.1, right) were distinctly paramilitary, very similar to the garb required when La Flèche had been a military school open only to the sons of aristocrats (see figure 2.1, left). Both styles required blue coats with gold buttons and contrasting bright red facings with matching collars, wide bands of red at the wrist, and white stockings.[11] Under the Doctrinarians, the boys wore the far less flashy uniform pictured on the right. This more civilian style featured a black rather than a military blue *culotte* and much shorter red facings on a more modern, cutaway coat. Day pupils, by contrast, turned up in whatever they could afford, which would have been neither high-quality nor fashionable. For the poorest, this would have meant wooden shoes and a humble *pantalon* (loose trousers) and loose shirt with a short jacket made of rough fabric. Powdered hair, let alone a wig, would have been unthinkable unless it was the cheapest kind. As a result, the school enforced and reinforced traditional social distinctions—whether that resulted in jealousy, enmity, or subtle imitation.

FIGURE 2.1 Military versus civilian student uniforms at La Flèche: More alike than different. Pen and color ink drawing: Left, Ecole Militaire at La Flèche, 1764–1776. Right, Collège des Doctrinaires at La Flèche, 1777–1793.

Source: *La Flèche: Quatre siècles d'éducation sous le regard de l'Etat* (La Flèche: Prytanée National Militaire, 2006), 77. Copyright Bibliothèque du Prytanée

In these ways, the places where the boys studied and Father La Mésangère and the other Doctrinarians taught them, were truly "class" rooms. In this mandatory public spectacle of high birth and affluence or lack thereof, the teachers and students were both actors and audience.[12] Even in schools like Napoleon's cadet academy at Brienne, where social differences were mostly hidden by look-alike uniforms, educational institutions could prove a breeding ground for pride, resentment, and shame.[13] Again, as at Brienne, the all-male education at La Flèche sometimes worked at cross-purposes to the school's supposedly normalizing objectives and ideals.

BOYS TOGETHER, BOYS APART, SOME IN DRESSES

In Napoleon's military school, as in Father La Mésangère's and his compatriot Besnard's schooling, up to and including the seminary, the absence of women and girls was a constitutive principle, not an accident.[14] In the Doctrinarian middle school in La Flèche, five nuns oversaw meals, and there were several female nurses. Nevertheless, the six hundred or so students, teachers, domestics, valets, tutors, cooks, and groundskeepers were male. While the wealthiest students could pay for private accommodations, the other boarders slept together in large rooms in which "thirty, forty, and sometimes fifty beds" had been piled, "separated by wooden partitions that formed alcoves or cells," intended to prevent close relations.[15]

In addition to strict regulations and physical barriers at La Flèche, surveillance was believed essential to maintain order both physical and moral.[16] No fraternization was to take place unless "the warder or the *préfet des mœurs*" was there to monitor what went on. The boys "were forbidden from going into another's alcove or cell under any pretext even to ask for papers, quills or books." When something untoward happened, "the curtain had to be opened entirely."[17] Thus, a space that seemed to promise privacy and safety could instantly become a stage for public humiliation.[18] At night, "a servant would make uninterrupted rounds of the dormitory from bedtime to one o'clock in the morning, at which time he would be relieved by another who continued the watch until dawn."[19]

As in Greek mythology, where Argus is the perfect watchman for the jealous goddess Hera because his hundred eyes allow him to see everything, this system was to guarantee surveillance.[20] As a consequence, boys in boarding schools grew up thinking it was normal to be monitored day and night and to suspect that a simple request or gesture of friendship in the dormitory was a slippery slope into mischief, cheating, roughhousing, or sexual relations. Nevertheless, the fact that close relationships among boys, as with Besnard and the handsome young seminarian, Craon, were deemed illicit and had to remain closeted did not banish intimacy, curiosity, fantasies, or desires at Brienne, the seminary, or the school at La Flèche.

The Doctrinarians' Jesuit precursors, who had been in charge of the school for 169 years, from 1604 to 1773, took a very strict line on gender distinctions: They forbade the schoolboys anything of the kind, including taking on female roles in theatrical performances.[21] By contrast, Father La Mésangère's order, which ran the school beginning in 1776, expanded the boys' homosocial world to permit, and sometimes even require them to play everything from "nymphs and dryads, bacchantes and furies" to juicier parts such as "goddesses and queens," and to do so in dresses or robes, not trousers or breeches. To boost wealthy students' chances on the elite marriage market, the school also offered dancing lessons at a price and under similarly paradoxical conditions. Without girls or women with whom to learn and practice, the young men were compelled to take the lady's part or to play the gentleman to a lightly bearded "lady."[22]

As clear exceptions to gender rules, drama productions and dance instruction reinforced dominant ideas about "natural" differences even as they suspended, temporarily, fixed and narrow definitions of what young men could be, do, and want.[23] Being the "female" dance partner, playing the huntress Diana or the disconsolate Dido, or just watching other boys and young men do so, showed that it was possible to assume the "wrong" gender roles, affects, values, and costumes even if these might suggest or provoke same-sex intimacy. Despite the institutional, logistical, practical, and moral impediments to aberrations, in this all-male setting, flirting with deviations from the conventional norms was crucial to instructing boys in heteronormativity.

By the 1780s, when Father La Mésangère entered the Doctrinarian order and was hired to teach at La Flèche, this idea of mild yet permissible divergence from the straight and narrow was even more apposite for men who sought ordination—especially teaching priests. They had always been hybrids—clerical but also secular—but their profession was gradually permitting modest secular luxuries and liberties.

LESS DOCTRINARIAN

About a century after the Church suppression of finery for its regular priests, teaching orders continued to urge their brethren to hew to "clerical modesty."[24] However, the understanding of that term grew more capacious over the decades.[25] In Paris, between 1753 and 1786, the amounts of clothing and allowance allotted for Fathers of Christian Doctrine was still humble, but it doubled. In Toulouse, between 1768 and 1780, they tripled.[26] Earlier in the century, changes in the amount of footwear permitted were even more remarkable. From 1708 to 1718, all Doctrinarians were strictly limited to two new pairs of shoes every five years. For those who had grown up as members of the higher classes, this would have constituted a significant renunciation of comfort and pride. By contrast, thirty years later, which was still before Father La Mésangère's day, Doctrinarian priests' allowance paid for two pairs per year for a total of ten pairs every five years.[27] Although hardly a consumer frenzy, this change represented a 400 percent increase. It was an investment not only in individual Doctrinarians' comfort and pride but also in the order's ability to attract and retain future novitiates.

Over the course of the mid-eighteenth century, the pressure from the religious teaching orders to liberalize their orders' rules brought about an incremental revolution. The young men of some social standing who were drawn to teaching sects were no longer keen to give up all their privileges. Meanwhile, those lower down on the social ladder counted on getting the advantages they dreamed of by joining the order. This made Father La Mésangère who took holy, lifetime vows to obey the order's rules, wear its costume, live with his brethren, teach, and practice chastity, in the minority. Eighty-five percent of Doctrinarians in his day made a simple promise, which is to say something on which it would be easy to renege.

Doctrinarians' religious obligations no longer included attending prayers "every morning and evening." They simply had "to attend mass on Sundays and saints' days."[28] In their personal time, Father La Mésangère and his peers could go out unaccompanied and unchaperoned and take one meal per day away from their brethren. They could "even receive women in [their] room[s]."[29] There is no mention of receiving men. Perhaps this meant that there was a presumption that nothing untoward could or would happen. If so, the idea of greater liberty had been extended to individual privacy: What went on in a Doctrinarian's room presumably stayed there. In these later years, the new secularism extended to Doctrinarians' pedagogy, which favored new and often controversial Enlightenment ideas and values, including nondogmatic approaches to Church teachings and respectful and more egalitarian attitudes toward students.[30]

Doctrinarians of Father La Mésangère's generation knew that teaching would be "arduous." Nevertheless, like their recent predecessors, they also expected to live "in comfort" rather than practice constant self-abnegation.[31] The order had by then abolished the vows of poverty that had been in effect for hundreds of years and even refused to use the word "poverty," preferring to speak of "clerical modesty."[32] Just as important, the new regulations allowed Doctrinarians who had access to private money to inherit, keep their income, and spend it as they pleased. From that point on, all Doctrinarians were part of the larger fraternity, but distinctions in wealth and status would be visible in their attire and in their private furnishings.

DRESSING UP: OLD AND NEW HABITS

Under this new, more moderate regimen, a Doctrinarian now had choices. The traditional cumbersome ankle-length cassock with a small stand-up collar and a rosary hanging from a cord at his waist (see figure 2.2) was no longer required. The other option was a dark, fitted, knee-length cassock with black breeches and stockings. This choice gave a Doctrinarian a sleek, "two-legged," columnar look more in line with what secular men of the elite wore. Not only did the short habit show they *had* legs; it also displayed them. Whether the teaching priest wore a robe or breeches, the traditional splash of clerical white at the neck would never be mistaken for a fashionable man's knotted white ascot, but it had a similarly

FIGURE 2.2 Traditional Doctrinarian priest's cassock. Colored engraving: "Doctrinairian," M. l'abbé Thiron, *Album historique des costumes religieux depuis l'établissement du Christianisme jusqu'à nos jours* (Librairie générale, 1869), 167.

Source: HathiTrust

dignifying effect. Insofar as women and nuns did not generally wear those particular collars, it also looked manly.

By the time Father La Mésangère was ordained in the mid-1780s, wigs, the ultimate upper-class luxury, which had been banned by the Doctrinarian order forty years before were now permitted.[33] As we saw with Besnard's comments on Father Limonas, if the wig was "short, modest, and uncurled," it was no longer a scandalous vanity.[34] Despite the purchase price and the cost and trouble it took to maintain them, a *perruque* came to be considered a teaching cleric's right. By the 1790s, it was a standard part of Doctrinarian dress, a sign of the wearer's corporate fidelity and class identification—if not necessarily his class identity at birth.[35]

As a result of these changes, on the one hand, the ordained teaching priests of the 1780s were still hybrids and identifiable as such; on the other hand, they looked much less like pastoral clergy or friars. Yet they would not be confused for worldly, style-conscious abbés either. If Doctrinarians pushed the boundaries, it was usually subtly and only at the edges—sometimes literally. Thus, in 1763, when the young Doctrinarian priest, Father Augustin Miquel, ordered six shirts from his tailor, he made two requests, the first for comfort, the second for aesthetic purposes: That "someone wear them first so that the cloth would not chafe" and that the shirts have "a pretty little edging and the customary pleats to wear when I go out."[36]

Life was easier in other ways as well. By 1780, each Doctrinarian school had an average of three domestics per ten teaching priests.[37] Well-to-do Doctrinarians could now bring their own furniture, have a private room with a fireplace, and engage a personal servant. Even those living in the country "did not walk anymore; or as little as possible." Rather than trudge along rough and often muddy byways, as commoners still did, they had the costly luxury of a carriage.[38] This was quite a different version of "renunciation" than previous teaching priests had known.

Under these more affluent conditions, Father La Mésangère and his colleagues would have experienced paradoxes familiar to consumer societies: Indulging in material wealth and pleasure can feel like an act of personal freedom and is often perceived as such. However, it is also a social constraint, as it was for Carlo Buonaparte at Louis XVI's royal court, where clothes did and should make the man even if it bankrupted his family. The Doctrinarian fraternity in the 1780s put so much stock in its members' proper appearance that for all its relative leniency, it explicitly forbade members from *looking* impoverished. To keep up the order's appearance of egalitarianism and clerical respectability, the Doctrinarians devised a universal clothing allowance so that all members could look the part.[39]

Given many Doctrinarians' personal wealth and their relative freedoms, one might expect them to have lorded their social superiority and greater wealth over their less fortunate brothers. That was what their precursors had done just decades before, in the 1740s, with ribbons, jewels, and short cassocks before the Church imposed the Great Religious Renunciation. Nevertheless, Jean de Viguerie, the order's historian, writes that Doctrinarian archives from the 1780s reveal few complaints about members dressing lavishly. By this time, Doctrinarians did not appear to covet the pastel silks and satins, delicately trimmed and embroidered waistcoats, frilly lace, and silver buckles that were still de rigueur for noblemen and those who wanted to pass as such. Instead, short cassocks and a wig turned out to be a good fit—neither too aristocratic and "feminine," like the dress of affected, ostentatious abbés in high society, nor too monkish and austere, like the garb worn by the Minim friars at Napoleon's middle school in Brienne. This form of moderation became the golden rule.

Father La Mésangère and his fellow Doctrinarians, a self-selected lot, were held in check not so much by rules and regulations, which had been essential in the decades after the crackdown, but rather by a common ethos of relative—but only relative—restraint as seen in their understated and uniform attire. In this sense, these secular-clerical hybrids were in sync with their secular counterparts who were already adopting similar looks in the name of other, related ideals: masculine, bourgeois, and, eventually, far more shocking, revolutionary ones as well.

The higher-ups in the Doctrinarian order continued making occasional reports about what their brethren were wearing, but the purpose had changed. No longer interested in condemning their peers' vanity and self-indulgence, these bulletins instead provided mild-mannered guidance about the newest acceptable kinds, amounts, and styles of consumption. By the 1780s, Doctrinarians were no longer constrained by the threat of punishment. They appear to have stayed voluntarily within the limited room for maneuvering they were given. In this sense, they were like others who were already following, or would soon follow, the principles of secular forms of masculine renunciation. Consider the irony. Even under the newly lenient clerical regime, teaching orders were still supposed to be at antipodes to the secular realm of fashion. Nevertheless, those clerical reports resembled nothing so much as the bare-bones factual descriptions of the latest styles in Donneau de Visé's *Mercure gallant* (1672–1724) renamed *Mercure de France* (1724-1825); however, this periodical also featured occasional rudimentary black and white illustrations of them.

A year after La Mésangère began teaching at La Flèche, François Buisson (1753–1814) made a name for himself by producing *Cabinet des Modes*, the first fashion magazine to feature elegant, hand-colored engravings in every issue. Perhaps it was unlikely that La Mésangère would have subscribed in those early days—it was an expensive, niche enterprise. However, early on, it was clear that this priest from the rural countryside was fascinated by everything that had to do with the French capital: its monuments and mores but also Parisian-style dress.

PARIS DREAMS AND DISCONTENT

Father La Mésangère first book was an anonymous, two-volume, 604-page small-format doorstop, published in 1790 or 1791 while he was still teaching at La Flèche. *Le Voyageur à Paris* [The Paris Traveler], subtitled "Picturesque and Moral Tableau of the Capital," offers an alphabetical guide to everything about Paris—from "Actresses (indispositions of)" to the famous Paris pleasure garden, "Waux-Hall in the Summer."[40] While most entries are short, warmed-over commonplaces and platitudes, some are lively and opinionated—even a tad risqué. This is especially true of the passages where Father La Mésangère mocks men in effeminate clothing overly eager, in his view, to put themselves on display. For example, he comes down hard on *les mignons*, the storied favorites of Henri III who continued to have a strong hold on the French imagination, were infamous for their "effeminate and unchaste apparel" and the lavish gifts and attention the king bestowed on them.[41] Father La Mésangère describes what the original *mignons* wore—"slit sleeves, hair pulled off the forehead and parted in the middle, a little hat adorned with a feather plume, [and] long, pointy shoes"—as a "burlesque getup." He also underscores the moral: Excess and peculiarity are never appropriate for (real) men. "You will see that a supposedly elegantly dressed man back then was not that different from those who want to claim the same distinction today."[42]

For all his prudish conventionality, criticizing fops and defending proper masculinity as moderation in *Voyageur à Paris*, Father La Mésangère also has an eye for excess, glamour, intemperance, and immodesty, which he delights in describing.[43] In the entry "Tight Breeches" (*Culottes étroites*), he again takes up men's fashions in the Renaissance—in this case, the codpiece. He writes: To cover the gap between "the two sheaths for the legs, a third was added," which "represented *au naturel* objects that modesty bids us not to name." "The codpiece," he continues, "was prettied up with fringe and bundles of ribbons surrounded by 'shoulders' called *mahoitres*," rolled-up padding that served as protection in military clothing.[44] Rather than condemn this practice, he calls attention to it and other things about the capital that he finds *piquants* (unusual, odd, peculiar, tantalizing). Certainly, writing about Paris while living in a backwater provincial town on the storied but staid campus of fellow Doctrinarians surrounded by students in uniform gave him a way to escape, even if it was mainly in his imagination, to what he saw as the naughty but exciting world of the capital. On this score, his views were at almost exact antipodes to Napoleon's.

In 1784, two years before Father La Mésangère moved to La Flèche, Napoleon, age fifteen, was already in Paris, living at the famous Ecole Royale Militaire. Like the other students being groomed to become military officers, he had a full class schedule and a demanding routine that gave him relatively little time for extracurricular outings in the city. This did not dissuade other cadets from urban escapades, but Napoleon saw relatively little of Paris and appears to have been mostly immune to its attractions and repelled by what he saw as moral degeneration and luxury outside the Ecole. Inside the famous school, however, he and his schoolmates had their first taste of strict regimentation but also conspicuous lavishness and surprising leniency. This, at any rate, is how the late nineteenth-century Napoleon biographer Arthur Chuquet represents Napoleon's time there, especially with respect to "improper" relations among the cadets.

But, first, how luxurious was the Ecole Royale Militaire? Chuquet describes the accommodations on the public floors as "tasteful and attractive." The parlor, used by visiting dignitaries and family, featured "benches and chairs offering short-pile upholstery patterned with green and white roses."[45] He notes that the school's staff of 190 far outnumbered the 150 cadets. Employees included Maurice the tailor and Derridole the wigmaker who "gave the young gentlemen [elegant] sticks of pomade rather than [cheap] candle ends" to style their hair.[46]

The students who boarded there were of two kinds. The first group, which included Napoleon, had survived the crucible of provincial military schools and passed difficult entrance exams. They received full royal scholarships to pay for tuition and board and the expensive livery that marked their rise in military rank. The second set of boarders were young noblemen who had no military training and had not had to take an entrance test, but their parents could afford the high costs of tuition, board, and the costly uniform. Unlike La Flèche, where Father La Mésangère's pupils' garb clearly separated the rich boarders from the poor boys living cheaply in town, the gentleman cadets and the wealthy aristocratic boarders with no military training were all "lodged, fed, and dressed alike, as junior military men."[47]

In this version of high-status egalitarianism, the habit did not make the monk. Those who were destined for a military career and those who were biding their time and living off their parents wore the exact same clothing. Nevertheless, the Ecole Royale Militaire brass took this uniform very seriously, sometimes changing the regulation garb as often as once a year, at tremendous cost. For example, when Napoleon first arrived, the yellow collar and white facings of the blue jacket uniform the year before now had to be red. Silver stripes on the sleeves had replaced trefoils. There was a new hat too, either "embroidered in silver or decorated with goatskin edging and a uniform button."[48] For barely adolescent boys, like Napoleon, who were unused to opulence at home and had been living in tawdry conditions in provincial military academies, the expensive fabrics, lavish accessories, and ostentatious display required of them were heady and perhaps also intimidating privileges.

The administrators and military brass at the Ecole Royale Militaire were of two minds about how lavish and lenient it should be. Many resisted the largesse being lavished upon the cadets, and they fought to establish serious reforms. In 1776, eight years before Napoleon enrolled, military authorities had shut down the Ecole for that very reason. They would do so again in 1797, eleven years after he left.[49] The war minister, Philippe Henri, marquis de Ségur (1751–1801), alleged that the Ecole Royale Militaire spent six times what military *collèges* in the provinces did with almost nothing to show for the prohibitive cost. Others continued to insist that ostentation was a necessary part of the cadets' education.[50] Still others objected to the school because it favored sons of the elite who had money and connections but not necessarily intelligence or talent.[51]

Although the Ecole Royale Militaire embraced material luxury and fancy uniforms, Chuquet states that rules were strictly enforced to ensure that the young boys being turned into men would have the right military stuff. This meant, in large part, the ability to obey orders.[52] According to Chuquet, "the school resembled a wartime town."[53] The cadets were awakened and called to meals and classes not by church bells but by the soldierly and heart-pounding rat-a-tat-tat of drums.[54] Everyday there were "drills, patrols, [and] sentinels," and constant, uninterrupted work, precisely calibrated by the minute for exercises, and by the second for everything else."[55]

This daily regimen lasted from reveille to lights out when servants locked the cadets in their cells. Like seminaries and single-sex boarding schools, the Ecole Royale Militaire prohibited close relations, let alone homosexual behavior, among boys and men. For such infractions, very harsh punishments—"prison, detention, and a diet of bread and water," were spelled out.[56] However, in case after case of this kind, War Minister Ségur preferred cover-up to penalties.[57]

UNDER WRAPS/IN THE OPEN

Two years before Napoleon arrived at the Ecole Royale Militaire, the superintendent of the barracks strongly urged Ségur to discipline three cadets. Since neither surveillance nor punishment had been effective restraints, he argued, they should be demoted and sent back to their provincial middle school. Ségur demurred. He let the cadets stay on campus under what he said would be heightened surveillance that may not have materialized.[58] Not long after, however, he rewarded the wayward cadets by authorizing their early transfer into the army, which amounted to a quick promotion. Explaining why he kept their misdeeds under wraps, Ségur took the high road, claiming he wanted to protect the cadets from false allegations, save them from public humiliation, and avoid inspiring "unhealthy ideas in their comrades."[59] According to this twisted logic, "don't ask, don't tell" was the byword—even though regulations demanded otherwise. Did the war minister turn a blind eye because he feared the allegations were true? It would appear so. To give any credence to them would cast shame on the cadets, which was also to say the school. Even stating their misdeeds would seem to have been regarded as infectious. However, concealing the facts also had another function: It saved face and honor for the Ecole Royale Militaire and Ségur personally.[60]

Chuquet's research into the surveillance and punishment of same-sex desire in the eighteenth-century French military confirms just such contradictions the better to blame Ségur for the hothouse same-sex environment and moral laxity of which the historian heartily disapproves. When it comes to Napoleon, however, Chuquet rushes to protect him from any possible charges of homosexual misconduct, let alone desires, during his time at the Ecole Royale Militaire.

Chuquet sets up a scene between the young Corsican and Laugier de Bellecour (1770–?), who had been one of the "nymphs" at Brienne, as a confrontation between good, "the grave, serious, austere Corsican" and evil, "the frivolous boy from Lorraine with dubious morals."[61] Chuquet writes that Laugier "conducted himself well [at the Ecole Royale Militaire] for the first six months of 1785" but "then degenerated" so much that "officers and teachers complained about him on a biweekly basis."[62] While leaving the exact nature of his wrongdoings vague, the moralizing language Chuquet and other historians use, along with complaints from the time, suggest gambling, sexual misbehavior, or both.[63] In this case too, believing that extra monitoring and punishment were not enough, army superiors urged the war minister to penalize Laugier by ordering him back to Brienne. Ségur once again chose to paper over the allegation, deferring punishment "provided that [Laugier] mend his bad behavior."[64]

At this point, Chuquet drops entirely what had been a fact-filled account based on official military archives. He offers instead an apocryphal, moralizing scene complete with dialogue ripped from the melodramas of the late eighteenth century. First, he recounts the circumstances and conveys the dialogue in indirect discourse: "Having noted that Laugier de Bellecour was falling out of line and degenerating," Chuquet writes, Napoleon "admonished [Laugier], ordering him to wrest himself away from his dangerous companions."[65] Chuquet then pretends to quote Napoleon's remarks directly, giving him the stilted, formal diction and absolute authority of a superior and a harsh moral judge: "'Sir, you have liaisons of whom I do not approve.'" Napoleon adds, "'I managed to keep your morals pure, but your new friends will ruin you.'" Having Napoleon set himself up as savior, Chuquet then has him issue an ultimatum: "'Choose between them and me; I give you no other choice; you must be a man and decide.'"[66] After the third time Laugier refuses this appeal to his male and military honor, Napoleon haughtily declares, "'Sir, you have scorned my advice, which is to say renounced my friendship; never speak to me again.'"[67]

In Chuquet's fictionalized account, the young Napoleon is a clear foil to Ségur's ostrich in the sand approach to scandal. The young man's take-no-prisoners version of manliness could not even countenance speaking to one of "those" kind of boys. Having branded Laugier immoral, Chuquet allows Napoleon to play not only "normal" but also moral to the nth degree, untainted by the "crime" of desire let alone sympathy, vulnerability, or even curiosity about his friend.[68] There are two villains in Chuquet's telling of the story: Ségur for his cowardly leniency and Laugier de Bellecour for his depravity. The hero, without a doubt, is Napoleon, whom Chuquet situates safely on the "right" side of what is to him a clear moral divide. Regardless, Napoleon had to leave the Ecole Royale Militaire the following year, 1785, for family and financial reasons.

AFTER SCHOOL

His father having died of stomach cancer the year before, regulations stipulated that under these circumstances, the orphaned Napoleon was no longer eligible for a royal fellowship. Squeezing the work of the final two years into one, he graduated in September of that year, barely in the twenty-fifth percentile of his class, "forty-second out of fifty-six students."[69] The egalitarianism that the Ecole Royale Militaire uniform seemed to promise cadets proved illusory for the boy named Napoleon. Although promoted to the rank of second lieutenant, as a son of the lower nobility, Bonaparte was relegated to the lowly artillery division.

Even there, the sixteen-year-old Bonaparte had the right, which was also an obligation, to suit up in a uniform even more gilded than that of the Ecole Royale Militaire cadet he had been. In addition to a "silver clasp at the throat," Bonaparte's new costume featured a "blue jacket with embroidered red cuffs, a muslin shirt with lace collar and cuffs, and the inevitable blue army breeches." He was also awarded the "much-coveted epaulet with gold fringe and a bright red silk cordon."[70] Other regulation gear included the black military bicorn (a hat with the brim turned up sharply on two sides) trimmed with a flat, round badge of gathered ribbons called a cockade. It was white—the color of the Bourbon royal line and a compulsory sign of allegiance to the French sovereign, thirty-one-year-old Louis XVI.

Napoleon's eye-catching second lieutenant uniform, the far more modest versions he and his peers had worn at Brienne, and the highfalutin varieties worn by the wealthy boys studying at La Flèche were a sharp contrast to the uniforms of a very large segment of the adult male population: the plain, dark costumes of judges, doctors, lawyers, parish clergymen, seminarians, and teaching priests, including Father La Mésangère. Despite the differences among them, all these versions of regulation attire marked boys and men as parts of all-male corporations—a mark of prestige and belonging but also a sign of livery. It was, in addition, a way of making the wearer conform to a norm and ideal that served to camouflage both conscious and unconscious deviations from it.

Once they were out of school, the majority did not and could not continue wearing the corporate attire of the army, the king, or the Church. Most probably reverted to civilian dress and the habits and values they had adopted growing up. Having lived in a highly regulated and uniformed all-male world, the return to "normalcy" would have been a big change—a relief to some and a loss to others. Leaving boarding school, privileged young men returning home were no longer expected to cohabit exclusively with men. At home, there were usually some female members of the household and, for moneyed families, female as well as male servants. In this "after-school" world, the copresence of the sexes (and sometimes different social classes) was not always de rigueur everywhere, but it was certainly requisite for many social activities. Eligible young men on the marriage market were expected to socialize in contexts where the second sex was not only present but often held sway as, for example, in elite gatherings called *salons*. Other points of continuity with their previous school life were the omnipresence of Catholic figures of authority. Abbés circulated in polite society, and parish priests could regularly be seen going about their business at Mass and in town. The teaching priests and friars who had earlier supervised these newly adult men would later teach some of their former charges' sons.

For boys and men changing back to civilian and secular attire meant freedom from institutional regulations. On the other hand, like everyone else on the social spectrum, they were expected to wear clothing that conformed to their line of work, social status, and gender—just as they had at school. Yet change was in the air.

MORE GOODS, MORE CHOICES

In 1776, Louis XVI issued an edict abolishing the French guilds, which had long restricted, regulated, and monopolized the production of French goods. Although revoked soon after, the restrictions on guilds were partially reinstated the next year.[71] Eventually, pressures to open markets further increased the production of goods, including clothing and accoutrements, and sometimes at more affordable prices.[72] This began to change consumers' expectations and desires. For the elite, wearing the exact same clothing and style day after day or week after week would begin to seem odd, if not downright déclassé. Especially in urban areas, for men and women who could afford it and were anxious to prove their worth and social status, dressing properly would increasingly require more than a modicum of originality and inventiveness or, at the very least, some fashionable variation over time.

Choosing one's civilian dress *could* be pleasurable, but it might also be fraught. In the absence of hard and fast rules, especially during a time of changing mores and social tensions, such a decision exposed a person's individual taste, ambition, personality, disposable income, and class status. In addition, notions of good taste, let alone fashion, were famously unpredictable and not universally shared. Few of the changing rules of attire were set down in print during this period. The well-to-do might wonder how tightly men's *culottes* were supposed to hug their thighs, how big was too big for silver shoe buckles, and how high was too high for a woman's wig. One obvious way to find out was observing what one's equals and betters were wearing in town, at Mass, and on social occasions. Gossip and correspondence with friends and relations supplemented firsthand knowledge, albeit with varying degrees of reliability. Given the increasingly rapid change of styles, elite dressmakers and tailors began sending monthly packages to their customers containing small beeswax dolls decked out in the latest fashionable and court styles.[73]

Loosening guild restrictions also "opened the market to a flood of illustrated fashion material."[74] For the upper crust, large-format anthologies offered hundreds of fine engravings showing the "diversity of costumes of various social classes and nations" or the latest styles for both genders. However, the volumes were exorbitantly priced and unwieldy.[75] In addition, published as infrequently as twice a year, the fashions highlighted in these anthologies might be out of style by the time they were in print.[76] There would be no modern fashion magazine, which is to say regular and timely updates about *la mode* with color illustrations, until 1785. These were *not*, as readers today might assume, a periodical for, about, and by women.[77] The job was almost entirely one for men, and the magazines were for and about men too.

THE FASHION PRESS: MEN'S WORK, PRECARIOUS BUSINESS

As it happens, the first modern fashion magazine, *Cabinet des Modes* [Fashion Cabinet] was sent to subscribers in Paris, the provinces, and outside France in October 1785. That same month, Napoleon left the capital to join his regiment in Valence, in southwestern France. Had the young officer heard of this new kind of magazine, he would presumably have dismissed it out of hand as something for women and for suspect men, like his brother Joseph, who cared too much about frivolities. Nevertheless, many men, among them fellow officers of Napoleon who took pride in their own appearance and interest in others', would have disagreed. So would the men behind the new kind of magazine, even if they were unlikely to have had the means to buy the new styles featured in it.

Journalism in France was an almost exclusively male hardscrabble job that paid a pittance.[78] Like priests and soldiers in their respective domains, men associated with the leisure press were often small cogs in a vast system devised for the pleasure and profit of others. Their job was to serve as intermediaries between members of the wealthy classes and those who designed, made, and sold stylish clothing to them. They were, like Napoleon and Father La Mésangère, almost always outsiders from the provinces come to Paris to seek their fortune.

The first modern fashion editor, Buisson came from Grenoble where he had spent almost two decades as an apprentice and then a journeyman in the book trade before moving to Paris. In 1785, at the age of thirty-one, the fledgling but ambitious bookseller and publisher had secured funding from the French textile industry, among others, who were willing to invest in a potentially lucrative business.[79] However, for Buisson and his financial backers, it was also a risky enterprise. The exquisite engravings on offer in every issue required a multistep, labor-intensive process. The women who colored the engravings by hand were not terribly well paid, but the operation was a significant expense.[80] The sole source of advertising income consisted of occasional product placement and the promotion of particular stores, tailors, dressmakers, *modistes*, and haberdashers. As a result, an annual subscription was a steep, twenty-one livres, which meant that readers primarily consisted of the affluent and the elite tradesmen and women who served them.[81] Those who could afford the lower subscription fees for entrance to a commercial library would have swelled the ranks of readers, although not the editor's or publisher's profits or subscription numbers.

Published every ten days, the magazine was a small-format, eight-page publication that featured three high-quality colored fashion engravings. The first two to four pages of each issue offered detailed descriptions of the styles shown in the images as well as others supposedly spotted on the street or featured by designers or modistes. The remaining content consisted of short, generally anonymous articles, from reviews of books or plays to amusing or newsy anecdotes, and some light poetry. However, the images and the news about the latest styles were the main novelty, visual appeal, and selling point.

Except for the publisher Buisson, who was listed along with his address, no one else involved on the editorial side of the operation was named. In the fashion bulletins, a detached voice spoke as a neuter *on* (one, people) or *nous* (we) or, occasionally, a male "I" with masculine adjectives.[82] The result was an editor who had, or took on, a male voice but remained invisible to his readers. I call this stance typical of journalistic prose Invisible Man.[83] As was common practice, the short miscellany, poems, and the like were sometimes signed. However, these signatures ("Mme P***," "le marquis de C***") were often so vague or truncated that they appeared to be pseudonyms and could, in any case, easily hide the identity, gender, and class status of the authors.

On the one hand, authorship in this magazine was just one of many "closets" in which anyone might hide but over which men ruled. On the other hand, neither the editor nor the journalists evidence self-consciousness or discomfort about being "in" fashion, which readers at the time might have seen as a "feminine" domain. As *Cabinet des Modes* proudly announces: Caring about how one looks is the very essence of being human and, especially, French.[84]

WHAT'S IN THIS *CABINET*?

Buisson's title for the magazine, *Cabinet des Modes* implies the class status of the readers he sought to attract and his own high ambitions for the journal. The French word *cabinet* referred to furniture for storing and displaying precious objects, as in English, which for the fashion periodical would be its fine, color engravings and perhaps the pearls of information and leisure reading the magazine offered. As we have seen, "*cabinet*" could also refer to small, enclosed spaces such as dressing rooms, studies, and privies in upper-class homes or a sovereign's residence, which were only accessible to insiders and servants (see the introduction). In that sense, the periodical offered a "private" place to reflect, share secrets, and give and receive valuable advice. "*Cabinet*" could also connote foppish elegance and moral dissipation, as it did with Henri III's unofficial cabinet of favorites. In sum, the word *cabinet* evoked many of the meanings we now associate with closets: luxury and privilege, exclusivity and privacy, confidentiality and authority, along with basic bodily necessities and potentially licentious freedom.[85]

Despite some of these louche associations, the editorial voice in *Cabinet des Modes* mixed the high-mindedness of a would-be *philosophe* with the hype of a huckster. Fully pro-luxury, the magazine ambitiously pitched the high life and consumption not only as naturally human but also as guarantors of happiness and prosperity for the "civilized world," which is to say the continent. With this new kind of periodical, Buisson boasts, "All the Nations of Europe will have the pleasure of being educated quite expeditiously about the most convenient, newest, and most tasteful fashions."[86] Furthermore, he claims, this little magazine with big aspirations is of universal interest because caring about how one looks has been, "in all times, in all places," the most fundamental of traits for both "savage" and "civilized" alike.[87] Caring about one's attire was, moreover, tied to definitions of normalcy as heterosexuality: "The two sexes have always dressed up in the desire to please the other through adornment."[88]

As if to prove it, the editorial voice frequently pronounces itself thoroughly, happily, and explicitly male and heteronormative. For instance, it goes so far as to encourage fashions for women that were inspired by men's styles. Speaking in the first-person plural, "We freely admit that this way of dressing pleases us enormously."[89] In another case, speaking for himself and others, the editor gushes about one woman's attire: "We saw an attractive woman 'of the highest quality, a perfect woman' in a stylish outfit and decided to represent her in the issue's first fashion plate." Shielding her from intimations of vanity, the editorial voice states that she "was assuredly unaware of the effect she was having [on us]." He avows that "There may be a little bit of overenthusiasm in our reaction. But there were several of us, and we all had the same feelings. May that excuse us."[90] The editor usually plays it straight in just these ways. However, his definition of normal is not narrow. *Cabinet des Modes* saucily declares that men had an additional reason for wanting to look good: "to attract the attention of [their] male companions."[91] Was the motivation one-upmanship, appreciation, envy, desire? Or all four?

Cabinet des Modes lasted a year (October 1785 to October 1786)—a strong showing for a costly, brand-new kind of magazine. Its replacement, from the same publisher in a very similar format, was a close variation on the theme but with a cosmopolitan twist.

DISIDENTIFICATION WITH THE FRENCH

The new title as of November 1786 was *Magasin des Modes Nouvelles Françaises et Anglaises* [The Magazine of New French and English Fashions] and it went beyond general cosmopolitanism. On questions of *la mode*, the two countries had long been engaged in a snarky rivalry. The typical French attitude in *Cabinet des Modes* had been that "the French," which in this case meant French men as much as women, had a natural genius for steering clear of somber, look-alike, unchanging, and understated attire. Englishmen's styles were stodgy, dull, and uniform by comparison with Frenchmen's ever-changing, inventive, and elaborate fashions.[92] The magazine's motto, "One day, uniformity gave birth to boredom," which appears on the first page of every issue, could even be read as a slight against upper-class Englishmen.[93]

However, *Magasin des Modes Nouvelles Françaises et Anglaises* grudgingly admitted that "today," in France, "the only real variation [between the two countries] is in the color."[94] In effect, the fashion magazine editor Buisson was complaining that the Great Masculine Renunciation of fashion, which had begun across the English Channel, was beginning to contaminate French men's attire.[95] As if to prove this point, just six months into the journal's run, in the May 20, 1787 issue, and without forewarning or follow-up, *Magasin des Modes Nouvelles Françaises et Anglaises* did the unthinkable. It trumpeted the highly heretical English notion that fashion historians now associate with the Great Masculine Renunciation. Men, even French men, it confidently asserts, are *not* "called upon by nature or by their social rank to work at being attractive." The journal added, "God forbid we should reproach [men] for this!" After all, "Their sex, too inept at this, would be all too ridiculous."[96] Instead, men "should leave these cares to the other sex, naturally finer and more pleasing" who "seem to have been born for no other purpose." It concludes that "any other responsibility [for women] seems to us entirely *unnatural*."[97] In sum, there was to be no room for anything that smacked of femininity in a man, and, as a corollary, women were the only ones who should care about being appealing—and fashionable.

This view was an aberration in the journal. Previous issues and later ones, too, often asserted the exact opposite: Fashion was naturally French and for men. Nevertheless, the statements in this single issue were a bellwether of the Great Masculine Renunciation that would eventually become not only the new norm but the new ideal in France. Throughout its two-year run, *Magasin des Modes Nouvelles* often recommended "English" restraint in men's styles in contrast with aristocratic French extravagance in dress. For example, the editor offers the following advice: "The best, undoubtedly, would be to take the middle road between two extremes because that is the goal that one should always try to achieve in everything."[98] Here, we find an echo of teaching priests' compromise with the secular attire of the male elite: the new, short black cassock and breeches with a powdered wig as their only costly luxury. This kind of choice made them part of the lay world, but not too much a part. In line with the magazine's anti-luxury attitude, *Magasin des Modes Nouvelles* often trotted out French popinjays as examples *not* to follow. The December 10, 1786 issue reproaches French men for wearing so many layers around their neck they look strangled. Eleven months later, the magazine ridicules fops whose gloves feature satin embroidery in a contrasting color.[99]

Magasin des Modes Nouvelles praises men who avail themselves of their masculine privilege as observers. The editor notes: "Try finding a young man who, upon seeing a woman who looks good from behind, has not run around immediately to see what her face looks like."[100] But the following sentence makes a ninety-degree turn: "Who among us has not been seduced by the elegant figure of a young woman, or even of a young man, whom we have only seen from behind?"[101] The question is rhetorical. A man, or presumably even a woman, getting a good look at someone good-looking, no matter their gender, is an equal opportunity pastime.

Despite the lip service it gives to cosmopolitanism, *Magasin des Modes Nouvelles* also exhibits French chauvinism. The periodical sometimes uses French *petits maîtres* as foils to show the inferiority of *English* gentlemen. One typically catty pronouncement: "Our *petits maîtres* should not be counting very much on the help of Englishmen" on new fashions: "If the English are wearing some form of attire today, they will be doing the same in six months."[102] Sometimes, a new French style, even one featured as an engraving, could be a target of attack for overdoing it. This is the case in the July 11, 1789 issue of *Magasin des Modes Nouvelles*'s fastidiously detailed description of the dapper young man pictured in the illustration: a white silk *culotte* lined in white taffeta, a white waistcoat with polished steel buttons, and white stockings featuring "sky blue embroidery on the sides."[103] Rather than elevate this style, the periodical makes a sardonic rebuke: "Steel [buttons] on silk!" and "a double-breasted jacket"; this might "keep the chest warm in winter, but in the middle of July? Good Lord, what capriciousness!"[104]

As *Magasin des Modes Nouvelles Françaises et Anglaises* underscores, although Dame Fashion's imperatives changed less often under the "English regime," they were also far subtler. This meant that outsiders would have a harder time getting the details right. For example, the width of the English jockey cap's very narrow brim, which had been "two to three inches at most," this year has none; last year, the crown was very high, now it is medium; sometimes "the band is silk or velvet or there's no band at all." Hats these days are "cinched with a medium-sized black ribbon."[105] Paradoxically, even the simplifying trend in men's clothing presumably made male readers more, not less, dependent on the self-declared "missionaries of fashion" behind the fashion press who could, and did, spell out all these fine points for them.[106] One thing these "missionaries" stayed well clear of, however, was radical politics.

KEEPING MUM

The occasional mockery of French fops and praise of English styles in *Magasin des Modes Nouvelles* made it an outlier, but it was, like *Cabinet des Modes*, almost entirely pro-French. In both magazines, there were only occasional and very tame allusions to political events or debates. The editor was not about to risk its French readers' displeasure, let alone the wrath of the king's censors. Thus, in the first months of 1789, *Magasin des Modes Nouvelles* makes no mention of the calamitous drought, colossal debt, or violent social unrest in the country, which included a popular riot in April in Seurre that Second Lieutenant Bonaparte and a detachment of about a hundred men successfully put down.

As of May, the political and economic dissatisfaction had become so dire that Louis XVI was forced to call a meeting of the Estates General, which is to say representatives of the three orders of French society, the clergy, the noblemen, and the

Third Estate for the first time in 175 years. *Magasin des Modes Nouvelles* says nothing about this either, even though much of the controversy was sartorial. Initially, all three estates were required to wear uniforms according to their class status: First Estate (the clergy), Second Estate (noblemen) and Third Estate (commoners). Art historian Richard Wrigley notes that many protested that sartorial distinctions of this kind were "false distinctions of identity" and "invidious" insults to the Third Estate's freedom, an "indecent masquerade," and a "superfluous distraction from more serious matters of political debate and legislation."[107]

Instead of citing any of these fighting words, the June 1, 1789 issue of *Magasin des Modes Nouvelles* reported the following, which passed for news fit to print: "Summer approaches; fruits are abundant in summer; Ladies gather them; they need pretty little baskets to put them in."[108] Meanwhile, the convocation of the Estates General solved little, and popular riots exploded all over the country. These too went unmentioned.

On the other hand, the same issue includes two short, comic anecdotes. Although set safely back in the distant past, they had direct implications for these tense political times.[109] In both, what elicited a public flare of resentment was *not* what a woman, or women, wore but the attire of male *parvenus*. The first story involves a man at the opera who finds his view of the stage blocked by another man's hairpiece. Taking justice into his own hands, he grabs the wig and throws it to the floor. The de-wigged man retorts, "Six months ago, you wouldn't have done such a thing." "And why is that?" demands the exasperated operagoer. "Because I didn't used to wear a wig," comes the reply.[110] This privilege, traditionally reserved for those of rank or specific professions, was being claimed by those wealthy enough to own a *perruque* but "unworthy" of the honor. The anecdotes underscore that wigs and other signs of privilege could be mere social pretention easily exposed.[111]

In June and July of 1789, just such conflicts among the classes were occurring around the country, albeit on a grand scale and with far more serious consequences. None would be more cataclysmic than the series of events that began on July 14. These shocking developments put *Magasin des Modes Nouvelles*—not to mention anyone appearing in public in France—on notice. The idea of curbing fashion and luxury, which had long been the practice among many of the provincial elite, regular clergymen, and teaching priests, was about to become one of the few, officially sanctioned new looks for members of the elite who hoped to keep their heads. Yet, for a long while, all it took to pass patriotic muster was the ultimate new French accessory: a badge in red (it was actually nacarat, an orange-red), white, and blue.

Chapter Three

FASHIONING UNIFORM MEN FOR THE FRENCH REVOLUTION

THE UNPRECEDENTED events of July 1789 and the ten years of radical social and political upheaval that followed forced approximately twenty-eight million to change at the very least how they dressed—if not what they believed. Bonaparte would try to play it both ways—France and Corsica, the monarchy and the Revolution—but eventually he would have to choose sides. Like all other clergymen and women, Father La Mésangère was forced to abandon his clerical robe and renounce his vows or risk exile, political violence, or death. Meanwhile, Buisson's *Magasin des Modes Nouvelles Françaises et Anglaises*, France's only fashion magazine at the time, went through its own makeover. For six months, it celebrated the Revolution as an opportunity for French men and women to buy luxurious, revolutionary-themed clothing and urged upper-class men to go easy on the new passion for uniformity and uniforms so as not to lose their "innate" French flair for *la mode.*

But by early 1790, under a new editor, Le Brun, who renamed the magazine *Journal de la Mode et du Goût* [Journal of Fashion and Taste], started taking the exact opposite tack. He insisted that true male patriots keep their distance from fashion and anything else considered potentially effeminate. The journal so politicized this "apolitical" genre meant as leisure reading that it mixed illustrations and descriptions of the latest elegant attire with anti-revolutionary screeds, mean-spirited caricatures, and anticlerical pornography.

■ ■ ■

In 1789, the 14th of July fell on a Tuesday. So did the infamous Bastille prison in Paris and more than ninety French soldiers and civilians killed during the bloody confrontations that day.[1] Neither Second Lieutenant Napoleon Bonaparte nor Father La Mésangère were in Paris during the early months of the Revolution.[2] Yet, like millions of others, they would have heard about, seen depictions of, and, in Bonaparte's case, participated in some of the most shocking events of the period. These were harbingers of a future in which the smallest details of costume could be a matter of life and death, and gender would become more strictly defined and monitored than social class.

WHAT TO WEAR TO THE REVOLUTION[3]

Early in the day on July 14, 1789, a ragtag group of about one thousand gathered around the docks on the Seine near the town hall in Paris. Fearful that Louis XVI's mercenaries would soon enter the city to crush the fomenting rebellion against the monarchy, they set off on a quixotic mission. With nothing more than rifles, pikes, and improvised weapons, they marched to the Bastille prison to seize the sizable cache of arms and ammunition there. A crowd of insurgents was already starting to pull down the fortress stone by stone. To their surprise, the governor of the Bastille, Bernard-René Jourdan Marquis de Launay, finding himself surrounded and outnumbered, eventually agreed to a ceasefire.

Meanwhile, suspecting that they were being double-crossed, other insurrectionaries marched the Marquis de Launay to the town hall. There, he was stabbed repeatedly and shot several times, after which an unemployed cook named Desnot took a knife and severed de Launay's head. Nearby, an unknown assassin shot the mayor of Paris, Jacques de Flesselles, an aristocrat who was believed to harbor royalist sympathies. By evening, both noblemen's heads had been mounted on pikes and were paraded through the streets of Paris.[4]

An engraving from the period (see figure 3.1) offers a traditional portrait of the Marquis de Launay in his powdered wig, lace cravat, and frock coat, looking elderly, stern, and resolute. Underneath, on a very diminished scale, we see his balding head on a pike, still bleeding, without his wig. Below his name and title, the caption reads: "Decapitated 14 July 1789 after ordering that the crowd be fired upon even though they were waving a white flag of surrender"—a statement that does not fit most historians' accounts of the incident.[5]

FIGURE 3.1 "The Marquis de Launay: In Life and After Death." Engraving. Portrait of the Marquis de Launay painted by Count Cagliostro, engraved by Chenon père; below, an etching of his balding, decapitated head on a pike.

Source: Chenon, "Le Marquis de Launay," Bibliothèque nationale de France, 1789

That day, de Launay, de Flesselles, other royal officers, and many less notable Parisians were assassinated because of what they were doing. But sometimes it was simply a matter of how their political views and class status were perceived based on their wardrobe. In this new era, all clothing was taken as a rallying sign, which made it a high-stakes political gamble for everyone in France, even the king.

Just three days after the siege of the Bastille, throngs of French men and women assembled in front of the town hall for another unprecedented occasion. As one of his first official acts as Paris's new mayor, Jean-Sylvain Bailly (1736–1793), a commoner, astronomer, and mathematician, did the unthinkable. Defying centuries of royal protocol, he approached His Majesty without permission, presumptuously handing him a new cockade that had been devised just days before.[6] Eager to herald a new order, insurgents had added to the all-white Bourbon cockade concentric circles of ribbons in blue and orange-red. The latter colors symbolized the city of Paris and, by extension, the citizens who had defied the king's authority and made rubble of his royal fort.[7] At any other time, Louis XVI would probably have ignored the gesture or stepped on the offending cockade with his elegant, heeled pumps. Instead, wildly outnumbered by his rebellious subjects, he held the tricolor cockade up high, plainly visible against his royal white hat. The assembled crowd reportedly erupted in cheers.[8]

However, just a few days later, on July 19 and 20, 1789, there was rioting in the town of Auxonne in eastern France. Second Lieutenant Napoleon Bonaparte was ordered to lead a detachment of artillery soldiers to put down the "boatmen, porters, and peasants" who were attacking "the tax offices and the homes of the wealthy."[9] In a letter to his brother, Bonaparte underscored and deplored the benevolence of the officer in charge. General du Teil "did not want to fire or do too much harm" to the rioters, and "only three of the thirty-three imprisoned would be hung."[10] However, the violent, popular uprising did not end there, and it would be met with ever fiercer royal crackdowns.

The third astonishing event took place less than three weeks after the fall of the Bastille. In early August, the self-declared National Constituent Assembly abolished noble privileges and feudal rights. By the end of the month, it had proclaimed freedom of religious opinions and freedom of speech. It also adopted the *Declaration of the Rights of Man and of the Citizen*, which begins, "Men are born and remain free and equal in rights. Social distinctions may be founded only upon the general good."[11] The notion of being the subject of a monarch was giving way to an idea of citizenship as a matter of individual rights and freedoms. Furthermore, an increasingly activist and powerful legislative assembly was supposed to hold the king in check. These and other new notions of Frenchness, masculinity, and patriotism would eventually alter the costume and badges that all French men and women would be allowed, encouraged, and obliged to wear. Later, women were prevented from wearing some of them. As corporate men, neither Father La Mésangère nor Second Lieutenant Bonaparte had the right to refashion or accessorize their regulation attire without the official permission of their superiors.

For those who feared this brave new revolutionary world, the fact that boys in boarding schools, parish priests, seminarians, teaching clergy, military cadets, and officers were *not* immediately required to alter their costume would have been reassuring. It was a sign that two pillars of traditional French society, the Church and the army, were holding firm against the waves of upheaval and uncertainty sweeping the country. For those of a revolutionary bent, however, clerical and military garb made those wearing it both suspect and loathsome. Thus, facing the populist rage of the rioters in Auxonne, the second lieutenant's blue officer's uniform, far from a matter of prestige and respect, made him an ideal target. Similarly, for those convinced that the Catholic Church was the Revolution's mortal enemy, Father La Mésangère's teaching costume, a black cassock (or the more secular equivalent, a black frock coat and *culotte*) and white collar, would have made him a target of insults or worse.

And yet being middlemen identified with powerful institutions had an advantage. Bonaparte and Father La Mésangère, forbidden to make their own decisions regarding the revolutionary tricolor cockade meant that the responsibility lay with the corporation that gave the orders. However, as with generations of boys and men with religious or military affiliations, regulation attire did not *necessarily* make the boy or man what he appeared to be. Thus, Bonaparte's Royal Army officer attire allowed him to pass as a loyal subject of Louis XVI even as he continued to feel deep antipathy for the French occupiers of his homeland, which is to say officers and soldiers dressed in the king's uniform.[12] During the first three years of the Revolution, between 1789 and 1792, Bonaparte spent two-thirds of that time in Corsica. At some points, he was on military leave, but for most of it, he was still officially in service to His Majesty, the French king.[13] Nevertheless, neither Bonaparte's uniform nor his position stopped him from conspiring to oust the French from Ajaccio on June 25, 1790.[14]

Historian Patrice Gueniffy notes that back on the mainland with his regiment—first in Auxonne, then in Valence, where he was promoted to lieutenant in February 1791, Bonaparte "did not find the pleasant society he had frequented before the Revolution." While "he had not long before tried to learn the manners of the Old Regime's social world," now he frequently "met with bitter comments from former friends, all hostile to the Revolution. A full-fledged 'patriot,' he bravely stood up to them," but he found himself in a nation bitterly divided.[15]

Father La Mésangère's situation was also advantageous and dangerous but in different ways. On the one hand, his status as a priest protected him from military conscription. On the other hand, the same month that the National Constituent Assembly declared the rights of man, it abolished the Catholic Church's considerable tax privileges and lucrative tithing practices, diminishing its powers considerably.[16] A few months later, the National Assembly started selling off Church treasures, buildings, and property to fill the nation's empty coffers. From that point on, Father La Mésangère's Doctrinarian costume, like that of countless other ecclesiastics, was no longer a sign of his privileged and protected position but rather his increasingly precarious social and political status.

Those in the costumes of state and Church were not the only targets of wrath during this period of intense factionalism and violence. Everything anyone wore, said, or did could be considered an expression of political partisanship. Thus, throughout the revolutionary period, donning the tricolor cockade (or not), choosing luxurious or ostentatious clothing, or even, as historian Lynn Hunt writes, wearing "a color . . . a certain length of trousers, certain shoe styles, or the wrong hat" could incite "a quarrel, a fistfight, or a general street brawl."[17] No matter what side one was on, during the Revolution, everyone had reason to find fault with others' appearance.

Could *Magasin des Modes Nouvelles Françaises et Anglaises*, a periodical that had been promoting luxury, taste, and elegance to its wealthy subscribers since 1786, survive a Revolution that urged upper-class and wealthy men to give up caring about all three and their wives and daughters to ease up on their taste for *la mode*? Its publisher, Buisson, hoped so.

REVOLUTIONARY CHANGES

The first issue of the periodical to appear after the fall of the Bastille on the 14th, was dated just seven days later, July 21, 1789, although it was probably several weeks late.[18] Buisson's magazine utters not a word about armed resistance or wigless heads on pikes. However, the periodical does abruptly change its tone and tune. Abandoning the gallant flattery and braggadocio of its first two and a half years, the journal takes on a more serious tenor, more in line with the new political realities, although it treats these gingerly. Referring to "the all-too-famous and unfortunate circumstances that Paris finds itself in" and the "dire catastrophes that have happened to us," the vague wording and passive voice neither assign blame nor take responsibility. But the editorial persona in Buisson's *Magasin des Modes Nouvelles Françaises et Anglaises* also makes a daring move: officially embracing the bloody and polarizing revolt. Using the pronoun "we/one" (*on*), as if speaking for the entire nation, it declares: "We no longer want these [class] distinctions in France. Only Citizens remain."[19] For many of the magazine's wealthy subscribers, this shocking egalitarian stance would have appeared premature, foolhardy, even abhorrent.

Buisson appeared to be in favor of the Revolution. Yet what this really meant for anyone—especially during the early days when absolutely everything was in flux—would vary greatly and change rapidly. Buisson appeared to assume that if his wealthy subscribers paid lip service to the Revolution by adopting appropriately themed clothing and accessories, indulgence in luxury would continue to be the order of the day. Thus, the October 21, 1789 issue proudly announces that the Revolution has not prevented young adults from pursuing their taste for finery and their desire to please nor from continuously inventing new clothes or coiffures, especially hats and bonnets.[20] The article touts the gauze hat in the accompanying engraving as the height of politically correct fashion, featuring "olive branches embroidered in green silk" as an emblem for the peace that was now to reign among the three orders. "On a very high white taffeta headband, there is a cross [for the clergy] and a sword [representing the nobility] embroidered in gold, and, in blue silk, a spade [for the Third Estate]." In case the bonnet's bounty of insignia does not make its bearer's presumed political affiliation clear enough, the description points out that it also features "on the left side, the national cockade."[21]

There was only one problem, a serious one. It had been going on for a while, but under revolutionary conditions, appeared to take on new significance. *Magasin des Modes Nouvelles Françaises et Anglaises* reports again with baffled dismay but increasing apprehension that upper-class men were no longer acting "French." Instead, they were abandoning fashionableness and ostentation. Some refrained from wearing new styles or accessories. Others adopted an austere look in keeping with revolutionary (and bourgeois) values: modesty, practicality, comfort, frugality, and health.

In the first few days of the Revolution, a civilian militia, the National Guard, was formed, composed of active citizens who volunteered for duty and could afford an expensive, custom-made paramilitary uniform.[22] The editorial voice comments that some "young men [who] are no longer in [military] service are still wearing their uniforms with passion."[23] The periodical acknowledges that there was a reason for this un-French behavior but describes it in the most anodyne terms: Given "what is going on at the moment," men have other things on their minds.[24]

In schools, seminaries, the Church, and the army, requiring uniforms had long worked to mold boys and men in the image of something larger than themselves and make them willing to represent, serve, and even die for it. This highly visible form of collective allegiance presumably heightened the status of both the institution and the individual. This was certainly the case with the revolutionary National Guard uniforms, which "symbolized the link between political rights and duties" and civic virtue.[25] However, this attire also signaled a paradox common to patriotic groups throughout history. In "fighting for 'freedom,' variously imagined," they have tended to devise "uniforms for themselves" that constrained them physically or restricted individual choice.[26]

Revolutionaries decided early on that only men and only certain kinds of men would represent and constitute the state. "In the fall and winter of 1789–1790," writes historian Timothy Tackett, "the majority of the Assembly made the fateful decision of limiting suffrage and the pool of potential officeholders to 'active citizens'"—those men who "paid a certain minimum amount of taxes."[27] Even though men who did not meet that income standard were subject to forced conscription, they could neither vote nor serve as representatives. No woman, even a wealthy, well-connected aristocrat, could put herself up for election to the National Assembly. No female could serve in the army either. Forbidden from "having legs," they were also prohibited from wearing male costume (a *culotte* or *pantalon* [trousers]). In these ways, women of all ranks made up a separate underclass. It is true that the revolutionary uniform branded men as subordinate to a greater whole, but it also elevated them and enshrined them as superior to women—no matter the latter's class, patriotic acts, or sacrifices to the nation.

Ironically, revolutionaries fighting to dismantle and abolish the Church and battle the royal army nevertheless borrowed some of the practices of both institutions: the requirement that fashion be renounced and the promotion of, even insistence on, uniform badges and attire are notable examples. In the clerical and revolutionary cases, renunciation functioned as a form of gendered belonging that constructed a wide swath of middle-men for the institutions in question. This idea also fed into a "popular conception of citizenship" in which uniforms and citizenship were "literally equivalent," further reinforcing the masculinity that inhered in each.[28] Indeed, when the October 1, 1789 issue of *Magasin des Modes Nouvelles Françaises et Anglaises* states that "ever since we have all become soldiers in France, our attire, or rather its ornamentation, has been very simple," there is no doubt that the first person plural is male. "We have all become soldiers" was, however, a big overstatement. Half the population of France, i.e., women, was not allowed to wear these uniforms, and a large percentage of men did not have the social status required nor the money to have a uniform made for them. Presumably to ward off accusations of counterrevolutionary sedition, the editorial voice hastily adds, "God forbid that we should ever regard uniform dress with distaste!"[29]

The magazine acknowledges the current necessity and appeal of military uniforms, but its explanation ties privileged French men to *la mode*, as had long been the case: "For Frenchmen, a military habit is too novel *not* to be a new fashion. We see our young men practically always in one. The same goes for the rifle, military parades and exercises. We're certain that this uniform will change neither in form nor in color," which was to say that it will never reflect "the French character."[30]

The magazine also chastens its readers that this sober, unchanging style could not last. Once the necessity and novelty of wearing a uniform have worn off, it predicts: "We'll end up only wearing [the uniform] for military service, while going back to all our city clothes as often as we used to. That is how the French character will reemerge."[31]

Yet in that very issue and the following one, *Magasin des Modes Nouvelles Françaises et Anglaises* bows to the fashion of the moment. Rather than the "city clothes" it hopes French men will pick up once again, it offers engravings of two uniforms. The first, military, is meant for male readers to emulate. The second, an abbé in his "uniform," is meant for all readers to belittle.

THE UNIFORM THREAT: DOS AND DON'TS

The description of the October 1, 1789 fashion plate of a National Guard officer in full regalia in *Magasin* (see figure 3.2) is easily twice as long as the one given for the woman's dress (also in red, white, and blue) pictured alongside it: "[His] uniform coat is royal blue, lined in white wool with crimson piping, a crimson collar, and golden buttons displaying the city's coat of arms with the division and company numbers."[32] Even the standard sword and scabbard get their fifteen seconds of fame. The officer's accessories were also far more elaborate, expensive, and flamboyant than those in any of the other female fashions illustrated that year. Yet, the man's rank and quasi-military uniform worked their usual magic, protecting this figure from

FIGURE 3.2 What was à la mode ten weeks after the Revolution? Three foldout fashion plates: two button patterns, a woman in a dress, a man in a National Guard uniform. *Magasin des Modes Nouvelles*, October 1, 1789
Source: Gallica

the derision traditionally leveled at fops for caring too much about their looks.

Although it is unlikely that it was intended, there is some irony in the placement of the figures and accessories in the three-engraving foldout. The elegant, wasp-waisted lady, her head in a book, appears to pay no heed whatsoever to the officer's confident, wide-stanced and muscular display of festooned virility. Is he in fact looking hopefully at her, or is he coveting those gigantic, stylish buckles in sharp close-up "behind" her, one edged in diamonds, the other made of silver plate?

The engraving of an abbé in the following issue highlights a similarly comical heterosexual disconnect (see figure 3.3). Ordinarily, no man of the cloth would be either fashionable or manly enough to be granted full citizenship in the fashion press. However, *Magasin* explains, there was no better alternative. Real men were "occupied with military service or the arts or sciences," making abbés who, like other Church men, were exempt from military conscription, the only men in town "engaged in society" and therefore obliged to "take care to be found pleasing.[33] There being nothing particularly new in the cut or style of the abbé's clothing, *Magasin Des Modes*

FIGURE 3.3 How the Revolution did and did not affect fashion. Three foldout fashion plates: three ladies' hats, a woman in a colorful dress, and an abbé all in black. *Magasin des Modes Nouvelles Françaises et Anglaises*, October 21, 1789
Source: Gallica

Nouvelles Françaises et Anglaises notes that "detailing his attire won't take long. [The abbé] is entirely in black velvet, silk, or wool. His coat is made of black taffeta. His collar is black silk. His clerical skull cap (*calotte*) is a very shiny black."[34] The rat-a-tat repetition, black, black, black, and, for variation, a very shiny black, is derisive. The curled and powdered wig does not even get honorable mention, but the hat under the abbé's arm does: "On his hat is the national cockade, which is worn, or must be, by absolutely all the men in the capital who can carry arms."[35] As with the images of *petits maîtres* [fops], the abbé's fashion plate shows readers that for any French man worthy of the name, effeminacy was to be avoided.

Like the officer, the abbé appears in a triptych. On the left are three ladies' bonnets in the latest styles. In the middle, there is a woman in a green dress with lavender trim and a hat featuring a flurry of pink bows and three white plumes. What the magazine calls a "very elegant young abbé," who holds a sprig of wild roses in one hand and a lorgnette up to his eye in the other, seems about to crash into the well-dressed lady, who points to her chest coyly as if to say, "Are those flowers for *me*?" Yet the abbé appears to look not at *her* but at the three frilly hats "behind" her, seen in giant detail as if through the lens of his lorgnette. The magazine coolly dismisses what it calls abbés' "usual" flaw: being "*coquets*," that is, seductive, elegant, overly concerned about their looks. It labels the figure's "highly ornate" lorgnette another "kind of affectation."[36] The implication is that if this was the only man *à la mode* worthy of a fashion engraving in the October 21 issue, the country's fashion standard had indeed fallen to a new low.[37]

So had *Magasin des Modes Nouvelles Françaises et Anglaises*. It ceased publication two months later, with an issue dated December 21, 1789, six months and one week after the fall of the Bastille. What replaced it, despite its frivolous-sounding new title, would leave no doubt as to the source of the nation's problems or who could fix them: the new editor. His main targets for a compulsory makeover? Not women but the wrong kind of men.

THE EFFEMINACY THREAT

Three months after the shutdown of *Magasin des Modes Nouvelles Françaises et Anglaises* and seven and a half months after the Revolution began, the country was still convulsed by turmoil of all kinds, which showed no sign of slowing down. January 25, 1790 saw the first issue of a new periodical to replace it, *Journal de la Mode et du Goût, ou Amusements du Salon et de la Toilette* [Magazine of Fashion and Fine Taste, or Entertainments for the Salon and the Dressing Room]. Buisson was once again the publisher, but its day-to-day operation was in new hands. The first page of every issue announced "M. LE BRUN" as the editor.

Yet another commoner from the provinces, Jean-Antoine Brun (1760–1837), later known as Le Brun and sometimes Le Brun-Tossa, was just one year older than Father La Mésangère. He was born in 1760 to a hatter and his wife on the other side of France, in a small town near Grenoble. Like Father La Mésangère, Le Brun was a small-town provincial who attended the seminary. Unlike him, Le Brun, who was much influenced by the works of Voltaire, Rousseau, and other proto-revolutionary thinkers, left the seminary because he found clerical, academic, and provincial life wanting.[38] Following countless others, including Bonaparte and La Mésangère, Le Brun eventually moved *up*, to Paris. At age thirty, he took over the third French fashion magazine not only to make his fortune but also to help foment revolutionary change. It was his personal bully pulpit for promoting suitably manly versions of revolutionary masculinity. His main aim was to eradicate foppish dress and behavior, which, he maintained, had no place in this brave new man's world.[39]

In the beginning, however, the new periodical appeared to share the same objective as *Magasin des Modes Nouvelles Françaises et Anglaises* had: To advise the upper classes on how to be good patriots while remaining *à la mode*. In many respects, Le Brun represented the progressive side of revolutionary masculinity as, for example, when he defended women's honor and rights, preached the moral obligation to help those less fortunate (October 5 and 15, 1790; January 25, 1791), and underscored the importance of standing up to despotism (September 15, 1790). However, he had no use whatsoever for the kind of patriotic bromides ("We are all citizens now") that his publisher Buisson had earlier offered as editor.

Instead, for six months, Le Brun fairly burst out of the anodyne and apolitical fashion magazine closet. He pressed his readers to organize vigilante groups (September 25, 1790), accused noblemen of stupidity, pride, untrustworthiness, and sloth (March 15 and May 15, 1790), and attacked what he characterized as their indolent and sybaritic lifestyles (April 25, 1790). He explicitly took aim at two-faced aristocrats pretending to adopt austere, republican dress and monks, priests, and friars whose robes, he claimed, hid lives of shameful lasciviousness. He touted republican family values as the solution to all ills. The first six months of Le Brun's *Journal de la Mode et du Goût* resembled a shooting range where potshots flew in every direction.[40]

While his predecessor and publisher Buisson had gently chided his male readers for failing to dress like true French men (i.e., fashionably), Le Brun took a hard line, berating and mocking them for anything that he found affected or unmanly, which was also to say unpatriotic, in their attire, comportment, and habits.[41] Thus, the double engraving in the October 5, 1791 issue (see figure 3.4) looks more like a caricature than a fashion plate. It takes aim at the male figure's frilly neckwear, tight clothing, curled wig, and excess rouge, not to mention his simpering expression, ballet-like stance, thin build, and limp wrist—as far from the muscular, no-nonsense male revolutionary ideal as it was possible to be. The contemptuous description of all such foppish and unmanly men underscores this point: "For some time now, our young men have become Hercules. It is quite amusing to see their weak arms lugging along heavy bludgeons whose only use is to kill flies and frighten children." Dismissing the "boastful posturing" of these *faux* Hercules and would-be Adonises, *Journal de la Mode et du Goût* predicts that they will soon be felled by their own cowardice: "Soon the north wind, blowing on [their] fingers, will force them to tuck their hands into their waistbands and throw their clubs on the fire."[42] Le Brun's periodical seems to say that if ever there was a time when men of means should check their privilege and renounce feminizing foppishness, it was now. Virility was all.

Yet the magazine also indicates the opposite. As social historian Richard Sennett observes, a properly republican male body during the Revolution was to be "desexualized—that is, no 'frills' were to be worn to make it attractive or remarkable."[43] By contrast, the magazine says nothing about the loose morals that the illustration attributes to the female counterpart of the false Hercules: A very busty young woman who appears

FIGURE 3.4 What the counterrevolutionary opposition was wearing. Double fashion plate: *Journal de la Mode et du Goût*, October 5, 1791.
Source: Gallica

to give a brazen come-hither look to the viewer. What mattered far more in the magazine was what men did, and should not, wear.

Le Brun explicitly identifies France's problem as a question of *men's* appearance and attire in highly derogatory terms. For example, "When you see a man walking around the capital in beautiful white silk stockings when wet weather has muddied the streets, you can boldly assume he is a popinjay, a conceited ass, or a fool, and perhaps he is all three."[44] Some of his most spiteful and seemingly ill-advised attacks target his presumably upper-class male subscribers. Reporting on the official ceremonies marking the first anniversary of the Revolution, the journal accuses aristocrats of shirking their patriotic duty: helping build a grand altar to the nation. Instead, they have been spotted "running through the streets of Paris, walking in the public gardens, a wooden shovel in hand, wearing . . . a work coat that had been made expressly for the occasion the night before."[45]

Under the coat, the description continues, their true colors showed: "an elegant waistcoat . . . with trousers made of twill, under which silk stockings peek out over well-polished, very shiny shoes adorned with rosettes." None of this would be sullied by physical labor: "Come evening, neither their curls, their round hats, nor any of the rest of their get-up suffered any alteration, and the wooden shovel is as clean as it was when it was purchased."[46] The message was clear: If these men's patent failure to pass as patriotic citizens made them risible, their disinclination to engage in their civic duty made them despicable.[47]

The idea that men might not just dress but *act* like women was especially abhorrent to Le Brun. *Journal de la Mode et du*

Goût notes with distaste that female theatrical roles in Rome are played by "smooth-cheeked young men."[48] The implication is that this dangerous trend will reach France. Yet Le Brun also tries to assure his readers that natural gender differences can always be discerned. Although such men may be "as similar to women in their figure as they are in their voice, [they] can never have the gracious posture, gestures, and walk, which are the exclusive endowment of that most amiable half of humankind." As was typical in such moments, the compliment to the ladies is followed by a warning to men. The detestable "half-men" in Rome, the magazine adds, "are even more ridiculous in ballets-pantomimes."[49]

In any historical period or culture, erogenous zones are notoriously labile and sometimes outright nonsensical to outsiders. In this case, today's readers might be struck by the fact that breeches worn with a frock coat in a contrasting color often formed an upside-down "V" that both framed and exposed the groin area. In addition, those breeches could, and often did, fit snugly, potentially revealing the shape and size of his genitals, especially if they were in a state of arousal. But for Le Brun, this aspect of men's dress was the way things simply were, unworthy of comment.

The same was true on June 15, 1790, in an image appearing in *Journal de la Mode et du Goût.* The pose taken by the woman (see figure 3.5) highlights her breasts and bustle to an extraordinary extent, but there is no hint that this might be outré. By contrast, the magazine derides the English-inspired male attire on the left for being so tight that the two coattail buttons in back touch. Walking around in such a frock coat, the

FIGURE 3.5 A "scandalous" split-tail coat, a fashionable lady. Fashion plate: *Journal de la Mode et du Goût*, June 15, 1790.
Source: Courtesy of Rijksmuseum, Amsterdam

magazine complains, a man's tails and pockets look like a lump "of crumpled-up fabric, ballooning out from the back and leaving a part of the buttocks indecently exposed up to the waist."[50] Was this shocking backside exposure also considered suspiciously homoerotic in the early 1790s? Le Brun does not say. Yet calling attention to parts of the male body that were usually kept covered was clearly perceived as a violation of sexual norms, and hence a moral threat.

One hundred years before, in the early eighteenth century, clergymen rained down hellfire and brimstone on vanity in men and women both. One Doctrinarian priest Father Jean-François

Maugras (1680–1726) thundered against those who spent all morning "getting adorned like an idol" and all day going about "seeing and being seen."[51] His primary target was women. Le Brun, by contrast, targeted proper, patriotic-minded men who did not hide their "goods" even as he highly approved of women who displayed theirs. "There is absolutely no indecency," he opines, about simple, fitted women's skirts and jackets, as seen in the accompanying female fashion plate in the October 5, 1790 issue, under which "every movement of the body can be discerned. . . . Even a round, ample [female] figure, if it is not excessive, poses no problem." The woman simply needs to put "all the folds of the skirt behind in such a way that the arch of the back is still visible and the rump that juts out is perfectly shaped."[52] While women's duty was to engage in exhibitionism, presumably for male observers like the editor, men were to be sleek, phallic columns, preferably in a uniform.[53]

Buisson's *Magasin des Modes Nouvelles Françaises et Anglaises* had decried men's new passion for unchanging attire and uniforms as an insult to Frenchness, but Le Brun's *Journal de la Mode et du Goût* hailed upper-class men's abandonment of aristocratic frivolity and adoption of revolutionary ideals of masculinity. He saw the combination as a patriotic solution to a very dangerous problem.[54]

THE UNIFORM SOLUTION

Unlike Buisson whose *Magasin des Modes Nouvelles* had lamented French men's preference for uniform, Le Brun's

Journal de la Mode et du Goût lauds the trend and in terms bordering on the homoerotic. Men, he writes, were lining up to demonstrate their patriotic valor and, when applicable, their muscles and build. "Hale and hearty citizens of an impressive size," *Journal de la Mode et du Goût* declares, "have donned the military badge, the bearskin hat, and the red epaulette" of the grenadiers, and a special uniform was being designed for an eager "battalion of old men" over age sixty.[55]

Wearing military uniforms and renouncing fashion were presumed to enhance revolutionary ideas of masculinity such as strength, rectitude, morality, frugality, and propriety—qualities that also reinforced bourgeois, patriarchal, and heteronormative notions of manliness. Yet these had implications for both sexes. Thus, reporting in 1790 that two Capuchin friars had enrolled in the National Guard as firefighters, *Journal de la Mode et du Goût* made it a lesson to male readers that they should be appropriately manly and to female readers that they should desire virility in men. Now that these friars "carry hatchets and wear fur skin bonnets," Le Brun proudly claims, "our lady patriots look on them even more favorably . . . than they ever had done for *les petits maîtres* . . . or for powdered up and mincing abbés in their perfumed attire."[56]

For Le Brun and the increasingly vocal and powerful Jacobin faction of the National Assembly at the time, sartorial conformity was supposed to guarantee a republican future. Decrees about the tricolor cockade and, later, the "red bonnet of liberty" made them compulsory for men. For these revolutionary legislators, a man's patriotic renunciation of "frivolous" attire and behavior shows that he shuns decadence and performs his proper role as soldier and/or father/husband: someone who would not let his wife wear the trousers/breeches in the family.[57]

Meanwhile, Le Brun approves male civilians who choose manly restraint and seriousness over hair powders and oils and "ridiculous," unhealthy styles, like overheating their necks and chests with "the puffiness of several yards of muslin or batiste."[58] Even fops are seeing the light, Le Brun claims. "In the past, what we called a *petit maître* could be identified by his sumptuous garb in gold or silver and a hairstyle that was ridiculously *recherché*. Today, he wears only the simplest attire."[59]

The new patriotic male simplicity did not necessarily mean subtlety—sometimes quite the opposite. Per the March 20, 1790 decree by the National Assembly reported in *Journal de la Mode et du Goût*, along with the relatively discreet tricolor cockade, city officials were now required to wear a long, bright tricolor sash to display their loyalty to the regime and their rank in it. No other specifications for their attire were laid out. However, rather than feature a municipal officer in working-class trousers, which is to say *sans culottes* [without a *culotte*], the fashion engraving depicts the mayor in a bourgeois or aristocratic frock coat and breeches in black, which is labeled the most "decent" color (see figure 3.6).[60]

This idea of decency recalls that of moderation, which, for two centuries, had been part of bishops' edicts on the clerical dress of pastoral and teaching priests. In both contexts, this look of moral rectitude implied sexual as well as personal modesty—whatever the wearer's actual desires or behavior. Unlike the abbé who had been mocked in *Magasin des Modes Nouvelles* for his black, black, and black attire, here, the model

FIGURE 3.6 Mayor's formal revolutionary uniform and lady's high fashion. Fashion plate: *Journal de la Mode et du Goût,* May 5, 1790. *Source*: Gallica

engages in no effeminate posturing or affectation; he appears upright in all senses of the word.

Black was associated with dignity, as seen in mourning clothes as well as juridical, bourgeois, and everyday clerical costumes.[61] Less than a year before, in one of the catalyzing events that preceded the Revolution, representatives of the Third Estate had made black, to which they had been relegated during the Estates General meeting in May 1789, a matter of pride rather than an indication of their status below both the clergy and the nobility. For some, the plainer and shabbier the black garb the better: These were to be the signs of superior probity and patriotism.[62]

The official mayoral costume depicted in the fashion plate was plain. However, as with the abbé, there were many ways of dressing up black and dressing up in black: the fabric quality, the fit, and, especially, the accessories, as we saw with eighteenth-century teaching priests and their wigs, silk stockings, and modestly pleated shirts. Rather than a wholesale repudiation of fashion, these black uniforms refashioned what male exhibitionism and distinction looked like.

Despite his basic black "suit," which was derided when worn by the abbé in 1789, the male figure in the May 5, 1790 fashion plate is far from unadorned. The new, obligatory over-the-shoulder sash, jauntily knotted at the hip, was about five feet in length and ended in gold fringe, making the municipal officer a flashy political banner whether he was coming or going.[63] As if the bright, phallic sash were not enough, the fashion engraving gilds the revolutionary lily with political symbols and high-class status markers galore. Dressed in a white powdered wig with a medium-sized curl at the front and another smaller one below on the sides and at the back, a lacy neck ruffle and frilly cuffs, yellow garters, and patriotic shoe buckles, the officer's signs of political allegiance and class, or at least wealth, are easy to discern—and hard to ignore.

If we read away the mayor's wig, lace, and yellow garters in figure 3.6 and the earlier abbé's lacy collar and cuffs (see figure 3.3 from 1789), this sleek, decidedly vertical and somber look with splashes of white at the throat and wrists prefigures what would become *the* silhouette for men of the haute bourgeoisie and upper classes in nineteenth-century continental countries and their (former) colonies, including the United States. Even the patriotic sash, despite its length, fringe, and diagonal position, is recognizably modern. The pop of color against the much plainer suit functions very much like the contrasting striped, patterned, or plain tie typical of conventional male office workers and politicians today. Then and now, in the secular and civilian variants of men's formal wear, the overall colors are often somber, but, for the upper classes, the fabric is supposed to be of superior quality and the accessories are often luxurious.

To underscore the mayor's supposed prestige and authority, the image depicts him holding an oversized book, described as "a volume of the proceedings of the National Assembly" in expensive, "red Moroccan leather," inscribed with the words "NATION, LAW AND KING" in gold. The new interest in renunciation as a sign of revolutionary patriotism most affected the very small percent of the population who could afford the ostentation, luxury, and fashion that "everyone" was supposed to be giving up.

For Le Brun, the former seminarian-turned-fashion editor, revolutionary ideals would never be achieved until the Catholic Church, which he believed to be riddled with despotism and sexual immorality, was eliminated for good. In revolutionary France, he was far from the only one to take this position.

DOMESTIC ENEMIES: ALL STATE, NO CHURCH

Having plundered the property, prestige, personnel, and power of the Church, the National Assembly continued to rain down new indignities on the tens of thousands of clergymen and women in France, including Father La Mésangère. On February 13, 1790, that legislative body abolished clerical vows and contemplative religious orders both. In July, it passed a Civil Constitution of the Clergy, which divested priests, nuns, and secular clergy of their special status by making them state functionaries. In October, another decree banned outright the long religious robes of priests and nuns as a sign of divided, even counterrevolutionary, loyalties. Another month later, the National Assembly took an even more radical step by decreeing that all clergy must swear fealty to the nation. About half of the clerical population refused—a decision that would cost them their position, salary, and any future pension. Beginning in January 1791, all around the country, those priests who took the oath were required to do so in public. Teaching priests, including the Doctrinarians signed the oath in greater numbers than their parish brethren who were generally less progressive, and Father La Mésangère eventually followed his colleagues' patriotic lead.[64]

Despite thousands and thousands of nuns and priests' official submission to revolutionary authority, anticlericalism, which had long thrived in France, became even more virulent, salacious, and pornographic. For the first time ever, a fashion magazine followed suit. Le Brun's *Journal de la Mode et du Goût* combined traditional themes of anticlerical literature (the clergy's holier-than-thou attitude cloaked unnatural depravity and cruelty) with the Jacobin insistence that ecclesiastics' vows of celibacy and their single-sex communities prevented them from fulfilling their foremost patriotic duty: marriage and procreation.[65]

From April 5 to June 5, 1790, ten consecutive issues of the "Magazine of Fashion and Taste," featured lengthy excerpts from what was then, and still would be, a rather shocking source: a pornographic diatribe in verse called "La Liberté du cloître" [Liberty in the Cloister]. Writing anonymously, Charles-Albert Demoustier (1760–1801) accuses bishops, priests, monks, and the occasional abbess of being lascivious predators of nuns. However, Demoustier's depiction of all nuns as young, beautiful, and nubile victims makes the subject's treatment less moral than titillating.[66] The poem tells of a convent visited by a deity who announces to the priests and nuns assembled that they are now ordered to do the very thing that had always been strictly forbidden: marry. The kicker: They had to marry each other.[67]

One of the characters, Sister Agnes, objects, saucily pointing out that all priests were not equally desirable marriage partners. As a good patriot, she explains, she would gladly marry a humble postulant but never a man who gadded about in "miters, short vestments, crosiers [bishops' ceremonial shepherd's staffs] or hats."[68] The moral was clear: In the new revolutionary order, there would be no room for men who paraded their "female" vanities or feminine proclivities. All men would be forced to be manly.

Despite the bombast of these and other pronouncements and with no forewarning or explanation, four months after the last installment of the salacious poem, in October 25, 1790, Le Brun slunk back into the safe, apolitical fashion press closet. He stayed there for three years.[69] Gone were the deeply partisan commentaries and condescending judgments of others' attire.[70] The periodical even took to pleading with its readers to abandon the political fanaticism *Journal de la Mode et du Goût* had so stridently promoted. It offered a confident prediction that matched its new approach: "Soon, the Frenchman, fed up with politics and plots, pamphlets and revolutions, will turn toward the quickly vanishing consoling arts whose total absence would lead us to barbarism."[71]

The magazine turned a corner on the question of gender too. Rather than continue to bait effeminate men and expose their attire as inappropriate, *Journal de la Mode et du Goût* gave far more attention to pretty women in fashionable dress as eye candy for its readers, who were male and female alike. Protest and resistance were entirely expunged. It was as if someone else entirely had taken over or Le Brun had changed his mind about making a radical fashion magazine that would still attract readers. The periodical's new, almost entirely anodyne content might have pleased some subscribers. However, it also made the journal very much out of step with the times, during which *philosophes*, magistrates, and a vocal and powerful majority of the National Assembly continued to decry the Church as anathema to revolutionary ideals.[72] Indeed, with the approval of the Constitution of September 3, 1791, the anticlerical nightmare Demoustier had concocted for his poem "Liberty in the Cloister" and Le Brun had published in *Journal de la Mode et du Goût* the previous year became law. After fierce debate and much controversy, the penal code made clerical vows of chastity illegal. Friars, monks, priests, and teaching priests would be forced to protect the state by joining the army and/or reproduce it by becoming fathers. Nuns, ineligible for military service, had no choice: They would become wives and mothers. Later legislation sweetened the deal with a financial incentive: Men and women of the cloth who entered holy matrimony could keep their pensions and salaries.[73] In 1793–1794, their choice to marry became a legal obligation from which there was little chance of reprieve.[74]

During that period, two of Father La Mésangère's Doctrinarian colleagues at La Flèche went down the matrimonial road. Father La Mésangère and four others did not. Whether for lack of opportunity, interest, or desire, he would remain a bachelor until he died.

As for First Lieutenant Bonaparte in the early 1790s, love and marriage were of far less interest than his twin desires to save his native Corsica from French rule and to pursue his financial, military, and political ambitions.

BETWIXT AND BETWEEN

By October 1791, Bonaparte believed he was back in Corsica for good. He spent most of his time there angling to restore the family fortune and become a Corsican volunteer for the French army "without losing either his rank or his pay," a plan that was thwarted by a recent French law.[75] To stay, he had to stand for election as a departmental representative. Making use of physical intimidation and some shady election dealings, he won. Bonaparte was part of a resistance effort to put loyal Corsican troops "back in the citadels occupied by the 'French,'" but they failed to seize the fortress that he and his troops had been assigned.[76] Having "lost all credibility" as a leader, he was convinced that his best hope was getting back into the good graces of the French military brass.[77]

Fifteen months later, in February 1792, Bonaparte once again left his politically divided island for Paris.[78] Thanks to his careful politicking and shading of the facts, the military brass ignored his seditious ambitions and his unauthorized six-month desertion. Timing was everything. Historian Patrice Gueniffey writes, "The army . . . needed all its officers, even those least worthy of confidence."[79] In the end, Bonaparte managed to finagle a promotion to captain. This meant that he would be issued another, even showier army uniform. It also appeared to identify him as a patriotic French man despite all the evidence to the contrary in the preceding three years alone.

Meanwhile, La Mésangère would be forced to wear new clothes. On April 6, 1792, a decree by the National Legislative Assembly ordered clerics of all kinds—rank and file, prelates, even secular clergymen—to forsake their traditional religious dress, which was now illegal.[80] Male clerics who previously donned long cassocks were now obliged to become two-legged creatures, wearing either the loose trousers of the lower classes or the *culotte* and stockings of the more affluent. François-Yves Besnard, Father La Mésangère's contemporary and fellow teaching priest, whose memoirs immortalized Limonas and the seminary's *mystiqueurs*, wrote how discomfited he felt in secular clothing. At the time (he was forty-one) and for decades after, he avowed, looking like a layman and being one again was not a relief but a painful encumbrance, obliging him to cloak who he really was inside: "Required to embrace secular life externally, I saw myself as an amphibious being in the world."[81]

No published accounts allow us to know where Father La Mésangère stood on the question of masculinity, fashion, or even his own sartorial preferences. Now that he could no longer wear an ankle-length cassock, did he feel half-naked? Or, like Father Limonas, did he enjoy showing off his legs, his physique, his financial resources, and his taste. The new look might also have made him self-conscious, worried that his stockings might be unclean, that his knees looked knobby, or his legs were swollen with gout. Perhaps early on, living as a secular man, the former Father La Mésangère too felt like an amphibian who needed to conceal the fact. Yet, as a teaching priest, he had already been amphibious—half clerical, half secular. It is also possible that he was delighted to be seen no longer as a man of the Church but as a man of some quality.

However, in the months that followed, the wheels of the Revolution began to turn even more quickly and in previously unimaginable ways. In the spring, Louis XVI continued to veto the radical measures the National Legislative Assembly sent him. On June 20, 1792, a revolutionary mob stormed the Tuileries Palace and forced him to put on a red, revolutionary cap. Caricatures of the rotund king, looking inebriated and wearing his seditious subjects' droopy "liberty cap" adorned with a tricolor cockade, circulated widely. Fifteen days later, "on 5 July 1792 the Legislative Assembly ordered all men to wear [the cockade]."[82] The idea was that the mere act of wearing a badge, in this case the cockade, "made" a person patriotic and proved that they were. But the wearer might just as easily be using it to closet his real views. Given that this set of decrees did not issue a long list of specifications about the fabric, position, or size of approved uniforms or accessories, there was no guarantee that these would always pass muster with fellow citizens or the authorities.

Against this background, even more highly consequential events were unfolding. All but one of the sections of Paris demanded the king's removal from the throne. Less than two months later, on August 10, 1792, the National Guard of Paris and soldiers (*fédérés*) from Marseilles and Brittany stormed the Tuileries Palace. Hundreds were killed in the mêlée, including many of the Swiss guards who were there to defend the royal family. The only way Louis XVI, Marie-Antoinette, and their children were able to escape the massacre was by fleeing to the National Legislative Assembly for protection. It did not last long.

Emmanuel de Las Casas's version of Bonaparte's memoirs claims that Napoleon recalled this time as follows: "Everywhere the anger was extreme; rage was in every heart, it was seen on every face, even though these were not at all people of the common kind." He also noted he was being perceived differently. "Although there was nothing peculiar about my appearance, or perhaps it was again because my face was calmer, it was easy for me to see that I was the object of many hostile and defiant looks, as if I were someone unknown and suspect."[83] The era of suspicion based not only on patriotic insignia but also on bodily affect was in full swing and would grow even more feverish.[84]

Just six weeks later, elected representatives to the new National Convention voted to abolish the monarchy and declared the king and queen prisoners. The very next day, September 22, 1792, they pronounced France a republic and voted by a majority of one to put the king to death. Four months later, on January 21, 1793, the former Louis XVI, stripped of his costume, wig, and the other appurtenances that used to "make" him a king was taken in a grubby *charette* to the newly named Place de la Révolution in Paris. There he was guillotined and his head help up before a loud, cheering crowd. In October, Marie-Antoinette would meet the same fate.

As of July 27, 1793, the most powerful man in France was Maximilien François Marie Isidore de Robespierre (1758–1794), the leader of the Jacobins. A thirty-six-year-old lawyer who had served as a representative from the north of France since 1789, Robespierre joined the notorious Committee of Public Safety, which had granted itself executive powers. A king he certainly was not, but neither did he resemble the usual Jacobin *sans-culottes*. Those men were generally unkempt and uncouth and favored loose trousers over expensive, often tight breeches: hence their nickname "without culottes." Their messy and coarsely cut hair and their red liberty caps were the other conspicuous indications of their radical politics. By contrast, Robespierre and other Jacobins of his kind "stuck by their middle-class forms of dandyism."[85] Thus, although known for his austerity, Robespierre had a barber come daily to shave him and powder his wig, and he wore his large, frilly cravat tied just so, with silk shirts, striped and colored frock coats, waistcoats, breeches, and silver-buckled shoes. It was as if the new Jacobin ideals of revolutionary male costume and, for that matter, republican masculinity, did not apply to their notoriously authoritarian leader. Over time, this costume, a somewhat more modest version of the male attire of the Old Regime elite, would be understood as a sign of manly, middle-class authority rather than suspect aristocratic foppishness or, as in Robespierre's case, dandified ruthlessness.[86]

For Bonaparte, the social and political tumult during this period gave him yet another chance to head back to Corsica to play a key role in what he hoped would be the independence of his homeland. However, by early 1793, his past military and political fiascos convinced him that it was time, once and for all, to place his bets on France and remain there. This turnaround would be a fortuitous realignment for him and, initially at least, the Revolution.

It was not lucky for Le Brun and his *Journal de la Mode et du Goût*, the only French fashion magazine of its time, or for those who might have wanted to follow Le Brun's lead by whipping up pro-revolutionary and macho fervor against the Church or simply offering the glamorous soft sell of leisure reading and images of beautiful ladies wearing the latest styles. On September 2, 1793, freedom of the press was repealed. *Journal de la Mode et du Goût* was already in dire financial straits. Although his magazine had much earlier reverted to fashion facts, cultural platitudes, and apolitical distractions, this was not enough to save it. The journal folded seven months later on April 1, 1793.[87]

By the end of its run, Le Brun's *Journal de la Mode et du Goût* had become a throwback to its tame, prerevolutionary precursors. However, the magazine was quite modern in one important respect. Even though men were still the owners, editors, most of the writers, and many of its readers and the periodical continued to offer articles and engravings about the latest styles for men, it helped further naturalize the Great Masculine Renunciation of fashion by offering a disproportionate number of images of women. No longer its predecessors' moderately equitable ratio of two female fashion plates to one male engraving, *Journal de la Mode et du Goût* offered ten times as many engravings of fashionable women for a ratio of ten to one.[88] Perhaps women's fashions dominated the magazine at this time because they were changing far more quickly than men's, but the lopsided numbers certainly underscored the idea that fashion was women's business.

In sum, in its three iterations over the course of eight years and one Revolution, the French fashion magazine no longer considered *la mode* a fully human and pleasurable pastime, a natural expression of heterosexuality, an engine for commerce, and a point of French national pride for both sexes, as was the case in *Cabinet des Modes* in 1785. Fashion was represented instead as a plaything for the "vain" and "frivolous" sex. The apparent reason was that men had more serious things on their mind—a foretaste of men's even more dramatic pull away from fashion in later decades.

In 1793, the state of the fashion press would have been the last thing on the mind of the former Father La Mésangère. Having outlawed the Church and sold off most of its properties, the revolutionary government ordered that Church-run schools, including the *collège* in La Flèche be shuttered. La Mésangère was asked to take care of the boys who remained and secure their transfer elsewhere. He stayed until the bitter end.

LAST PRIEST STANDING

In the early 1790s, France was riven by internal division and threatened by foreign powers who were allied against the Revolution and preparing to invade. In August 1792, the National Legislative Assembly abolished religious nursing and teaching orders, which included Father La Mésangère's Doctrinarians. When the paper money issued by the revolutionary government and valued on state-confiscated Church property became worthless, the *collège* at La Flèche, like other Catholic institutions, was bankrupt. In March 1793, La Mésangère was appointed director of the boarding school where he had been teaching.

What was he wearing within the confines of the campus? The revolutionary cockade was required of all Frenchmen and even visiting foreigners. Failing to put it on in public would have made him a target of revolutionary partisans and authorities. Yet wearing a cockade would have riled up a substantial majority in this western province who were fiercely loyal to the monarchy and the Catholic Church.[89] This no-win situation for him was about to become a wholesale catastrophe for the country.

The same month Father La Mésangère was appointed to manage his school's closure, counterrevolutionary royalists and fervent Catholics in neighboring Brittany and the Vendée revolted against the National Convention's forced conscription of three hundred thousand men from these provinces. In response, the "Convention sanctioned the use of extreme violence and brutality . . . and ordered the death of all priests involved in the uprising."[90] Not far from La Flèche, near

Angers, eighty-three refractory priests "were shot in one day during the Vendée revolt." In the following sixteen months, "as many as 300,000 people went to prison as suspects between March 1793 and August 1794. . . . Some 30,000 to 40,000 clergy who refused the oath emigrated, at least 2,000 (including many nuns) were executed, and thousands were imprisoned."[91] Under these circumstances and these legislative orders, which applied to the entire country, Father La Mésangère's most recent assignment was not to save the two-hundred-year-old school but to shut it down.

Only two published articles about this period tell us how Father La Mésangère may have been perceived and represented at this time. Neither pretends to be objective. The first depicts a sentimental and thoroughly anti-republican Father La Mésangère; in the second, he comes across as a good civilian "soldier" of the Revolution—a kindhearted but dutiful revolutionary patriot who obeys orders.

WHAT TO WEAR AT THE END OF AN ERA

Jules Clère (17??–1860) was a tutor at La Flèche in 1808 after it reopened as a military school under Napoleon's order. Sixty years after La Mésangère managed its closure, early in the Second Empire, when Napoleon's nephew reigned, Clère wrote a history of the school. In it, he offers a fictional re-creation of Father La Mésangère's "last stand," based on the unpublished recollections of M. d'Hennezel, a "retired commander" at the school. In 1793, d'Hennezel was a twelve-year-old pupil at La Flèche, which had, by then, been renamed the Collège National.[92] Clère does not quote d'Hennezel directly. Nor does he hide what may well have been his own pro-Napoleon political perspective, which was very much in sync with the presumed aim of d'Hennezel's memories: To portray the horrors of republicanism by evoking its innocent victims, among them Father La Mésangère.

Clère's highly idealizing account depicts Father La Mésangère as the ultimate benevolent paternal figure saying farewell to the young d'Hennezel and the seven or eight other remaining pupils whom the school had been sheltering because their parents had died, emigrated, or been taken prisoner. In his telling, a man-made disaster, the Revolution, threw innocent boys and Father La Mésangère from their natural, all-male pastoral and familial "nest." Clère begins, as if recounting a fairy tale, "One day, around the first of May, when the trees on the grounds were covered with a tranquil greenery, and the birds sang as they always had, on their branches, next to their nests, Father La Mésangère was choked up, and his young audience had tears in their eyes."[93] In this dewy-eyed account, no dissenter, malcontent, or prankster makes an appearance. Instead, Father La Mésangère and the students are solemnly united in heartbreak, innocent victims of a common enemy: revolutionaries of all stripes. Their brutality destroyed the Doctrinarian *collège* at La Flèche, which Clère reveres as a place that had, for centuries, made boys of the upper classes (along with some lucky social inferiors) into the right kinds of men.

The second version of this story, told by Roland Houlier, author of a short article on Father La Mésangère published in

1988 and apparently based on Clère's depiction, also stresses Father La Mésangère's Old Regime dignity. However, Houlier portrays the former priest's grace under fire as that of a loyal and manly partisan of the Revolution, not that of a nostalgic mourning the prerevolutionary past, as in Clère's telling. As Houlier recounts the scene, Father La Mésangère says to his young charges: "'My children, we are going to have to take leave of one another; the government of the Republic demands it. Let us submit.'"[94] Houlier also has Father La Mésangère express deep regret that he cannot remain as father to them *in loco parentis*: "'I do not want to abandon you like this, but I have no resources and will have to seek my fortune in Paris. Unable either to take you with me or stay with you here, I entrust you to an honorable townsman of La Flèche, your neighbor, my friend Brossier,'" who, we are told, "ran a small boarding house near the school."[95]

Given the extreme political conditions of 1793, were the school boarders still in their white stockings, blue waistcoats, jackets with red, buttoned facings, black breeches, and black shoes with buckles? Or had this dress code already gone the way of so many other traditions during the Revolution? For La Mésangère, ecclesiastical black would have been fitting for such a sad leave-taking. However, something a bit more colorful and nonclerical would have been safer politically—perhaps a frock coat in cornflower blue (which would later be his signature color), contrasting breeches, and traditional white stockings. Maybe he would have thought it best to leave the silk ones, if he had any, in his room and wear modest cotton ones instead.

Whatever the former Father La Mésangère wore that last day, this cataclysmic turn in national events and personal circumstances may have felt and, in lucky cases, turned out to be liberating: He would soon be free from his former responsibilities as a father to his young charges, a *confrère* in his order, and the director of a school. Since his relationship with his own father had long been strained, leaving the area would mean he no longer had to be a dutiful son within easy reach.[96] La Mésangère may have welcomed the chance for a taste of independence, far from his family, his Doctrinarian peers, and the schoolboys in his charge, and well outside the campus's twenty-foot-high walls. Nevertheless, a big question loomed: What was he free to do or be exactly?

In this era of general suspicion with political tensions high, saying, doing, or wearing something the "wrong" way could make a person subject to disproportionate punishment. Monsieur Guillotin's "humane" invention, the guillotine, meant that there was now a much more efficient way than the axe or the noose to assassinate people, especially a long line of them. The shadow of Guillotin's killing machines in the public squares of cities all over the country along with the rise of vigilantism and street riots made the stakes clear: It would be easy to run mortally afoul of revolutionary law. Nowhere were these reminders more numerous and visible than in Paris.

A more fortunate cleric than many, at age thirty-two, La Mésangère was too old for the universal conscription of 1793. By that time, having published the two-volume *Paris Traveler*, in 1789 or 1790, and his four-volume *Géographie historique et littéraire de la France* [Historical and Literary Geography of

France], which was applauded by the National Assembly in 1791 and republished in 1792, one could imagine that La Mésangère dreamed that a new life would give him more time to write. Yet his Church pension was a mere 160 livres a year and being a writer was not highly lucrative; nor was his success assured.

If he had been a confirmed royalist, La Mésangère might have stayed in western France with like-minded counterrevolutionaries. However, he was not. By late December 1793, getting out of town appeared to be a matter of life and death. The pitched civil war between royalists and revolutionaries had left 100,000 dead in the region, many of them noncombatants.[97] According to Clère's decidedly anti-republican account, the streets of La Flèche "were obstructed by dead bodies, and houses were filled with the sick and dying."[98] The *collège* had been requisitioned by the French Revolutionary Army, which held nothing sacred. Some of the soldiers could have been graduates of the venerable school, conscripted against their will or fighting proudly, some wearing the ragtag costume of the rank and file or, for those of higher rank, much fancier officer uniforms. In the classrooms, "dead horses were stretched out on straw" and the great painting gallery, which had also served as the library, had become "a shoemaking workshop for the army."[99] The "sacerdotal ornaments, paintings, epitaphs, [and] statues" in the chapel "were profaned or surrendered to destruction," and "the library, rich in precious works" including, perhaps, La Mésangère's own tomes, "was also pillaged."[100] Many soldiers took their last breaths in the great rooms that La Mésangère and his pupils had frequented in the main building, which had been transformed into a hospital for the wounded.

No place in France could guarantee safety to anyone—let alone a former priest. However, like many of his clerical colleagues and so many of the men in this study, La Mésangère took the upending of everything he had ever known as an opportunity to try his fortune in the capital. His timing was terrible. He arrived in Paris in December 1793, three months into the Reign of Terror.

Chapter Four

MAKEOVERS: MEN, REGIMES, MAGAZINES

DURING THE Reign of Terror (September 5, 1793 to July 28, 1794), the slightest slipup of word, deed, or accessory could make someone a target—especially anyone suspected of being a royalist, priest, or hoarder. The former Father La Mésangère would be liable on the first two of those counts. Vigilantism, street riots, and the prominent presence of the guillotine were clear and chilling evidence of the climate of public shaming and state violence. It was easy to run afoul of revolutionary law. Nowhere were these reminders more numerous than in Paris, where the volume of public executions was so great that the Jacobins set up several other prominent sites.

Despite these dangers, for La Mésangère with his eclectic interests and fascination with all things Parisian, moving to the capital would still have a decided advantage: the opportunity to live among a large, diverse urban population. Unlike the campus of the all-male school at La Flèche, in Paris women made up fully half the residents, and they were visible almost everywhere. In sharp contrast to the uniforms of the wealthy boarders and teachers at La Flèche that concealed to a certain extent the social distinctions within each cohort, Paris was a place where the classes mixed and members of the fashionable set in the capital delighted in showing off what they had. To the extent that La Mésangère was free to roam unobserved and unimpeded, he could pretend that he was *le voyageur à Paris*, the traveler in Paris, whom he had imagined in his book of that title. "Content to do without fame," this early flaneur goes about the city anonymously, seeking to "amuse and educate himself" by observing the dress, behavior, and follies of others.[1]

During the Terror, however, the byword was not freedom but survival. La Mésangère would probably have needed to disguise his status as a minor nobleman and former priest, his prior position at the cushy Doctrinarian *collège* at La Flèche, and his provenance from the western provinces where armed counterrevolutionary insurgents were wreaking their own form of terror.[2] La Mésangère's challenge was to become, or at least appear to become, a very different kind of man. No longer a half-clerical, half-secular hybrid, he would have to learn to look and act like a layman—and a fervent republican one at that. There would be severe consequences if he didn't.

In April 1792, a year and a half before La Mésangère's arrival in Paris, legislators gave authorities the right to execute anyone caught wearing a clerical costume. New decrees also outlawed men dressing in public as women. The reason given was that wartime exigency required punishing anyone who shirked military duty, but a fear of (manly) women taking over was never far from general revolutionary misogyny. Meanwhile, civilians who impersonated soldiers were also declared illegal. Such attempts at disguise were viewed as acts of rebellion so heinous that many of them were punishable by death.[3] Article 16 of a July 5, 1792 decree declared that whether a man was French or not, "any man residing in, or traveling through, France, is required to wear the national cockade." Article 17 stated that "any person wearing an emblem of rebellion . . . if found guilty . . . shall be put to death. . . . Any cockade other than the revolutionary cockade," was also declared "a sign of rebellion."[4]

As long as La Mésangère desisted from committing these counterrevolutionary acts, he was presumably free to choose to wear what he liked and could afford. Months before his arrival, on October 29, 1793, the National Convention had also passed legislation declaring a new universal right: "every individual is free to wear whatever attire or adornment of their sex they see fit." While truly revolutionary in its conception, the law was not in fact a declaration of absolute freedom of dress. First, absolute gender boundaries had to be respected: Each sex was to wear the attire of that sex. Second, the law, which was meant to inhibit public vigilantism and suppress women's exercise of political power, made the legislature, not the individual, the arbiter of inappropriate political attire and the police, not fellow citizens, those who were to enforce it.[5]

If La Mésangère and others took some comfort in this new declaration of relative sartorial freedom, it might be because the explicit proscriptions and prescriptions in the 1793 laws took much of the chilling guesswork out of clothing choices. In principle, if the former priest rid himself of signs of his ecclesiastical past and religiously wore layman's clothing, a cockade, and a red revolutionary bonnet (depending on the laws in force at any given time), he would be safe. Whatever his true or mixed political sentiments, these badges would mark him as a right-thinking citizen loyal to the revolutionary regime.

■ ■ ■

Roland Houlier, a twentieth-century author summarizing previous biographical sketches of La Mésangère's early days in Paris, writes that the former priest was in financial straits, which may have required him to perform manual labor to survive. As Houlier imagines the scene, "every morning, the solemn *philosophe* could be seen waiting for the stagecoach to arrive so that he could pick up travelers' bags on his shoulders and haul them to their lodgings."[6] Under such circumstances, the drab clothing and loose trousers of the working class were the only kinds of attire that would have fit the bill. However, these relatively coarse forms of manliness would not have entirely disguised what could easily have marked La Mésangère as suspect: soft hands, an educated way of speaking, a western accent, ink stains on his fingers or clothes, or an ecclesiastical manner.[7]

The same month La Mésangère arrived in Paris, December 1793, the twenty-four-year-old Bonaparte was appointed head of the artillery regiment at Toulon on the Mediterranean coast. The populace had revolted against the brutal Committee of Public Safety and handed over its port to the Anglo-Spanish warships that lay anchored between the city's two harbors. Twenty thousand anti-revolutionary foreign allies were poised to invade. To repel their advance, Bonaparte had to barter with "military and civilian authorities until he had at his disposal the sixty artillery pieces he needed."[8] Although outgunned and outnumbered, Bonaparte and his troops prevailed. After five days, "the British were defeated [and] they evacuated Toulon the next day," December 23, 1793.[9] Just three months after his previous promotion, Bonaparte was made brigadier general of the French Revolutionary Army. This meant an even finer military uniform and more regalia to signal his rise in the ranks.

Napoleonic legend often claims that this marked the beginning of Bonaparte's fame. Historian Patrice Gueniffey maintains, however, that at this point, his renown was limited to a "small group who were lavish in their praise of him."[10] Nevertheless, Bonaparte did not fit the image of someone who might go far, let alone conquer the world. Unprepossessing, of medium stature and frightfully thin, with a pale complexion—"yellow," some witnesses say—he looked worn-out, ill, and in truth a little pathetic.[11] His hair fell on his shoulders, he was unkempt and poorly dressed, and his clothes were threadbare. According to most observers of the time, he lacked the desire or the wealth to care about stylish, let alone clean or tidy, civilian clothing. According to the memoirs of the Duchess of Abrantès, who was no fan of Bonaparte, as late as 1795, he was wearing "badly made and badly polished shoes" and "a shabby round hat pulled down over his eyes from which two badly powdered 'dog ears' [pigtails, fashionable at the time] fell over the collar of the [plain,] iron gray greatcoat that would later be his banner of glory."[12]

Yet, she admits, "he impressed people."[13] He also continued to move rapidly up the military chain of command.

■ ■ ■

For most of their childhood, adolescence, early adulthood, and early career both our protagonists wore institutional garb as a matter of course. However, once La Mésangère lost his livelihood and it was illegal to wear his clerical habits, Bonaparte was the only one still in uniform. To see him was to know his rank and, in theory, which political side he was on. As for his career, despite the victory at Toulon, Bonaparte complained that the army had not found him a suitably prestigious and important assignment.[14] He was similarly betwixt and between in his political views. He hated the revolutionaries and wanted, above all, a stable government, but at that juncture this would have seemed impossible.[15]

In the mid-1790s and after, Bonaparte, La Mésangère, and millions of French men and women would discover that the quickly shifting winds of revolutionary change meant that neither a cockade, a uniform, nor even proximity to the powerful were guaranteed to save one's skin. This would take luck, sometimes lots of it.

LUCKY AND UNLUCKY STARS: THERMIDOR

Maximilian Robespierre, the powerful Jacobin on the Committee of Public Safety, had been lying low for some months, but in late July 1794, he showed up at the National Convention. There, he gave a thunderous tirade, making threats and accusing representatives of conspiring against him. Deputies, decrying his dictatorial rule, shouted him down. In this counterrevolutionary coup, called Thermidor, the name for July on the new revolutionary calendar, Robespierre and dozens of his allies were summarily arrested and imprisoned for treason. The next day, without further ado, they were guillotined. Bonaparte, who admired Robespierre's authority and power, was also a loyalist. He was held in detention in Toulon and stripped of his army rank. Yet luck was once again on his side.[16] Eleven days later, the war ministry not only released him but also regularized Bonaparte's position and assigned him to a group of officers devising plans for France's conquest of Italy.

Meanwhile, the Thermidorean regime quickly disbanded the Committee of Public Safety, released political prisoners, and outlawed Jacobin clubs. As tight strictures on morality and social life eased, fashion and other forms of luxury exploded, as did expressions of personal freedom. Three highly influential women, Josephine Bonaparte, Térézia Tallien, and Juliette Récamier, revolutionized female fashion by renouncing restrictive Old Regime dress with its bone-crushing corsets, thick, heavy fabrics, six-foot-wide skirts and high, teetering wigs in favor of loose dresses in light fabrics, and cropped hair—shocking for the time.[17]

Political corruption was extreme and barely concealed and the overall situation was extremely dicey. In October 1795, the revolutionary factions of the National Convention made a particularly brazen move. Fearing they would lose the upcoming elections, they declared by fiat that two-thirds of the current legislative seats would no longer be in play. Outraged, thousands of moderate and royalist insurrectionists began amassing in Paris. The National Convention's representatives appointed Paul François Jean Nicolas de Barras (1755–1829), a former viscount, army officer, and member of the National Convention, as commander of the Army of the Interior (Paris and its adjoining provinces). He, in turn, chose Bonaparte as his second-in-command. Bonaparte had served Barras well when they defended Toulon against a populace in rebellion. Now, years later, in the early hours of October 5 (13 vendémiaire) 1795, Bonaparte ordered three dozen cannons to be hauled to the Tuileries Palace. Desperate to secure an advantage against the insurrectionists, he insisted that Barras and the troops use "real bullets and not just blanks" against the civilians in revolt.[18] Bonaparte's lethal strategy went against the National Convention's orders, but it helped carry the day for the Thermidorian regime.

Just three weeks later, on October 26, 1795 (4 brumaire, an iv), however, there would be yet another consequential turn of the revolutionary screw. As the National Convention was disbanding, it passed a new constitution designed to prevent dictatorship in France, whether it came "from a Jacobin cabal manipulating a fickle populace, or from a single individual."[19] Under Barras's influence, the National Convention set up a new executive branch, the Directory. However, the system was ripe for abuse, in large part because the two newly defined legislative bodies, the Council of Ancients and the Council of Five Hundred, had very little authority over Barras and the other four members of the Directory.

The many men in Barras's pocket included Bonaparte. The two were, in many ways, an odd match. Barras was famous for graft, intrigue, sexual license, corruption, and expensive taste. Bonaparte, by contrast, was known for his stoic asceticism and for taking the moral high ground.[20] Nevertheless, once Barras promoted his young protégé to replace him as commander of the Army of the Interior, Bonaparte underwent an astounding makeover. According to the memoirs of his dogged detractor, the Duchess of Abrantès, once the shabby, unkempt young Bonaparte started circulating in loftier social circles and spheres of influence, he conveniently forgot his supposedly principled disdain for finery and luxury.

His new salary, "48,000 livres, paid for the most part in cash," certainly helped, as did the considerable perks of the new office: among them, "a personal carriage, a town house, [and] a loge at the Opera."[21] With his recent promotion and accession to wealth, the young general happily showed off his arriviste status on social occasions. In the anything-goes salons of Thermidor and the Directory, he was not alone. Nouveaux riches and "former revolutionaries in tousled hair and trousers or pantaloons" rubbed elbows with aristocrats. The latter, many of whom had recently returned to Paris after years as émigrés, tended to wear old-fashioned "powdered hair and a formal suit with knee-breeches," as if the Revolution and the Terror had never happened.[22]

It was in early 1796, in Barras's salon, that Bonaparte met the director's former mistress, thirty-three-year-old Josephine de Beauharnais, the mother of two children and widow of an aristocrat-turned-Jacobin beheaded during the Revolution.

Smitten by this older, worldly woman, Bonaparte, twenty-six, married her a few months later in a simple ceremony. Just two days after the wedding, as the newly appointed commander of the Army of Italy, Bonaparte left Paris and his new bride. In this latest assignment, he faced a monumental challenge that previous, far more experienced revolutionary French generals had failed: To drive the Austrian army out of the Italian peninsula and claim it for France. As part of his Italian campaign, Bonaparte waged war, but he helped sway French opinion in his favor by issuing deft propaganda bulletins from his various posts in Italy that highlighted his conquests and soft-pedaled his army's brutality, destructiveness, and defeats.

During his early years in Paris, the former Father La Mésangère experienced nothing like Bonaparte's social success at home or his high-stakes prominence as a general abroad. Nevertheless, La Mésangère too was moving onward and upward. Journalism, the new line of work he eventually took up, would require him to fight his own battles for predominance and territory albeit in the press.

NEW CONQUESTS

In 1796, at age thirty-five, La Mésangère no longer feared being persecuted as a former priest. He started signing the new editions of his books, which may have brought him some income.[23] By the following year, he was hobnobbing with the "right" sort. He paid 150 francs as annual dues to the Lycée des Arts [Art Lyceum], "which offered free public classes and prizes in the arts and sciences."[24] In light of the price of membership and the mingling of social classes during this period, La Mésangère would have seen a variety of male attire there—much of it bourgeois. Perhaps he would have worn a version of the newest civilian republican "uniform": a round hat and an everyday jacket with trousers rather than silk breeches—a way to avoid "the pretentions associated with the aristocracy of the Old Regime."[25] It had also become acceptable, however, for republicans to "wear elegant breeches, well-shaped hats, and hair styles in which the delicate and light touch of a wigmaker shines."[26] The new styles struck a moderate note, neither wholesale renunciation nor in-your-face exhibitionism. However, there was a great deal of the latter on the part of men and women who were unhappy with the revolutionary order.

According to art historian Ewa Lajer-Burcharth, the psychic aftermath of the Terror manifested itself in the intense individual, social, and state concern about the body and clothing, which resulted in public parades of fashion on promenades, and in public balls, gyms, and swimming pools.[27] The most fashionable upper-class women renounced the richly hued, highly accessorized, tightly corseted bodices and voluminous skirts and wigs that had been de rigueur. They chose bobbed haircuts, simple, light-colored, sheath-like dresses sometimes made of a sheer material like muslin that shockingly revealed their bodies.[28] What also captivated the public imagination and inspired ridicule was the outrageous clothing of the counterrevolutionary vigilantes, the *Incroyables*, as seen in figure 0.1 and also in the caricature "Café des Incroyables" (see figure 4.1). Here, again, we see earrings, tight *culottes*, calf-high boots, tassels, and high cravats up to and even over the chin. Parting their shoulder-length hair in the middle to make pigtails, it is pulled up in the back—a defiant reference to the ritual that preceded the guillotine.

Lajer-Burcharth notes "the ambiguity or the outright effeminacy of some of these figures" in the image and points out their "scopic engagement" with one another.[29] She notes that the café depicted is an all-male space and suggests that it may be homoerotic. I would argue that this depiction of men's intense desire to see and be seen, to touch and be touched in an intimate hothouse atmosphere is pointedly homoerotic. The image also ridicules the group's look-alike uniformity and the brazenly open way it polices admission based upon adherence to its dress code and also, perhaps, attractiveness.[30] A flood of social and political caricatures as well as boulevard plays and doggerel skewered such men for their sartorial excesses, effeminate air, and affected lisp that dropped the *r* sound, allegedly to avoid uttering the word *revolution*.[31]

▪ ▪ ▪

These consciously outrageous styles might have been illustrated in French fashion magazines, but France had been without a fashion press ever since *Journal de la Mode et du Goût* folded in April 1793, four years before.[32] By 1797, however, the French appear to have had their fill of revolutionary asceticism and, for those who could afford it, the time was ripe for the revival of luxury, personal freedoms, and pleasures, including fashion journals. Fashion was not just à la mode again; it was all the rage as La Mésangère would soon find out firsthand.

FIGURE 4.1 "Café des Incroyables: Like Meets Like." Hand-colored engraving: Anonymous, "Café des Incroyables" (1797). "Ma Parole d'honneur! Ils le plaisantent."/"My word! They're making fun of him." *Source*: Musée du Louvre

FRONT MAN, SHADOW FIGURE

Today, we might consider La Mésangère and his business partner Jean-Baptiste Sellèque (1767–1801), also from the provinces, highly unlikely candidates for bringing the fashion press back to life. Yet their predecessors had equally improbable backgrounds. Nor is there evidence to indicate whether either man was personally stylish, but that had not mattered before either.

In March 1797, La Mésangère and Sellèque's combination of ambition, education, skills, talents, modest connections, financial investors, and luck made them the first men to revive the fashion press for the postrevolutionary age. La Mésangère certainly had the academic qualifications and the publishing experience. Moreover, his *Paris Traveler* had proven him an adept and avid collector of information about the capital's lure, lore, history, sites, and trends, including fashions. Six years younger than La Mésangère, Sellèque was the son of a modestly wealthy tax collector from Normandy. He too had been a schoolteacher, albeit as a layman, not a priest.[33] When Sellèque and his wife left Chartres and moved to Paris, he found occasional work as a journalist and moved into his mother-in-law's house. There, he set up a bookstore, which is where their periodical's subscriptions would be managed.[34]

In the beginning, the two men named their new publication *Journal des Dames* [Ladies' Journal]. This unmistakable appropriation of a very famous French periodical of the same name, which ran from 1759 to 1779, revealed the newcomers' high ambitions and intended audience, women.[35] But using the earlier title was disingenuous on several counts. The original *Journal des Dames* was led by a succession of male and then female editors, whose stated purpose was to elevate and educate the second sex. For that reason, the earlier *Journal des Dames* assiduously avoided hoary associations of women with vanity and frivolity, said very little about *la mode*, and featured no illustrations.

By contrast, the fashion content of Sellèque and La Mésangère's "Ladies' Journal"—three full-color engravings, detailed descriptions of them and other new styles, reviews of books and plays, and miscellaneous leisure reading—followed the lines of their fashion magazine precursors. However, five months after the inaugural issue, on August 20, 1797, Sellèque and La Mésangère were the first editors ever to make the association between fashion and (elite) femininity official by appending "et des Modes" [and Fashion] to the title, making it *Journal des Dames et des Modes* [Ladies' Fashion Journal]. A harbinger of gendered assumptions to come, this name change reinforced the idea of *les dames* and *les modes* as a natural—and desirable—association. Downplaying men's involvement and interest in it,[36] the magazine bolstered masculinist revolutionary ideology about the sexes and the trend toward masculine renunciation more generally, shoring up ideas of *la mode* as a trivial, feminine subject.

Like its forerunners, Sellèque and La Mésangère's new magazine offered an eclectic mix of poetry, curious facts, and remarks about literary works and artistic goings-on. It also featured more serious fare: commentaries on the nature of womanhood, letters from readers (some real, most fictional), short theater and book reviews, excerpts from recent novels, comments about everyday problems, thoughts on social issues, and stories about commoners.[37]

Timing wasn't everything, but it helped. The journal's success was due in part to a series of historical changes that was finally making France, long after England and the United States, "a modern consumer society," writes historian Leora Auslander. These factors included "the definitive repeal of sumptuary legislation, the expansion of new forms of retailing, the urbanization of society, and the growth of a population with disposable income." More important still, "the acquisition of goods came to represent and even constitute people, groups, and institutions in a new way, that is, class, gender, nation, and even self were constructed through the acquisition and use of goods." In this new, consumer world, La Mésangère was one of a growing number of "taste professionals" who "earned their living" as such rather than by "actually selling objects."[38] Yet these editors, like others, did in fact sell objects: the magazines, prints of the engravings, and their own books.

For two years, La Mésangère's role in Sellèque's operation was anonymous. Nevertheless, Annemarie Kleinert, the expert on the man and his magazine, maintains that early on he exercised considerable influence on the publication's tone and style, choice of content and collaborators, design elements, and high-quality engravings. La Mésangère's invisibility during those years had an advantage: It meant that he got neither credit nor blame for the important role he played in a women's magazine unless it was from insiders.[39] Going unnamed also helped hide his past as a teaching priest, protecting him from disparaging stereotypes about clerical-secular hybrids (see figure 3.3), the vain, all-too-dapper and eager-to-please abbé from *Magasin des Modes Nouvelles* in 1789, a lorgnette in one hand and a spray of roses in the other. However, this "female" genre remained almost entirely men's business. In the beginning, the man in charge was not La Mésangère but rather the younger, thirty-year-old Sellèque.

ABOUT BUT WITHOUT LADIES, FOR, ABOUT, AND BY MEN

The first pages of *Journal des Dames*'s inaugural issue were dedicated to a lengthy, saccharine encomium to women signed by Sellèque. He pointedly distinguishes himself from what he calls the "tyrants" of the Revolution and their "appalling plan" to make the French barbarous cannibals by "annihilating the influence" of what he calls "the adored sex." To counter these despots and male journalists who, he writes, have not "two words" to say about the female sex, he promises that he and his staff will act as "valiant avengers of women's glory."[40] Typical of the cloying male tributes to female virtues during this period, the article extolls women's "physical attractiveness, gracious sociability, and emotional sensitivity." These qualities, he writes, have long tempered men's natural force and brutality and make women superior to men. Yet, in the end, Sellèque leaves no doubt that women exist to serve men: "*Mesdames*, make us always happy, and you will always be happy."[41] In these and other such passages, renewing male gallantry and setting women on a pedestal only appears to turn patriarchy on its head.

The same was true on the production end of the enterprise. The few female staff members had low-impact, low-paying positions: folding the periodical's pages and doing the mobile typesetting. The women who did the painstaking job of hand coloring each of the engravings may, however, have earned a little more. All the other employees, including "journalists, draftsmen, engravers, . . . binders, and those in charge of record-keeping and distribution," were men.[42] As for contributors, a good number of them were female—or at least writers who used female names/pseudonyms.[43] Between 1798 and 1802, a woman, Albertine Clément-Hémery, was part-owner and manager.[44]

Until mid-1799 when Sellèque was still in charge, the tone and content of *Journal des Dames et des Modes* were nothing like the polite, tempered appeals for patriotism and men's return to *la mode* in Buisson's *Magasin des Modes Nouvelles Françaises et Anglaises* from just before and just after the Revolution. Far from following Le Brun's scorn for unmanly men in *Journal de la Mode et du Goût* Sellèque does the exact opposite: He takes aim at the machismo politics and posturing of the Directory. The magazine quotes from an anonymous letter purportedly from a French soldier serving in the French Army of Italy in Venice. While acknowledging that the war might bring a more lasting peace for France, the writer notes pointedly that war "destroys men, often solely for the pleasure of their masters."[45] The masters in question were the government's five directors but, more directly in this context, its generals, including Bonaparte who was in charge of the Italian campaign.

Sellèque and La Mésangère were not waging war, but they learned quickly that to master their new domain, they needed to conduct civilian versions of conquest. In the early days, "immediately overwhelmed with work," writes La Mésangère's biographer Kleinert, the partners "would run to shops, theatres, political meetings, and public places where they observed *le beau monde* and picked up all the news and rumors they could."[46] Their mission was not going to be easy. While subscription rolls for their predecessors, *Cabinet des Modes*, *Magasin des Modes Nouvelles*, and *Journal de la Mode et du Goût*, had been passed along from one to the next, Sellèque and La Mésangère had to start from scratch. Despite their advantage, the three preceding fashion magazines had enjoyed only modest success, and none had lasted longer than three years. The third, Le Brun's *Journal de la Mode et du Goût*, had imploded and gone bankrupt.

However, there was another self-imposed difficulty. To convince readers that theirs was the periodical that offered the absolute latest in *modes*, Sellèque and La Mésangère decided to double the speed of production, from ten days to five. The downside was that this doubled the cost, labor, and pressure of getting issues out on time. The resulting delays frustrated the editors as well as subscribers.[47] The biggest concern, however, was the steep 92,000-franc investment that two wealthy entrepreneurs, the printer Mollet, and the bookseller (*libraire*) Dentu, had made in the magazine.[48] Within a short time, they had even more to worry about: competition. Francesco Bonafide, an Italian writer and editor living in Paris, was celebrating the maiden run of his once-every-ten-days *Tableau Général du Goût, des Modes et Costumes de Paris* [General Tableau of Taste, Fashions, and Paris Costumes] (March 1797–February 3, 1799); and it would remain Sellèque and La Mésangère's rival for two years.

To succeed, Sellèque and La Mésangère and their competitors made use of tactics not unlike those of General Bonaparte in Italy: Plunder and annex enemy territory while concealing from the public the often-unseemly machinations behind those conquests.[49] In journalism, as in the military, good timing and chance played no small role. For example, in August 1797, Sellèque and La Mésangère who were rapidly running out of funds, learned that yet another rival, *Journal des Modes et Nouveautés* [Magazine of Fashions and Novelties], offered far more fashion content and at a 20 percent lower subscription rate. Luckily, the owners Moller and Dentu managed to buy out the rival publication and annex it to *Journal des Dames et des*

Modes as a supplement.[50] Just one week later, however, France underwent yet another seismic political shift, in which Bonaparte would play a significant role.

■ ■ ■

Faced with a growing royalist backlash against the Directory, on September 4, 1797 (18 fructidor), four of the five directors plotted a coup. Emboldened by the armed troops that General Bonaparte had sent to Paris to prevent a popular uprising against them, the legislature voted to annul the elections that were to take place that spring, which favored the royalists. In addition, its members ordered the deportation of over fifty hostile deputies, journalists, and generals.[51] The directors also revoked many of the liberties promised in the Declaration of the Rights of Man eight years before, including freedom of the press.[52] Government censors made it clear that no aspect of the press would be impervious, even if the publication were "only" a women's magazine. Between November 1798 and November 1799, they found *Journal des Dames et des Modes* "quite reprehensible" for treating serious matters lightly, condemned certain "immoral" content (song lyrics and an article describing a scene of prostitution), and temporarily shut down Sellèque and La Mésangère's periodical.[53]

Draconian censorship laws ensured that newspapers and magazines remained strictly apolitical or dutifully parroted the Napoleonic line. If not, they would get the axe. Printers were arrested and titles banned outright. Bonaparte's tight reins on the press meant that journalists, editors, and printers had very little flexibility when it came to political subjects.

This was far from the last time the French press would be attacked. On January 17, 1800, just a few months after he had maneuvered to be named First Consul, Bonaparte shut down sixty daily newspapers. Only fourteen survived. Meanwhile, the state's heavy stamp tax on newsprint and a crushing rate of inflation hit newspapers and magazines very hard. Sellèque and La Mésangère had to raise the annual subscription price of *Journal des Dames et des Modes* from ten to thirty-six livres. Subscribers got double the number of pages and dozens of supplementary fashion plates, but this was an astronomical 260 percent rate hike for an already expensive periodical, shutting out consumers with more modest means.[54] Despite the cost, wealthy individual subscribers, those who were members of *cabinets de lecture* (subscription fee libraries), and many prosperous tailors, seamstresses, and milliners apparently felt the price was worth it.[55]

The growing success of the journal meant that more would-be players wanted in. Jean-Jacques Lucet, a well-published journalist and editor, bought one of *Journal des Dames et des Modes*'s major competitors, *Tableau Général du Goût*, in February 1799. Following Sellèque and La Mésangère's gendered lead, Lucet renamed it *La Correspondance des Dames*, making it only the second French fashion magazine to be titled as a work for "ladies." Yet it explicitly featured an authoritative male voice, that of a presumed gentleman in Paris ostensibly sending fairly patronizing letters about Parisian manners, gossip, and fashion to a female friend in the country. Five months later, Lucet refashioned the magazine around a more flippant character: Harlequin, the mocking servant in variegated clothing from the Italian *commedia dell'arte* tradition. *L'Arlequin* lasted a mere two and a half months.[56]

Whatever the gendered configurations of the magazines, all the male editors made it quite clear that this domain of "feminine" subjects and female readers was masculine turf—their chance to lob snide putdowns and cruel remarks against their male rivals. For example, *Le Mois* [The Month] (March 1799–August 1800) offers a sardonic eulogy for its competitor, *L'Arlequin*, stating that its eponymous figure, Arlequin, like the magazine itself, was "very nicely dressed, but a little thin, a little slight, and his innocent little blows with a bat, his little Bergamo [Italian] accent, and his little grimaces must have seemed a little too frequent, a little too monotone, and above all, a little too expensive."[57] In a word, *L'Arlequin* was a wimpy, emasculated, and foppish foreigner. By contrast, the men behind *Le Mois* declare themselves "faithful guardians of the temples of taste and glory," belittling still other competitors as "foreigners and thieves" who, having no ideas of their own, merely copied the other "dogs" in the pack, of which *Le Mois* was one.[58]

By contrast, Sellèque and La Mésangère generally refrained from meanspirited mockery of their rivals. This decency may well have made them appear to be above such low-class behavior, but it also hid from the public their ruthless business tactics. For example, shutting down *L'Arlequin* in 1799 was not its owner's idea. Sellèque and La Mésangère bought it from Lucet, whom they also poached as a journalist for their own staff. The following year, La Mésangère, by then the sole editor, would purchase the high-and-mighty *Le Mois* and hire away its talented draftsman and engraver, Labrousse. He also did away with *La Mouche*, a three-month, flash-in-the-pan edited by C. J. B. Lucas de Rochemont who, like Lucet, chose to write for La Mésangère's journal rather than compete with it.[59]

By August 1800, Sellèque and La Mésangère's strategy—selling what subscribers seemed to want, buying out competing publications, and stealing their talent—made *Journal des Dames et des Modes* the only French fashion magazine standing—the clear winner in this male-run, dog-eat-dog "women's" world.[60] Over that two-year period, Sellèque's editorial persona had shifted, from the fawning, supposedly enlightened praise of women in his opening letter to sassy flippancy and aggressive arrogance—especially toward his fellow men.

AN EDITOR WITH ATTITUDE

Whether to appear consistent with the magazine's "frivolous" content or to conceal his own and others' high personal and financial stakes in it, Sellèque largely adopts the fashion magazine convention of Invisible Man. However, his antiauthoritarian cheekiness called attention to this stance, which risked alienating well-heeled or high-placed subscribers, just as Le Brun had done with *Journal des Modes et du Goût* in the early 1790s. There, the similarities end. When in top form, Le Brun's Invisible Man editorial voice is earnest, pugnacious, and self-righteous; Sellèque's is distinctly cynical. His editorial persona takes few things seriously, least of all politics, politicians, or party lines, not even questions that would presumably be within his jurisdiction, such as class-appropriate clothing.

Early on, in 1797, Sellèque paraphrases at some length the recent, heated debate in the Directory's Council of Five Hundred about proper attire for its members. Should they wear breeches or trousers, square riding coats or short jackets? Should they sport bobbed hair like the radical Jacobin Jean-Paul Marat (1743–1793), assassinated years before in his bath, or follow the lead of the long-haired and bearded Moses from the Bible? Sellèque's pointed choice of comparisons and the bouncy rhythm of the oppositions puts him at an amused distance from those who cared too much about the wrong things, especially, but not only, politicians. Although Sellèque states that the legislators' deliberation about clothing was a matter "of highest importance" and deems the speeches made "solemn and sublime," his ironic tone would not have been lost on savvy readers.[61]

Sellèque offers a similarly cheeky putdown of men who, he claims, take macho militarism too far. In the May 3, 1798 issue, he comments on the Directory's recent announcement that General Napoleon Bonaparte would be leading an armada of 160 scholars along with tens of thousands of troops and tons of arms, in a bid to conquer Egypt.[62] Sellèque pronounces himself unconvinced that "Cannons, bombs, hails of bullets, generals, suppliers, [and] armies" would ever succeed in "dazzling [the Egyptians], subjugating minds, winning hearts, civilizing customs, softening mores, or instilling in them a taste for [Western] arts and proper [French] manners."[63] He also criticizes what he sees as a scandalous omission in the cultural component of the mission to Egypt: Why not fashion, he asks, which is "everywhere queen?"

Sellèque's biggest objection, although he makes it sound facetious, was personal: He, the self-declared reigning expert on style, had not been invited to head up this military/scholarly expedition. He boasts in mock-macho manner: "I would have already set sail on the Mediterranean with my thirty-three issues [of *Journal des Dames et des Modes*] on Parisian dress, along with a flotilla of all the latest French fashions for women and men alike." His cargo would include "Greek chignons, corkscrew curls, Titus-style hairdos, blond, black and chestnut wigs, [in styles] fluffy, bristly, fancy, unkempt . . . square-cut coats, octagonal buttons, waist coasts *en schall*, English-style breeches, clog shoes, flock cravats, etc. etc.!" as ways to civilize the "unenlightened" Egyptian population. Give me just "300 wigmakers, 500 hair stylists, 1,000 dressmakers and tailors," he boasts, "and I will answer for the conquest of Egypt, Abyssinia, the Niger, the Congo, and all of Africa."[64] This is just one of Sellèque's many remarks that today's readers might find surprisingly contemporary, even queer in tone and content: over-the-top exaggeration and snappy insults along with a campy insistence on his own fabulousness. Despite Sellèque's own cocky confidence, his personal dominance of the fashion press would come to an end much sooner than he would have imagined.

TAKEOVERS

By June 1799, Sellèque, at age thirty-two, a widower with three children who had remarried, was so ill that he had to pass the management and ownership of *Journal des Dames et des Modes* to his business partner, La Mésangère.[65] In the magazine, Sellèque announced his departure by slyly comparing his own exit with the infamously rapid turnover in the Directory's innermost circle: "Yet another DIRECTOR hands in his resignation."[66] Within a month, La Mésangère bought out Sellèque's 50 percent share of the periodical, which meant that after two years of anonymity, his name finally appeared on the last page of the magazine.[67] This was a career changer: the beginning of an even more impressive and far more public success. Meanwhile, General Bonaparte would triumph too, although in ways less aboveboard and on a scale that far eclipsed La Mésangère's: He would put all of France ever more directly under his thumb.

■ ■ ■

By October 1799, General Bonaparte had left Italy and returned to France. There, he could have been dismissed or court-martialed for deserting his troops in Egypt and for some of his defeats in Italy. Thanks in part to his brilliant propaganda dispatches and a starry-eyed public weary of war and political instability, his homecoming became an occasion for reviving the cult of revolutionary heroism. Bonaparte's return was also of keen interest to two rival French camps. Pro-Jacobin politicians counted on him to back the revolutionary army's ongoing battles in Europe. Meanwhile, Emmanuel Joseph Sieyès (1748–1836), the reigning director, believed that Bonaparte would be just the man to help him pull off a coup against the other four members of the Directory.

However, General Bonaparte had his own wish list: Rid France of the ineffectual Directory that he had been appointed to serve and, under a thin veneer of legality, replace it with a new government under his rule. In the early morning of November 10, 1799, having just been named head of the Directory's military forces, Bonaparte had devised the perfect cover for his covert operation. He secretly ordered high-ranking officers to show up at his residence on the rue de la Victoire in Paris in their full-dress uniform. Although the rank-and-file soldiers also assembled there did not yet know it, their military garb had a purpose: To make a show of Bonaparte's legitimacy and apparent loyalty to the regime in power while serving as muscle to overthrow it. Bonaparte led his forces to a site outside Paris where the government's Council of Ancients and Council of Five Hundred had been summoned. Standing before the government's representatives to plead his case, Bonaparte made several political gaffes that might have dashed his dream of taking over, but with last-minute help from his brother Lucien, the coup of 18–19 Brumaire succeeded. All five directors were forced to resign, and both legislative chambers were dissolved. The Directory was now history.

In its place, Bonaparte and his coconspirators wrote up a constitution for a new regime, which was to be called the Consulate. Bonaparte got himself named First Consul by cagily manipulating Sieyès, the principal director, during a supposedly secret legislative vote. He also managed to get his choice of co-consuls, two men quite different from each other and from Bonaparte but who would nevertheless do what he believed was their "real" job: Let him have his way.[68] In his

1799 proclamation to the French, Bonaparte declared that with the Consulate, the Revolution was over and, with it, "representative government [and] the sacred rights of property, equality [and] liberty."[69] While claiming that his reign would nevertheless be held in check by a "spirit of order, justice, moderation," Bonaparte was now essentially free to rule by decree, and he did. The hero quickly became a dictator.

What Bonaparte did *not* attempt to do, at least not immediately, was lord his new position over his subjects with fancy attire or other luxuries.[70] Instead, on his first day as First Consul, the head of France's government, Bonaparte is said to have arrived at the entrance to the Luxemburg Palace "as a 'citizen' wearing a 'greenish' frock coat and a bowler hat."[71] Later, in February 1800, when an official cortège marked his official move into the majestic, albeit pillaged and rat-infested Tuileries Palace, three thousand infantrymen and cavalrymen in uniform preceded him. Even so, the scene was nothing to write home about according to one early twentieth-century historian. "In place of carriages, the new regime's dignitaries had gotten into rented cabs 'whose numbers had been hidden beneath a strip of paper.' There were no servants, no liveries, no powder on people's hair, but rather an air of improvisation, 'poorly concealed poverties,' and, in short, a very republican simplicity." The sole exception was "a team of six white horses . . . that had been given to Bonaparte by the emperor of Austria."[72]

Just a year later, however, in 1801, the First Consul refashioned himself in high style for official events: "a red, embroidered, cuffless coat of Lyon silk, a black silk cravat, boots of

Moroccan leather, tight buckskin pants, a vest of white *bazin*, and yellow gloves worn to his elbows Crispin style and a saber worn à la turque, affixed to his tricolor silk belt, hanging very far down to his side."[73] Despite this impressive new look and in part perhaps because it appeared to represent a return to the bad, old, authoritarian days of the Old Regime, Bonaparte's coup d'état was far from cause for universal celebration.[74]

One of the most famous assassination attempts against him is often considered the world's first "car bomb" attack. It took place just a year after he was named First Consul, and its effects would be significant, not only for Bonaparte and the country but also for Sellèque and thus for La Mésangère.

On Christmas Eve 1800, not far from the Palais Royal in Paris, three *Chouans* (royalist insurgents from western France, where La Mésangère grew up and taught), disguised as workers in coarse trousers, set up a long fuse to a keg of gunpowder on a cart they had set up to assassinate the First Consul and his cortège as they passed by on the way to the opera. As legend has it, delayed by Josephine, who had gone back for a shawl and then took her own carriage, Bonaparte missed his date with death, as did she.

When the First Consul finally arrived at the opera, he is said to have received a standing ovation. What that grand hurrah really meant would have been up for debate. Those who might have cheered had Bonaparte been successfully assassinated would certainly not have dared show it. In the weeks and months that followed, Bonaparte's narrow escape further enhanced his aura of invincibility and convinced him that he should execute brutal political crackdowns against those he considered enemies. Even though the assassination attempt had in fact been a royalist, not a republican, plot against him, Bonaparte took the opportunity to deport no fewer than 360 Jacobins whom he accused of treason.

While the reigning First Consul came out of this incident even stronger than before, those near the site of the blast on Christmas Eve fared less well. The thundering explosion blew out doors and shattered windows, maiming, blinding, and killing dozens of residents.[75] Sellèque lived nearby on the rue Saint-Niçaise. His frail health and his fear that the bomb marked a return to further political violence and chaos appear to have contributed to the fatal stroke he suffered one week later, on New Year's Day 1801, at the age of thirty-three.[76]

After almost two years in the shadows as Sellèque's business partner, La Mésangère, now forty, could finally step into the limelight. Rather than focus attention on himself, however, he continued to adopt the masks of various editorial personae, all of whom claimed invisibility. For variety, however, he also added male and female characters. Blithely unaware of the foolishness of their opinions and behavior, their function was presumably to make readers feel superior to them.

INVISIBLE MEN AND CONSPICUOUS CHARACTERS

As the sole editor of *Journal des Dames et des Modes*, La Mésangère could have made himself and his views known in any number of ways, as some previous fashion journals had done.

While Le Brun had displayed his name in large letters on the front page of *Journal de la Mode et du Goût*, La Mésangère continued to list his in small letters on the back page. Nor did he mimic his deceased partner, Sellèque, by setting himself up as a loquacious and arrogant expert on the sexes and ideal gender relations. La Mésangère also eschewed aggressive self-righteousness. This meant that under his watch, neither Le Brun's avid Jacobinism and intolerance for effeminate men nor Sellèque's cheeky cynicism about men in power and blustery bullies got much play.

La Mésangère also avoided the narcissistic, "feminine" paths modeled by some of the male authors of women's health and beauty manuals during the early Napoleonic period, such as Dr. Marie de Saint-Ursin's *L'Ami des Femmes* [Women's Friend] and Joseph Lemaire's *Le Dentiste des Dames* [The Ladies' Dentist] (1812). Both writers worked to ensure that no prospective female would discount them as marriage material. The dentist even included a bust-length portrait of himself in fine clothes. The older man, Saint-Ursin, does so by including in his manual a long, one-page list of his medical honors. He also indulges in a great deal of obsequious fawning over women in "feminine" prose filled to the brim with puffed up curlicues and bows. Meanwhile, he reserved serious "male" discourse for the medical footnotes meant for fellow male doctors and male readers. Like the younger and more cynical Auguste Caron, author of *Toilette des Dames, ou Encyclopédie de la beauté* [Ladies' Toilette, or the Encyclopedia of Beauty] (1806), La Mésangère did not stoop to conquer in any of these ways.[77]

Rather, like his prerevolutionary antecedents in the modern fashion press and following a long tradition of scholarly and journalistic writing, La Mésangère chose to be Invisible Man.[78] He could see everything, it appeared, and he showed his readers what he saw, but he gave away almost nothing about himself. Rather than adopt Invisible Man as a single generic and indivisible entity as his forerunners had done, La Mésangère came to feature several Invisible Men in every issue. Their bylines ranged from the banal "Observer" to the mythological "Argus" or "One Hundred Eyes." Each had a different wheelhouse and a minimal but somewhat distinctive shtick.

None of them were marked female or feminine. Instead, they spoke as rational beings taking supposedly universal (and therefore presumably male) perspectives.[79] In other words, La Mésangère made his magazine a safe "closet" full of various invisible male personae with different names. There is no way to tell whether La Mésangère always wrote the texts attributed to his Invisible Men personae. However, their attitudes and tone are rather alike: Plainspoken, averse to conflict and risk, they tend to leaven their stuffy respectability with dry wit and self-deprecating humor. Thus, rather than rail against the clothing and follies of men and women, as his predecessors had done, La Mésangère's Invisible Men tend to favor what we might call a Doctrinarian perspective: more concerned with facts, common sense, middlebrow notions of good taste, and proper behavior than morality per se. This may or may not have been La Mésangère's own view.[80]

La Mésangère's Invisible Men have something else in common, which is unique to *Journal des Dames et des Modes*. Rather than assume and embrace heterosexuality, almost all his editorial personae hold it and women at arm's length. In France, male authors' and editors' distance and detachment from women were hardly new. However, La Mésangère's editorial personae go further. They bear almost no relation to bachelors looking for a member of the opposite sex to bed or to marry, like the doctor and dentist. They appear never to have experienced the pleasures (or constraints) of courtship, marriage, and procreation. They do not speak, even in jest, of desiring a woman or women in general—as if it were against their nature or religion. Neither hyper-gallant toward women, like the doctor, nor dismissive of them, as in so many others' works, La Mésangère's Invisible Men appear to have evaded two versions of conventional heterosexuality: fawning praise and harsh misogyny. Nevertheless, in what the Invisible Men write, there is still a trace, and sometimes more than a trace, of paternalism.[81] Was it by sidestepping desire that these personae avoided the late Sellèque's truculence, arrogance, and sardonic egotism?

For all their relative detachment from worldliness, La Mésangère's invisible personae were not above making, or quoting, an occasional catty putdown. For example, "One Hundred Eyes" remarks that a certain kind of fashionable man riding a horse "resembles a groom riding his animal to the slaughterhouse."[82] More commonly, one or another of the Invisible Men parries the attacks against La Mésangère, his magazine, or his readers not with a forceful smackdown but with cutting irony. Thus, one of the editor's personae, "*Le Compère*," which can mean accomplice, crony, godfather, good guy, useful connection, or self-interested man, mischievously reports that a recently published almanac dared call *Journal des Dames et des Modes* good only for "*frivolous* ladies and *young* gentlemen."[83] "Us?" Le Compère gasps in mock horror. "Good for foolish people?"

In another case, claiming to reject "frivolous" as an unjust slur against women, he nevertheless takes the occasion to remind readers of two *other* common "female" faults—inconstancy and shallowness—while claiming, facetiously, that the fair sex could never be accused of either.[84] Soon after, Le Compère appears to bite the hand that feeds him. He derides his own *Journal des Dames et des Modes* for its "solemn" debates over silk versus cotton stockings: "It's revolting, it's a scandal." Nevertheless, he saves the last laugh for himself and his journal: "We wouldn't be surprised if these were the reasons for our success."[85] Through his many multiple editorial personae and his "catch me if you can" turns of meaning, La Mésangère took neither himself, his magazine, nor even his defense of women too seriously.

Despite or because of this light tone, the editor sometimes found himself on the defensive. For example, his childhood friend François Desvignes wrote him to express his shock at what he considered the magazine's racy tone and content. La Mésangère replied, "You don't know public opinion. If I did less of this, far from gaining more subscribers, I would lose some. . . . I must avoid taking a more reserved tone; its sole effect would be boredom."[86] His strategy apparently worked. Just over a year after assuming the role of editor, in a December 1801 letter, La Mésangère told Desvignes, "With this magazine, I am very comfortably well off."[87]

One of the many ways La Mésangère found to produce a morally upright yet *piquant* "ladies'" magazine was to populate it with dozens of stereotypical but fully embodied fictional characters. Male and female both, they appear as the authors of (fictional) short letters to the editor pleading the righteousness of their points of view. One effect of their presence is to emphasize the invulnerability of the Invisible Men—and the foolishness of the caricatural characters, real people like them, and perhaps his readers. The characters write earnest, unwittingly comic letters to the editor, which would presumably have tipped off sophisticated readers that the point was to mock them.

Fretting, wanting, judging, and complaining, almost all the fictional letter-writers are explicitly gendered caricatures—often from the middle or lower classes: the henpecked, parsimonious husband; his compulsive shopper wife; the country bumpkin in the big city, etc. Each one confirms hackneyed ideas about age, occupation, marital status, geographical origins, class, and especially gender. To wit, female characters often admit that they are concerned about their appearance to the point of obsessive peevishness. By contrast, the fictional men generally express little concern about how they look. Together, these two stances frame the Great Masculine Renunciation of fashion and, with it, the Great Feminine Fixation on fashion as complementary facts of nature—not contingent and historical attitudes and practices.

Conversely, La Mésangère gives the lie to notions that women's attractiveness and flair for *la mode* are what make heterosexuality work—one of the claims of the first modern fashion magazine. In *Journal des Dames et des Modes*, by contrast, fictional husbands who talk about what their wives wear do not generally compliment them but bitterly protest the high cost of keeping them in the latest style. Meanwhile, Rosa, one of the fictional wives, bewails her husband's tight hold on the family purse strings: "Oh, what tyrants men are! How unhappy women are!" This is a far cry from the ideal, mutually respectful gender relations touted by Sellèque in the inaugural 1797 issue, not to mention Le Brun's starry-eyed promotion of the marriage of clergy to patriotic laymen and women in his radically revolutionary magazine from the early 1790s. If anything, in La Mésangère's periodical, the many grievances on both sides of the marriage gender divide appear to demonstrate that the idea of gender and heterosexuality as a matter of natural, complementary differences that was so pervasive at the time makes no one happy.

Far from a new theme, the unhappy marriage was a centuries-long tradition in French literature, popular song, doggerel, caricatures, comedies, farces, and even children's puppet shows. However, La Mésangère was the first fashion magazine editor to consistently represent traditional gender arrangements as comical at best, injurious at worst. In another writer's hand, this could have been the basis for a sharp critique of the patriarchal status quo. In *Journal des Dames et des Modes*, however, it is played for easy laughs as if it were simply inevitable.

Avoiding the political may in fact be part of what made La Mésangère's first two decades as the magazine's editor, beginning under Bonaparte's tenure as First Consul, so successful.[88] In his journal, the former priest generally gave Bonaparte what he wanted: attacks against English fashion, praise for French fashions and textiles, promotion of the flailing French silk industry, and mute acceptance of the state seizure of English merchandise in French shops and ports. La Mésangère certainly did not make the contemptuous digs against Bonaparte that Sellèque appeared to enjoy.[89]

Bonaparte appears to have understood that La Mésangère's *Journal des Dames et des Modes* helped keep women in line just as his official daily propaganda newspaper, *Le Moniteur universel* (1798–1868), did. Although Bonaparte claimed to eschew frivolity, when "the ladies in his entourage hesitated over a question of official etiquette, he is said to have advised them to 'consult *le La Mésangère*.'" In other words, *Journal des Dames et des Modes* was supposed to be women's *Moniteur*.[90] The idea, presumably, was *chaque sexe a son journal.*

Both publications purported merely to report the news but in fact skewed it. Each functioned as a version of the mythological Argus, the hundred-eyed creature whose ever-watchful surveillance readers were supposed to internalize. Whereas Bonaparte's *Moniteur* told the French what they should believe, La Mésangère's *Journal* let them know what they should be, wear, read, know, enjoy, and desire. In these ways as well, *Journal*'s light reading and "frivolous" fashion news served Bonaparte's purpose: It entertained the leisure classes and distracted them from serious and substantive matters. Its content and engravings also buttressed the cornerstone of Napoleon's regime by making gender distinctions appear both natural and glamorous. For almost two decades from 1800 to 1818, the mild favor that Bonaparte accorded the magazine, along with the First Consul's hard line against protest, which accounted for the stability of his regime, helped give the former Doctrinarian priest a virtual monopoly on the fashion press.[91]

In this mutually beneficial arrangement, the journal made a profit doing its own business and the regime's as well. Although *Journal des Dames et des Modes* comically skewered patriarchal arrangements that clearly weren't working, it also helped create properly gendered, docile, and disciplined readers, citizens, and consumers. During this period, the phantom of individual freedom and the chance to come up in the world were supposed to make up for the political liberties that had been lost. La Mésangère, the premier fashion editor of his day, appears to have accepted this bargain. For the next decade, his personal fortunes and influence would continue to climb. Bonaparte's would too—albeit to an infinitely greater degree and at a far higher cost to himself and others.

Chapter Five

THE EMPERORS' TRIUMPH AND DISGRACE

ON THE first day of December 1804, at age thirty-five, Napoleon Bonaparte, Consul for Life, was on the eve of realizing his most grandiose ambition: He would become the first French emperor since Charlemagne more than a thousand years before. Unlike his lifelong appointment as consul, this was to be a dynastic regime passed along the male line. Seven months before, in May, after months of scheming and horse trading, members of the Senate agreed to proclaim Bonaparte emperor. In November, the Senate set up a national plebiscite of propertied men to legitimize its vote. Pierre Joseph La Mésangère, the man who reigned over the French fashion press, may have participated in the referendum because he was a man of property, but his vote would not have mattered. The election was a sham: It gave only an illusion of choice. Napoleon already commanded the army and government and, having restored Catholicism in France in 1801, he effectively held the Church hostage to his demands.

But other aspects of Napoleon's rule had not gone so handily. A few years before, in 1801, Napoleon sent 30,000 troops to the country's most lucrative colony, Saint-Domingue to crush the revolt against France and its colonists by an alliance of slaves, *gens de couleur*, and free Blacks. However, in November 1803, the French army, diminished by battle losses and yellow fever, was dealt a humiliating defeat, proving that France could not necessarily establish an empire anywhere it wanted. By December, all French troops had fled the island. On January 1, 1804, the victorious revolutionaries pronounced their country's independence from France and restored its Taíno name, Ayiti (Haiti). In other words, just before Bonaparte founded his official "empire," he lost one of the jewels in its "crown."[1]

This clash between the facts and Napoleon's self-serving imperial mythology would be a challenge not only in the colonies but also at home. After the Revolution, which had upended the country's most venerable institutions and values in the name of liberty, equality, and fraternity, how would Napoleon convince his subjects and the rest of the world that he was emperor by rights?[2] To conceal or distract from his regime's fundamental illegitimacy required skillfully controlling optics. He did this, in large part, through fabulous costumes—not just for Josephine and other women of the court, but also for male courtiers, army officers, and himself. The ultimate expression of this cover-up as power play was his coronation, a grandiose spectacle that would set the pattern of uniform splendor for the rest of his reign. No longer would men at the highest echelons of state and court power be expected or even allowed to renounce or at least refrain from fabulous display as had happened at some points during the French Revolution. On the contrary, they *had* to dress up in spectacular uniforms following the dictates and taste of Napoleon the First.

SPLENDOR MADE TO ORDER

Despite the disdain for luxury that Napoleon had often expressed and shown earlier in life, his December 2, 1804 coronation and anointment at Notre Dame Cathedral featured unrivaled sumptuousness for both men and women. Napoleon put designers in charge of an army of artisans. Their goal was in effect to surpass the sartorial magnificence of Louis XIV, the seventeenth-century Sun King, as well as Napoleon's own predecessor, Louis XVI, guillotined just over a decade before. It cost the state millions of francs. Had Josephine, not Napoleon I, been the mastermind behind this exorbitant display, he and the public might well have vilified her as another example of natural female profligacy and vanity—the kind of scorn Marie-Antoinette had faced as queen. But this was another era entirely: One man, Napoleon, was fully in charge, and he would emerge largely unscathed from accusations of decadence and extravagance. He retained tight control over the army, police, legislature, arts, and the press, aggressively sought out French conquests elsewhere, and sent out a constant stream of propaganda. He also followed royal protocol but made it his own. Nowhere was Napoleon's new, imperial brand more visible and imposing than during his coronation ceremony, where he had the most to cover up, wanted most desperately to impress, and put up the most resources to do so.

For three dynasties, French coronations had always been self-conscious and politically freighted affairs. From the Merovingians (Clovis, AD 481) to the Carolingians (Charlemagne, AD 800) to the Capetians (Louis IX, AD 1226 through Louis XVI, AD 1775). Each new sovereign had to walk a tightrope: Hewing to tradition while putting a personal stamp on his reign. Given Napoleon's status as pretender to a new throne and his determination to secure an empire for himself out of whole cloth, it is no wonder he went to far greater extremes than his predecessors to secure his legitimacy. Insisting on jaw-dropping grandeur, he created a world-class spectacle, micromanaging how his royal forerunners' rituals, artifacts, regalia, and symbols would be refashioned for his own purposes.

A few years before, it is said that Napoleon had rejected the idea of holding a ceremony outside on the Champ de Mars, a large public space on the outskirts of Paris, which had been the site of revolutionary festivals. According to one source, he claimed that such a public spectacle would draw "the ignoble and corrupt populace of a large city," such as "twenty or thirty thousand fishwives or others of their kind."[3] His legitimacy would be a particularly tough sell for Parisians, he is reported to have said, who were "accustomed to seeing [the famous singer] Chéron at the Opéra and [the actor] Talma at the Théâtre-Français playing emperor far better than I could."[4] For similar reasons, Napoleon allegedly demanded that the coronation ritual be held indoors: "Can you imagine the effect if the emperor and his family were to be exposed in their imperial regalia to the ravages of the weather: mud, dust or rain?"[5]

The risk of exposure for Napoleon was not just having the wrong kind of people in attendance or that the emperor's men and women might be caught in a downpour or snowstorm. It was also about displaying himself partially unclothed, as royal protocol had dictated for centuries. Just twenty years earlier, during Louis XVI's ceremony, the would-be king's elbows, shoulders, back, and chest were bared.[6] After the French Revolution, however, a partly naked body could no longer be counted on to incarnate majesty, especially if the man in question had no royal blood.[7] It is no wonder Napoleon was adamant that every sumptuous layer of his costume remain in place.

More outrageously, the emperor-to-be insisted on breaking with the ancient Catholic tradition according to which the pope alone had the authority to crown the French sovereign. Although he invited the pope and high officials of the Church to be part of his imperial pageantry, he refused to be upstaged. He made sure that the prelates understood that their job was to demonstrate that they were under *his* thumb: He would crown himself. In addition, Napoleon arrogated to his made-to-order empire the country's most hallowed relics: a reconstruction of Charlemagne's scepter and gold-handled sword studded with diamonds, "symbolically carried during the [coronation] ceremony by his marshals."[8] Likewise, he ordered that all traces of the Bourbon white lily (*fleur-de-lys*) be replaced with the figure of a bee, a Merovingian symbol from the early days of French royalty in the fifth century. Some of the objects he wanted to use had been destroyed during the French Revolution as symbols of tyranny. In this way, the facsimiles he ordered of the gold, open laurel crown and the Hand of Justice, "a hand sculpted in ivory on a gold-plated baton, encrusted with cameos of rock crystal and amethyst," were meant to expunge from memory the Revolution and his own role in it.[9]

At the crowning ceremony, the regime took a totalizing approach to its self-fashioning. If something could be done once, it should be done everywhere and to the nth degree. Every imaginable surface and fabric were covered with the new and purloined symbols of the empire. The *N* for Napoleon, the Merovingian bee, the eagle (symbol of imperial Rome), and intertwined olive, oak, and laurel branches all appeared as exquisite, delicate gold-embroidered decorations on everything from the blue velvet that draped the inside of Notre Dame to the emperor's kid gloves, which were made expressly for the ceremony.

Even the articles of clothing that were completely hidden from public view featured symbols embroidered in gold thread: the entwined branches on Napoleon's delicate white, silk tricot coronation stockings (see figure 5.1) and the underside of his tunic and mantle.[10] The only person who might see these, aside from the women who did the delicate stitching and the valets who dressed Napoleon that day would have been the emperor-to-be. Embroidery inside a gown was not uncommon in high ceremonial costumes, but this time, the man-who-would-be-emperor had to be sure that more than the usual amount of smoke and mirrors would be deployed for the grand occasion.

The *Livre du Sacre*, a deluxe volume commemorating the coronation, gives an itemized account of the emperor's distinctive and splendiferous apparel. "White silk breeches and stockings; white shoes embroidered in gold; a white satin tunic embroidered and decorated at the hem with gold fringe, a

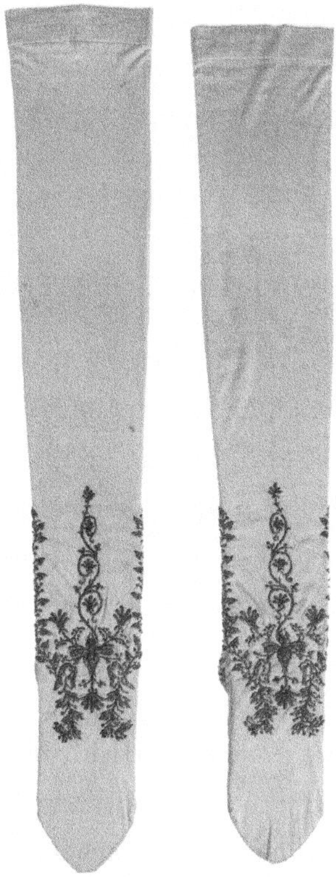

FIGURE 5.1 Opulence and symbolism on stockings. Photograph: The emperor's white silk coronation stockings embroidered with gold thread, 1804.
Source: Copyright Musée des Arts Décoratifs

mantle covering the shoulders and chest with a long train in crimson velvet speckled with bees in gold and edged in embroidery and ermine; white gloves with gold embroidery; a lace cravat; a gold laurel leaf crown; a golden scepter; the Hand of Justice, [and] a gold-handled sword studded with diamonds attached to a white sash worn around the waist and ornamented with gold fringe."[11] Napoleon's was by far the biggest personal makeover of all. The spectacle of power and majesty he orchestrated would be preserved for posterity in the highest art form of the period: painting.

WAS IT MAGNIFICENT?

Most famous of all is the monumental history painting by Jacques-Louis David, *Le Sacre de Napoléon* [The Coronation of Napoleon] (1807) (see figure 5.2). In it, the artist and emperor were almost wholly in sync. Napoleon gave David a rare amount of access to the coronation costumes and regalia, and he ordered those who had been present to sit individually for the painter.[12]

In the painting, most of the men and women of the new imperial court are grouped not with their family but rather according to their gender, rank, and function in his reign. Their costumes are also "his"—ones that Napoleon had made designers draw up according to his wishes. Behind the standing women are Napoleon's generals, the first in France to be elevated to courtly stature by virtue of their military rank even if they were not noblemen. In their hats topped with

FIGURE 5.2 Napoleon crowns Josephine. Painting, detail: Jacques-Louis David, *The Coronation of Napoleon* (1807).
Source: Courtesy of Dennis Jarvis

tall, exquisite white plumes, they look like swashbuckling sixteenth-century courtiers or, perhaps, well-to-do Parisians dressed for a costume ball. Anachronism was not unique to Napoleon's coronation, but it was a reminder that under his reign, almost anything could be, and would be, redesigned to serve his purposes.

Meanwhile, on the right side of the painting, members of the Church make a splendiferous display in their ceremonial dress. Pope Pius VII, seated on his papal throne, wears his traditional, formal white tunic with a simple gold-embroidered chasuble and gold accoutrements. For other prelates, outer vestments in lustrous fabrics featuring splendid, multicolored and gold embroidery were the order of the day. Not to be outdone, bishops wore their bejeweled miters. In this act of political window dressing, the more the pope and other ecclesiastical dignitaries glittered the better it was for both Church and state. Moreover, all were safe from accusations of personal vanity: Everyone had been ordered to dress to awe.

Lavish and exaggerated pomp had practical downsides for everyone, including male and female courtiers, prelates, and military men on parade, but perhaps no one more than Napoleon at his coronation. Without the aid of four male dignitaries to distribute the weight of his eighty-pound mantle, the emperor would only have been able to take a few small steps. Decades later, the ever-loyal valet of Napoleon, Constant Wairy, writing his memoirs, appears to want to reassure his readers that deep down, the emperor was neither vain nor vainglorious. Wairy states that the emperor favored ease and convenience above all. "On returning to the château, [the newly crowned emperor] freed himself as soon as he could from all that rich and uncomfortable apparel." This was far from a full masculine renunciation of ostentation, however. He replaced the gown with his royal blue grenadier uniform, with its decorative white and scarlet trim, gold-braided epaulettes, and white breeches. Wairy reports that "he repeated over and over, 'At last I can get my breath.' He was certainly much *more* at his ease on the day of battle."[13] Wairy's anecdote portrays Napoleon as a man's man, more comfortable weighed down by the anticipation of carnage than a surfeit of opulence.

Military uniform historian Raoul Brunon echoes Wairy's observations, emphasizing that Napoleon was naturally and fully on board with the Great Masculine Renunciation despite the huge amount of evidence that belies this. "By nature, Napoleon was a frugal man who kept the expenses for his wardrobe within a certain budget. . . . When the fashion was for tight-fitting, cramped styles, he had his tailors make clothes wide enough for him 'to be able to put on with the most ease,' as his valet Constant remembered. Constant adds that his employer's 'only concern in clothing was for the quality of the material and convenience.'"[14] If he couldn't get a piece of clothing on right away, he wouldn't wear it.

In the postrevolutionary era, however, French artists eager to represent the emperor in his *new*, opulent clothes needed to avoid the negative connotations of male pretense and excess.

HOW MUCH IS TOO MUCH?

Before the coronation, seeking to flatter the emperor-to-be with whom he was often at great odds, Foreign Minister Charles Maurice de Talleyrand-Périgord commissioned a full-length portrait of Napoleon I in his imperial robes. The artist he chose, François Gérard (1770–1837), one of David's most promising students, had already painted portraits of Napoleon, Josephine, and other members of the Bonaparte family. Like other artists of the time, Gérard took a page from the emperor's book. Just as Napoleon I had used his predecessors' coronations as a template for his own, Gérard borrowed essential conventions of royal portraiture to paint the man who had made himself emperor.

A large (89" x 57") canvas, *Portrait of Napoleon in his Coronation Costume* (1805) (see figure 5.3) shows the subject in a dignified stance in a regal-like setting. The work's splendor is certainly consonant with the image Napoleon had painstakingly created for himself. The trick was making the self-made emperor look as though he fit the part. In the portrait, Gérard made Napoleon look taller and more imposing by setting him on a short dais looking down at the viewer.[15] As in portraits of his distant predecessor, Louis XIV, the emperor appears here as "the individual who looms over everything with a single gaze, which no detail, however minute, can escape."[16] While Napoleon's head is bare except for the laurel crown, the emperor's body is enveloped in layer upon layer of rich fabrics, fur, and gold. His attire recalls what art historian Norman Bryson has called the "markers of virility" in military costume, which appear to provide the male body with layers of "protective encasements" against vulnerability and figurative, or literal, exposure.[17] On the other hand, overkill or anachronistic attributes of majesty could also signal something amiss in depictions of the new emperor. This was the case with his most unusual monumental portrait of him, which was completed a year later.

Jean-Dominique-Ingres (1780–1867), another of David's ambitious and prize-winning students, decided that he too would paint the emperor in his full imperial costume. Doing so was riskier and more difficult than it had been for David. The emperor had not asked Ingres to paint his portrait and did not pose for him (he rarely posed for portraits at all). In

FIGURE 5.3 An official royal portrait. Painting: François Gérard, *Portrait of Napoleon in his Coronation Costume* (1805).

Source: Courtesy of Rijksmuseum, Amsterdam

FIGURE 5.4 Napoleon enthroned. Jean-Auguste-Dominique Ingres, *Napoleon I on His Imperial Throne* (1806). Musée de l'Armée, Paris.

Source: Wikimedia Commons

addition, his coronation garb was not on public display so Ingres had to glean what he could from hearsay and previous images. Although the painter invested a great deal of time and money in the project, there was no guarantee that the emperor, his council, or the legislature would purchase it.

Finished in 1806, the painting is enormous at 102" x 64" (see figure 5.4). In *Napoleon I on His Imperial Throne*, the emperor in full coronation regalia is seated on a massive, gilded throne holding the Hand of Justice on his left and the scepter on his right. The highly compressed space in the portrait pushes him forward. The pose and gaze, with their clear references to Phidias's monumental *Chryselephantine Zeus* (ca. 432 BCE) and Jan van Eyck's (1390–1441) painting, *God the Father*, in the Ghent altarpiece (AD 1426), cast Napoleon as a deity. Yet, here, the "god" appears smothered by the amount and magnificence of his gold, satin, and ermine finery. All of it, captured in splendid detail, glows with supernatural allure, thanks to the triple glaze Ingres applied to the painting. In sharp contrast, the only human flesh visible—the emperor's face—appears small, pasty, and inconsequential.[18]

In the end, the legislature *did* buy Ingres's painting. However, the rest of Napoleon's government "orchestrated against it," and when it was initially exhibited at the Salon of 1806, critics and public alike greeted the portrait with "hostility and ridicule."[19] Disturbed by Napoleon's pale, deathly-looking face, some compared it to the figures in Madame Tussaud's famous wax museum.[20] Art historian Susan Siegfried summarizes the hostile reactions: the figure was rigid, the painting "coldly symmetrical," the style too Gothic. Especially germane here, critics maintained that the portrait represented the emperor as "nothing more than a splendid exterior," and they derided his costume's splendor, which they deemed effeminate.[21] It was as if the painting revealed that the emperor was not wearing his clothes; *they* were wearing him. If that was the case, the painting represented a kind of hollowing out, even an emasculation of this mere mortal, clearly unfit for his throne.

Nevertheless, Napoleon continued to triumph. From his time as First Consul in 1799 though his imperial regime, 1804 to 1814, he enjoyed a series of military and political victories that vastly expanded his personal power and France's hold on the continent. While fighting battles elsewhere, the emperor did not loosen his iron grip on the country lest dissent fester and intensify at home. His autocratic dominance over the press certainly helped in this regard. Napoleon's reign did not see anything like the explosion of nude and seminude pornographic caricatures that had humiliated Louis XVI and Marie-Antoinette before and during the Revolution.[22]

What happened across the English Channel, however, was another matter. There, disdain and hatred for "Boney," the quintessential French enemy, flourished. Even so, anti-French political cartoonists in Great Britain did not choose to disrobe the world-famous general and emperor. Rather, they greatly diminished his height, made him look like a French fop, and used the very clothing that had helped make him emperor and the uniforms that were supposed to make him look like a man's man to puncture his pretentions.[23]

SKEWERED

In some of the most infamous British caricatures, instead of occupying center stage as in David's painting or dominating the visual field, as he does in Gérard's and Ingres's paintings, Napoleon appears diminutive—even unmanned. In 1812, the popular English caricaturist George Cruikshank (1792–1878) represents Napoleon dwarfed by his oversized black bicorn, up to his neck in desert sand—an allusion to his failed Egyptian campaign. Even though it was his brother-in-law, Murat, who went all out for the trappings of rank, in this image, Napoleon, in a bicorn five times bigger than his head and equally outsized and extravagant plumage, plays the fool.[24]

In 1815, eleven years after Napoleon's coronation and right around his downfall, Cruikshank lampooned Napoleon's coronation ceremony by oversizing the other figures he chose for the foreground of the image. The Empress Josephine, on the left, and the archbishop in his ornamented chasuble look more than three times their actual size and girth. The emperor, on the right, looks youthful, fit, and muscular, but he is also puny by comparison (see figure 5.5).[25] The image also does something the French painters would not have dared fabricate: Napoleon flinging open his ermine mantle (minus his satin tunic) to expose far more of his diminutive figure from the waist down than any attire of the time would have done. This exhibitionist pose appears to allude to the famous *Portrait of Louis XIV* by Hyacinthe Rigaud (1659–1743), completed in 1701, a century before. In it, the king takes up a similar, attention-seeking posture as a presumed sign of his glory. Despite Louis XIV's aging face, the royal body

FIGURE 5.5 Napoleon's coronation by an English caricaturist. Hand-colored etching and aquatint: George Cruikshank, "Crowning Himself Emperor of France."

Source: Copyright British Museum

appears surprisingly youthful, striking a coy ballet stance that reveals his shapely legs, about which he was said to have been quite vain. His red pumps, which only the king had the legal right to don, also show him—and them—to advantage.[26]

Exhibitionism had confirmed the superiority of the earlier, seventeenth-century sovereign. By contrast, in the English caricature, Napoleon's cocky, splay-legged stance and the oversized red, white, and blue sash dangling at his crotch suggest overcompensation for any number of presumed inadequacies. These and other such images reveal the downsides of the in-your-face self-display that Napoleon I was reclaiming in postrevolutionary France: the potential for humiliating public exposure of his hubris.

DRESSING UP FOR THE EMPEROR, OR ORDER AND GENDER IN THE COURT

At court, Napoleon not only chose splendor for himself, he also demanded it of the men directly under him. Doing so demonstrated his power over them. As in the Old Regime, uniform exhibitionism was a right and privilege of the male elite, but it was also something a ruler could either confer or strip away. The most elegant uniforms were modeled after Napoleon's *petit costume* as emperor: "knee-length mantle, coat, vest, knee breeches, lace cravat, and plumed hat." This style revived the "habit à la française reminiscent of the elegant days of Versailles" but distinguished itself by the "extreme height of the standing collar and the more fitted skirt, the larger scale of the floral embroidery motifs, and the height of the cravat."[27] The idea was to dissuade men and their tailors from showcasing a personal style or other sartorial originality. What was supposed to be more impressive was wearing a uniform that allowed everyone to know one's own and other men's precise status in the imperial hierarchy. Napoleon even required that "men who did not have an official position, civil or military" wear a variation on the uniform in a particular color. "Made of rich dark silk or velvet, exquisitely embroidered in polychrome silk mostly in floral motifs," this garb would have made them a part of the majestic spectacle while revealing their inferior status (see figure 5.6).[28]

The fact that this new, resplendent uniform, like the far more modest uniforms of schoolboys, seminarians, and the clergy, was required had advantages for those who were, or had been, in the lower ranks, as it had for Bonaparte and La Mésangère. Writes one costume historian, "the universal wearing of . . . formal embroidered dress [even] by men with *no* official function when at court" helped "neutralize the differences in birth, rank and fortune"—at least within the imperial category they were assigned, which strictly delineated rank by color.[29] This outward uniformity occluded the often-nondemocratic favoritism on which that "equality" rested, including the uniform's prohibitive cost and the fact that it could *not* disguise all social differences. The effect might well have exacerbated feelings of inadequacy or imposture.[30]

Many men in Napoleon's court were delighted to wear the magnificent new attire. However, some wanted the freedom to personalize and embellish their court uniform as they would have been able to do during the Old Regime. They sometimes went "so far as to ask for richer embroidery or a mantle that had not been part of the original regulations."[31] Under Napoleon, however, permission for exceptions was rarely granted, and the price of unauthorized overdressing or underdressing was high: public shaming, even banishment from court.

For women—family members, courtiers, and visitors, the imperial court made luxurious garb mandatory, but there was no uniform per se, making it a minefield of personal choices. Their wardrobe was subject to the judgment of their male and female peers but also, most harrowingly, that of the emperor. Claire Élisabeth Jeanne Gravier de Vergennes de Rémusat, one of Josephine's ladies-in-waiting and a woman of letters, was no fan of Napoleon. At receptions, she writes, he made "clear his approval of those women . . . whom he thought dressed

FIGURE 5.6 Costume for a male courtier per the emperor's specifications. Photograph: Court suit (late eighteenth–early nineteenth century).

Source: Metropolitan Museum of Art

well," but he reprimanded "those who appeared too often in the same outfit" or wore what other titled women did.[32] In other words, Napoleon insisted that the ladies of his court be a constantly changing and varied spectacle. Their role was to showcase both the newest in French luxury and their own docile subjection not only to his rule but also to that of men more generally—a fact that would be made explicit and official in the Napoleonic Code of March 21, 1804, which locked in gender hierarchies.[33] By contrast, men simply had to wear the uniform he assigned them. There was no personalizing of it, therefore no risk of dangerous self-expression.[34]

Paradoxically, then, in the imperial court, female courtiers' relative sartorial liberty made them far more vulnerable to psychological degradation and political marginalization than Napoleon's male courtiers. If they were unequal to the new requirements of patriarchal self-fashioning, they could be personally shamed. At the same time, women were vying with each other for male approval, even if it was ill-mannered. As Rémusat notes, it was no secret that "the emperor scorns women."[35] He was fond of saying, "'Women must be as nothing in my court; they will not love me, but I will be able to rest.' He kept his word. We adorned his social events. That was about our only function."[36] The emperor's principal objection to women was their frivolity—most notably an obsession with *la mode*. Yet that was precisely the "superficial" but essential domain to which he had condemned them.[37]

Napoleon's regime owed much of its prestige to these "feminine" kinds of cultural superiority. But the emperor did not respect the male (or female) designers and craftsmen who helped his female courtiers achieve ever-greater heights of elegance and style.[38] Most notably, despite the considerable fame and success of Josephine's couturier, Hippolyte LeRoy (1763–1829), Napoleon openly derided him as his wife's "rag merchant."[39]

Despite this disdain and the control Napoleon exercised over his court, for about a decade, beginning when he was First Consul and then for some time as emperor, there was one set of men who got away with making their uniforms even flashier than what was required: the officers in his army.

LET THEM STRUT

After Brienne and the Ecole Royale Militaire, where he had been sloppy and neglectful about his cadet uniforms, Bonaparte is said to have begun taking pride in the new uniforms that came with his many promotions in the army. However, while his fellow officers added extravagant elements to the regular costume of their military rank, Bonaparte, reportedly still frugal and austere, did not. That said, the higher he moved up in rank, the more he understood how much showy uniforms meant to his troops' morale, discipline, and esprit de corps, which was also to say his control over them.

For the first eight years or so of his reign, the emperor let officers get away with adding variety and color to their standard issue costume—a striking contrast to his tight control over court attire. As a result, "in the army headquarters in the Consulate and Empire," it was common to see soldiers and officials in an amazing diversity of patterns and styles and a wide range of colors, including "royal blue, sky blue, green, scarlet, crimson, steel gray, and white"—whether these were officially sanctioned or not.[40]

Despite Napoleon's early reputation for caring little about the specifics of dress, he had strong opinions about them. He revealed a nostalgic attachment to the traditions of military dress and often bristled at changing them. In an 1803 letter to his chief of staff, Louis-Alexandre Berthier (1753–1815), he wrote, "I cannot imagine you would want to do away with the brigadier general's plume and baldric [a shoulder strap for a sword] or that you would change the color of the uniforms of the aides-de-camps."[41] However, he is also said to have "derived much delight from the excess and extravagance of certain uniforms," especially the new ones he commissioned.[42] The result, as one Napoleonic costume historian, voicing a widespread view, puts it: "In the days when the French imperial armies played their role on the European stage, there was an unparalleled deployment of rich costumes, a veritable explosion of panache."[43] Beginning as Consul for Life and throughout his time as emperor, particularly as of 1811, Napoleon "personally attended to the details" of the uniforms of his 2.4 million troops.[44] He believed that having them redesigned was crucial to their willingness to submit to discipline, hardship, and sacrifice. The emperor had a particular weakness for assigning fine accessories to his officers. Among the most costly and flamboyant were the thick gold braid and fabulous egret and ostrich plumes of marshals and generals. Although Napoleon especially spoiled the higher-ranking officers, some of the lowly ranks who were nevertheless essential for parades, such as drum majors, got truly extravagant upgrades (see figure 5.7). The rich, gold-braided embroidery, white breeches (displayed here as skin tight), flashy vertical decorative elements that highlighted the crotch area, gold-trimmed black boots, and the lofty poof above the elaborate high hat were typical of the revival. Napoleon's army remains famous for its "tremendous intensification" of old-fashioned elite masculine power as "macho spectacle."[45]

In sum, for any man interested in legitimizing his desire to dress up and be admired for doing so, the French army would be just the place. Humility and even practicality were very much beside the point in this apotheosis of military exhibitionism. In these respects, Napoleonic military uniforms, like his court's required imperial dress, were throwbacks to Old Regime masculinity and the traditional privileges of elaborate and colorful martial display—far from the variations on renunciation that were increasingly being demanded of male civilians and had been accepted by rank-and-file men in the Church.

For all the flamboyance of Napoleon's army, the uniforms also reinforced the idea of masculinity as a form of renunciation. In this circular logic, military uniforms were, by definition, sober, appropriate, and decorous rather than frivolous, exhibitionist, or ornamental precisely because they were required by a powerful male institution. Thus, rather than a suspect, feminizing tendency, luxurious dress for men in the military represented something transcendent: male superiority, the ruler's sovereignty, and, in this case, France's renown in the world. Empire style in the military helped masculinize and thereby

FIGURE 5.7 Parade costume for a drum major of the Imperial Guard. Hand-colored etching. "Drum Major of the Imperial Guard." *Troupes Françaises*, plate 176. Aaron Martinet, 1806–1812.

Source: Courtesy of Guy Dempsey

re-legitimize the display of male power over women and racial and class "inferiors" by providing elite, normative cover for what was in fact quite ostentatious attire.

The contrast between this foppish military masculinity and the demand for restrained self-presentations that the Church, after Napoleon's restoration of it, required of its regular clergy, teachers, schoolboys, and seminarians and that Jacobins had expected of "true patriots" could not be starker. Whereas the religious and the revolutionary versions of the Great Masculine Renunciation held that rejecting luxury and vanity was a higher good (especially and, often, only for those low on the hierarchy), Napoleon demanded that his military subordinates engage not only in old-style male exhibitionism but in its most recent, which is to say most fashionable, form.

No matter how flashy military attire was or how often individual officers' taste or the army brass altered it and Napoleon himself ordered it refashioned, he and most others still insisted that *l'armée* and *la mode* were fundamentally antithetical. Thus, Etienne Alexandre Bardin (1774–1840), an army officer charged with the administration of the new uniform order under Napoleon, writes, "Given over to the liberties and whims of civilian fashion, military attire was unrecognizable."[46] Lest there be any doubt, he states the point more baldly as a natural gender difference: "Military styles are not the same as women's fashion."[47] In his scathing indictment of officers for meddling in army regulations before 1812, Bardin insists that they dressed to please their egos and lay low their rivals. "The sole, but disguised, point of those regulations," he writes, "was to please coquettish, powerful colonels" who demanded that they be allowed to use the most complementary colors to avoid a sarcastic putdown by other officers. More often, Bardin writes, "it was a traffic in caresses and condescendence between great lords and lowly clerks."[48] It also had to do with the colonels' mistress; one loved pale blue, another was crazy about daffodil yellow or adored crimson, and still another wanted her lover's soldiers to be outfitted in the "colors of her livery."

Nonetheless, Napoleonic officers' attire was also sometimes consonant with civilian men's fashionable dress at the time. For example, the aides-de-camp uniform, which "had been strictly established in 1800, was all blue with some gold ornaments . . . [and] increasingly fanciful uniforms."[49] As with the most fashionable Parisian women and female courtiers, the emperor did not care if his male subordinates outdid him. They too were his arm candy. According to the new military ethos, which was a full-scale resistance to the Great Masculine Renunciation but with a paradoxical spin that reinforced it: The new fashion helped Napoleon I look even more manly in his more ornate but regulation uniform.

Among the most famous and outrageous of these real-life fashion plates was Napoleon's brother-in-law. A military officer at one of the highest imperial ranks, Marshal Joachim Murat (1767–1815) went to extreme degrees to be the center of attention. Yet even Murat who was, literally, in the family (he had married Napoleon's sister Caroline) risked criticism that he skirted the boundaries of gender-normal masculinity. Thus, one of the light cavalry officers who admired Murat describes what the marshal wore as so frilled up and over the top that it verged on ludicrous and nonsensical. Made of "rich fabrics, contrasting colors, furs, embroidery, pearls, and diamonds," the ensemble constituted a "pompous and flamboyant" mishmash of styles, "something between [Polish] and [Muslim]."[50] Yet so long as Murat and other military underlings channeled their narcissism into imperial exhibitionism, it was just the thing for Napoleon's political purposes—or it was until he decided to suppress this practice, albeit lightly and at a fairly late date.

Around 1812, battered by disastrous defeats on the battlefield in Smolensk, Borodino, Moscow, Krasmoi, and Berezina, starvation, disease, and freezing temperatures, and increasingly frustrated by his officers' lack of discipline, Napoleon I set out to prohibit the sartorial liberties he had earlier condoned and even encouraged. In other words, the surprising new order of the day was a variant on the Great Masculine Renunciation. Disobedience was now to be treated as a form of heinous insubordination rather than suitably imperial self-expression. Ironically, the emperor convened a military commission to systematize a return to the kinds of ideals, "comfort, economy, simplicity, and uniformity," that had been common in revolutionary rhetoric about true manliness and patriotism and in male dress more generally. In Napoleon's newly redesigned army, a uniform had to reflect an officer or soldier's place in the larger hierarchy and his subservience to it, not his ambition, personality, or preferences. Like a cassock or a school uniform, it began once again to signify, as it had before, a supposed renunciation of self. The only one allowed to break rank with official splendor in the army and even the court by drawing from the manly, "renunciation" side of his closet was Napoleon.[51]

DOWNPLAY, UPSTAGE, DOWNFALL

Despite his place at the pinnacle of French society, the emperor regularly dressed down, wearing low-level military uniforms, like the one in David's famous portrait, *Napoleon in His Study at the Tuileries* (see figure 5.8) of 1812. Far from a figurehead in magnificent, "timeless" regalia, he appears as a modern ruler going about the business of state in military apparel.[52] Although he wears the badges of the Legion of Honor and the Order of the Iron Crown, Napoleon's dark blue uniform with white facing and red cuffs, gold epaulettes, and white knee breeches and stockings is that of a mere colonel in his own Imperial Guard, a division whose sole reason for existence was to serve *him*. In the painting, a somewhat portly but elegant, erect, and unruffled head of state stands at ease. His scabbard rests on a nearby velvet chair in front of a desk covered with documents, and his right hand is tucked into a white vest called a plastron. The implication was that for everyday dress, his was a "manly" lack of interest not only in changing fashions but also in the excessive signs of wealth and rank that his position as emperor could have afforded him. However, Napoleon I did have limits in this regard: He never debased himself by wearing the rough, often ragged, and humble uniform of a common soldier. His renunciation only went so far.

As commander in chief on maneuvers and in battles, Napoleon did, however, make modest wardrobe choices, most frequently and famously, an unadorned gray overcoat and simple black bicorn. In such gear, he appeared the very image of

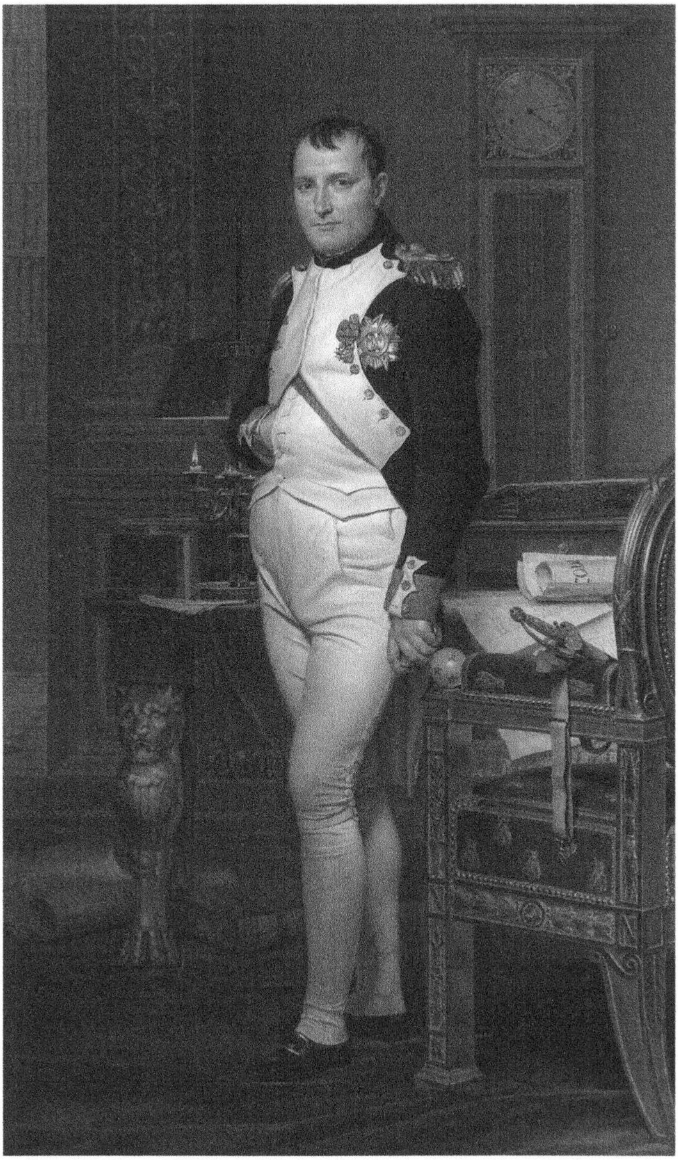

FIGURE 5.8 Emperor Napoleon in the uniform of a corporal of his Imperial Guard. Painting: Jacques-Louis David, *The Emperor Napoleon in His Study at the Tuileries* (1812).

Source: National Gallery of Art

down-to-earth soldierly manliness rather than the dandified military display of Murat and many of his other officers. It had the desired effect on his rank-and-file troops: Adulation for a leader who dressed more like they did and at least made a *show* of not pulling rank even though he held supreme command over them.[53]

In the end, no matter what Napoleon wore, he ruled over all. The man at the very top of the social, military, and political pyramid preserved a unique combination of sartorial power by reserving for himself three wardrobe options. First, he wore the spectacular, richly embroidered attire and elaborate, costly accessories of previous regimes to intimidate his subjects and arrogate the aura of France's royal past to himself and his reign. Second, unlike the preening officers who added tall feathers to their hats and colorful accessories to their uniforms, he treated his own military costumes as true regulation dress without embellishing them further. However, as we saw in battle, Napoleon also made himself the only man of the elite who had the right to choose from the "renunciation" side of his closet when he so desired. On this last point, Napoleon purportedly asserted that "the right to be simply dressed does not belong to everyone."[54] *Mutatis mutandis*, this idea represents the logic and values behind the renunciation of fashion laid out in the regulations for parish and teaching priests, prized by revolutionaries, preached in middle-class households, and, as when Rosa's husband censures his wife for her typically "female" vanity and spendthrift ways, touted in La Mésangère's *Journal des Dames et des Modes*.

Regulating others' dress was key to the emperor's power. For almost a decade and a half, from 1799 to 1812, it appeared that Napoleon could and would reign supreme indefinitely. However, and despite his new effort at keeping the troops in line by increasing constraints on what they could wear, the few years that followed turned out to be the beginning of the end. The disastrous campaign in Russia, begun in 1812, ended a year later with his army's resounding defeat by the Sixth Coalition (Russia, Prussia, Austria, and Sweden) at the Battle of Leipzig. An estimated 100,000 died in combat and around 200,000 others of disease and freezing temperatures. After French troops' ignominious retreat from Moscow, Coalition forces invaded Paris on March 30, 1814, took over the city and brought about the abdication of Napoleon. With them, they brought back to France the man next in line to the Bourbon throne, Louis XVIII (1754–1824), who had been living in England in exile for eight years. In May, his accession to the throne represented the restoration of the Bourbon monarchy twenty-eight years after Louis XVI was guillotined.

Humiliated and forced to abdicate, Napoleon was exiled to the island of Elba in the Mediterranean. The rest of his life can be summarized quickly. He attempted a comeback in 1815, but it endured for only one hundred days. As a result of his final, infamous defeat at the Battle of Waterloo, the United Kingdom of Great Britain and Ireland banished him to an even more remote location where he could do no more harm: Saint Helena, 1,200 miles off the coast of Africa. Although Napoleon's followers remained steadfast, their support changed little about his conditions of exile. After five and a half years on Saint Helena, the man who had conquered, then lost, most of Europe died on May 5, 1821 at age fifty-one. He probably succumbed to stomach cancer although rumors swirled that he might have been poisoned.

■ ■ ■

That same year, La Mésangère turned sixty. The fashion press "emperor" would never experience anything like the power or fame of Napoleon I. Nevertheless, over the preceding two and a half decades, he had managed to avoid the emperor's highly public defeat and continued to build up his journalistic and publishing empire. It was not to last.

THE OTHER EMPEROR: RISE AND FALL

In 1821, La Mésangère was at the height of his success. He published a 438-page dictionary of French proverbs, which was reprinted in two, much longer editions.[55] Six years later, he saw the publication of his *Galerie des femmes célèbres* [Gallery of Famous Women], a biographical encyclopedia of famous women featuring full-length portraits and remarks about their life and attire. The celebrated editor also continued commissioning engravings from the best illustrators of the day, 2,865 for his magazine and another 1,600 singly and in large series on a wider range of subjects from "regional costumes to satires of fashion and detailed renditions of carriages and decorative objects," for a lifetime total of 4,465.[56] La Mésangère's *Journal des Dames et des Modes* was so popular that it achieved a record-breaking 2,400 subscribers in 1821, making it the second most widely subscribed and distributed nondaily journal of any kind.[57]

However, after its eighteen-year near-monopoly over the French fashion press (1800–1818), competition again grew heated. From 1818 to 1829, rivals launched no fewer than eight new fashion magazines. As in the early days, the famous editor was able to buy out or annex some of them; others folded on their own. Yet those that survived were quickly catching up to La Mésangère's formerly indomitable magazine. By 1827, its subscription numbers had stagnated, and it fell to second place behind a brand-new fashion periodical, *Album des Modes et Nouveautés*, thereafter called *Le Bouquet*. Its gimmick was to offer artificial flowers with each issue, and it boasted three thousand subscribers, an unprecedented number.[58] Although *Le Bouquet* lasted only six months, the writing was on the wall. If La Mésangère wanted his magazine to prevail, he needed to up his game.

However, the famous editor did *not* appear to be up to the task. Every five days, *Journal des Dames et des Modes* gave visible proof that fashion was changing at an ever more rapid pace. But the magazine's format and tone never changed—neither did his attire.

AN ANACHRONISTIC UNIFORM FOR ONE

The earliest contemporary description of the "emperor" of fashion dates from the late 1820s. Writers and brothers Edmond de

Goncourt (1822–1896) and Jules de Goncourt (1830–1870) were too young to have known La Mésangère. However, they wrote a book about the life and work of Paul Gavarni (1804–1866), the illustrious draftsman who remained grateful to La Mésangère for having hired and mentored him at *Journal des Dames et des Modes* when Gavarni was just starting out.[59] The Goncourts write that Gavarni described his mentor/editor, then in his sixties, as an old-fashioned character: "a tall man in a powdered wig," a rarity at the time, "and white cravat, dressed from head to toe in cornflower blue [*bleuet*]."[60]

The Goncourt text gives no context to understand what, if anything, "cornflower blue" meant to La Mésangère. However, decades before, in May 1804, seven months before Napoleon's coronation as emperor and around the time the draftsman Gavarni was born, this shade of blue was featured in La Mésangère's *Journal des Dames et des Modes*. The periodical announced that fashionable men in search of the latest frock coats and trousers were "not choosing dark blue but rather a lighter shade reminiscent of the pansies and cornflowers that will soon be growing in our countryside. This is now the elegant color."[61] Whatever other meaning might have been attached to cornflower blue in 1804, for La Mésangère, that blue "of the moment" appears to have lasted for decades.

Although the editor clearly renounced the latest styles, it would be inaccurate to say that he did not care about his looks, that he would just wear any old thing. Quite the opposite: La Mésangère was determined to look like himself, which is to say always the same and always eccentric. The editor's refusal of both the perils and pleasures of being up to the fashion moment was deeply paradoxical. Although he made his name and his living off *la mode*, he pointedly disobeyed his magazine's injunctions to consume, repeat, continue. Perhaps La Mésangère considered thumbing his nose at the latest styles a feather in his cap, a sign of his frugality (although he had become quite well-to-do), or a matter of pride and a refusal to play everyone else's game—rather like Napoleon's "renunciatory" plain gray coat and bicorn. Such attire distanced both men from what their regimes characterized as the fair sex's inveterate fickleness and self-indulgence, which they derided, but on which their rule heavily depended.

Yet La Mésangère's dated costume would also have had distinct drawbacks. In the past, his Doctrinarian cassock had identified him as someone who enjoyed the blessing, authority, and financial largesse of a hallowed institution, the Church, just as military and imperial clothes did for Napoleon. Now a layman and in unconventional, old-fashioned garb, the editor risked being seen as a troop of one, leader of none.

The Goncourt brothers claim that La Mésangère's obsolete way of dressing did not bother Gavarni who would become one of the famous illustrators of the nineteenth century. On the contrary, the draftsman considered the renowned editor "the refinement (*politesse*) of the last century in the flesh."[62] But for most of those in Gavarni's generation, who came of age in the 1820s, La Mésangère's garb would have simply been ample proof, if any more were needed, that the old man's attire was antediluvian.

In the late 1810s and 1820s, fashion periodicals, including La Mésangère's, featured elegant variations on the Great Masculine

Renunciation as *le must* in men's styles. According to the engraving from the November 15, 1819 issue (see figure 5.9), for everyday wear, powdered wigs were out except for very formal occasions. They had been replaced by top hats, which showed off the man's natural, unpowdered hair peeking out underneath. In this fashion plate, being à la mode meant, among other things, a dark blue "woolen riding coat with velvet collar decorated with braided trim and olives, [beige] pants of woolen leather, with stripes on the sides."[63] Self-contained, sleek, unfussy, and covered from head to toe, all the elements of the model's attire—tall top hat, long sideburns, thin walking stick, calf-length coat with high, stand-up collar—contribute to an imposing and decidedly phallic verticality. There would be no confusing this version of masculinity with that of the mincing abbé with his lorgnon and spray of roses from 1789 (see figure 3.3), the prancing courtier showing off his shapely calves and ankles from the same year (see figure 3.4), or La Mésangère's top-to-toe cornflower blue and powdered wig. Everything about this sober male model, including his pointy black shoes and firmly planted walking stick make him appear recognizably modern especially compared to women's ribbons, flounces, and bows: rational, practical, restrained, "powerful, serious, and of singular, unified intent."[64]

As we have seen, to forswear "feminine" ornamentation is not always a way of fading into the woodwork or even hiding one's body. In this case, the male model's coat, inspired by the classical statuary that was then all the rage, nips, tucks, and stuffs the man into a "wasp-waisted" and "full-chested silhouette."[65] The point of wearing such clothing was to prove one's

FIGURE 5.9 A fashionable man, 1819. Fashion Plate: *Journal des Dames et des Modes*, November 15, 1819. "Woolen riding coat with velvet collar decorated with braided trim and olives, pants of woolen leather, with stripes on the sides."

Source: Gallica

manly superiority to women but also to any man who could not pull off this "effortless" self-presentation.

Perhaps because La Mésangère reigned supreme for almost three decades, he enjoyed relative immunity from public notoriety despite his obsolete attire. Journalists' and others' comments about him were usually limited to bland banalities: La Mésangère's magazine was a favorite of the ladies and the best source for the latest on *les modes*. His contemporaries also referred to him as if he *were* his magazine, calling it "Le La Mésangère," as Napoleon is said to have done.[66] Even the few journalists or authors in later years who dared to be snarky about the periodical did not expose the editor's sartorial eccentricity. Perhaps doing so would risk displeasing the ladies enamored of the magazine. Whatever the reasons, La Mésangère remained an "Invisible Man"—one who could avoid being judged on his wardrobe. What counted instead were the fruits of his labor and that of his staff. However, all this was about to change radically.

By 1830, many rivals were copying several of *Journal des Dames et des Modes*'s features and aspects of its format. Increasingly, however, the new approach, tone, and content of these copycats exposed La Mésangère's periodical as frightfully *démodé*. One of the magazine's most formidable rivals was *Petit Courrier des Dames* [Ladies' Little Courier] (1822–1868). Mme Donatine Thiery and its other female editors offered a "woman's" point of view on all manner of topics, including fashion (although it did not offer fashion engravings), and would outlast the journal La Mésangère helped found by thirty-one years.[67] However, a very recent competitor, *La Mode*, subtitled

Revue des Modes, Galerie des Mœurs, Album des Saisons [La Mode: Review of Fashions, Gallery of Mores, Seasonal Album], inflicted far more damage on the venerable *Journal des Dames et des Modes* and, especially, its editor.

BESTED BY *LA MODE*

Founded in October 1829 by two men, Emile de Girardin (1806–1881) and Charles Lautour-Mézeray (1801–1861), *La Mode*, a weekly artistic, literary, and society journal, offered only one fashion illustration per issue, but it revolutionized the fashion press and men's attire. The editors hired up-and-coming writers, journalists, and illustrators whose attitudes and opinions were distinctly modern. Unafraid of being provocative, they were a clear rebuke to La Mésangère's anodyne prose and the reflections of his fussy, old Invisible Men. Gavarni, the draftsman who admired La Mésangère's sartorial refinement while recognizing its datedness, and Honoré de Balzac (1799–1850), a soon-to-be best-selling novelist at the beginning of his career, would be the magazine's most famous early contributors. Although mentored by La Mésangère early on, they left his *Journal des Dames et des Modes* to join *La Mode*, which, for them, represented the future.[68]

The editors of the magazine, de Girardin and Lautour-Mézeray, were around Gavarni's age, which is to say in their twenties, thus about forty years younger than the reigning emperor of *la mode*. They were also, on almost all counts, La Mésangère's opposite. Unlike him and most other fashion magazine editors, who were of modest origins, de Girardin, the illegitimate son of a general and his mistress, was nevertheless noble, wealthy, and well-connected. In the late 1820s and 1830s, he and Lautour-Mézeray frequented the most fashionable salons and literary and journalistic circles where they joined other self-avowed dandies (also called *lions*, *fashionables*, and *la Jeune France*) to show off their fashionable attire—its exquisite tailoring, the impeccable white linen, and a maximum of refinement.[69]

For all their traditional signs of elegance, however, the young *lions* also adopted distinctive individual styles, which were often frilly or gaudy affectations—from small, black fans to Lautour-Mézeray's signature white camellia boutonniere to Balzac's gold-and-turquoise-topped cane.[70] In this way, stylish men were supposed to present themselves as liberated, albeit minimally since they were themselves a type, from the fashionable "uniform" of the moment. Rejecting La Mésangère's old-fashioned recipes for the latest styles, the new periodical expected and encouraged personal distinctiveness in fashion and in prose. Paradoxically, this meant these would-be originals tended to consist of variations on modern conformity.

Rather than hide behind the pages of their publication, as the venerable editor La Mésangère continued to do, de Girardin and Lautour-Mézeray were the first French fashion editors to make their gender, attire, and social cohort selling points for *La Mode*. Whereas the venerable fashion editor of the past decades appears to have considered his clothing a simple matter of personal preference, for many in the new world, a modern fashion editor had to be a player who intentionally dressed *up* as a man à la mode. In this circle, flashy fabulousness was, once again, fully masculine, upper class, and heterosexual although it flirted with ambiguity on the latter score.

Nonetheless, only certain kinds of variations would pass muster at any time, and one could never be sure which those would be—especially in the early days. The exclusionary nature of dandyism was, in fact, the point. So was haughtily calling out the inadequacy of those not able to meet its standards or play by its usually unwritten and fast-changing rules. This is how La Mésangère, the "invisible" fashion editor, came to be the target of a thoroughgoing and vicious public attack.

EASY TARGET

The article in the February 20, 1830 issue of de Girardin and Lautour-Mézeray's *La Mode* went right for La Mésangère's jugular and did not let up for over eight full pages. The article's title gives the sixty-eight-year-old editor of *Journal des Dames et des Modes* the minimal honorific "M." for *Monsieur*, but there, and twenty-four more times after, his name is misspelled as "La Mésengère" [*sic*]. This possibly unintentional slight was nothing compared to the article's willfully malicious content. The author, writing anonymously, was Jules Janin (1804–1874). At twenty-five, he was young enough to have been La Mésangère's grandson. Son of a lawyer, educated in Paris, Janin was already known as "*un élégant*."[71] For many decades, as a novelist, critic, and journalist, he would make a career of savaging publications, politicians, and authors. This early article set a high bar for contempt.[72]

Janin's criticism of La Mésangère was the first full-frontal attack on him in print. It was also a doozy. Flattering *La Mode*'s well-to-do readers as "the beautiful people" (*les gens de luxe*), he presumes that they have never heard of the obscure M. La Mésangère (which is doubtful). But, Janin informs them, they have seen him everywhere—and how could they not—for he was not just outmoded but downright peculiar: obsolescence incarnate. "A grotesque, stiff type, long and short, fat and slender, always taking styles to ridiculous extremes: a wide pocket, a wide snuffbox, a wide jacket, a vast hat, breeches, and something like the braided cords on military epaulettes; a wig, oh! a ratty red wig curled up over the forehead with a pony tail in back."[73] The mismatch of elements ("long and short," "fat and slender"), the insistence on excess ("ridiculous extremes," "wide," "wide," and "vast") and eccentric touches ("the braided cords on military epaulettes") underscore the point: All of this was laughably wrong. But the kicker is the wig: ratty, red, and in an Old Regime style. The latter might be that of the gentleman represented as highly effete in the comparison with the post-revolutionary *Incroyables* (see engraving 0.1). As if this were not humiliation enough, Janin then attacks La Mésangère's horse (ancient), his carriage (shabby), and his coachman (ancient and shabby). In this explicitly class-based attack, far from considering La Mésangère as an embodiment of old-time elegance (as Gavarni had done), Janin mocks La Mésangère as an "honest bourgeois" who is "too simple, happy, assured of his own good reputation and, above all, too virtuous and naïve" to realize that he gets elite masculinity and fashion all wrong.[74] In a word, completely *déclassé*, the venerable editor has no authority whatsoever to talk about *la mode*, let alone make sovereign edicts about it.

Labeling La Mésangère a fraud and imposter, Janin taunts him for his childish, low-class tastes and habits. These include using the informal "*tu*" with his tailor, loudly guffawing at puppet shows for children, and eating not at the best and latest stylish restaurant but at a tavern that had not been popular since the seventeenth century. On all counts, Janin brands La Mésangère the ultimate outsider: an "anachronism."[75] He urges *La Mode*'s well-to-do readers to shun this great pretender. "Not one of the upper crust," he knows nothing about "what goes on in your antechamber, where even his lackey would not be allowed to enter."[76]

At one point, turning the tables on La Mésangère, it was Janin's turn to play Argus, he who could see all. The critic pronounces himself ready to disclose a scandalous secret about the has-been editor—what this "virtuous gentleman [does] in the privacy of his *cabinet*," which Janin describes as being "as impenetrable as that of Bluebeard."[77] This reference to the French folk villain infamous for murdering his wives suggests that La Mésangère was hiding some salacious or criminal skeletons in his study. In the end, however, the "crime" taking place behind closed doors is nothing more than what Janin had already revealed: La Mésangère, the fashion world's most unlikely fashion maven, dares make pronouncements on "fashions for today, for tomorrow, for the day after, for the court, for the city, for Versailles, [and] for the provinces."[78] He is, Janin writes snidely, especially successful in Pontoise, a small town, northwest of Paris, where, apparently, no one important or elegant lived. Janin's takedown ends with a warning that this menace to society who "has been making fashions for thirty years" will not stop. "He will do so until he dies."[79]

Envy and resentment of the editor's three-decade reign over the French fashion press might explain some of Janin's complaints but not, perhaps, the violence and excess of his public exposure of La Mésangère. The fury unleashed resembles attacks on those who do not conform to sexual and gender norms. Along the same lines, Janin gives the editor's "impenetrable" *cabinet* decidedly sexual—or asexual?—overtones.

Janin appears willing to do almost anything to embarrass and undermine the once-popular editor. It is therefore noteworthy that he makes no mention of aspects of La Mésangère's job and life that might stand out to us today. Janin does not consider La Mésangère's profession as fashion editor gender-inappropriate, nor does he exploit the fact that the man had been an ordained priest, taught young boys, and lived among them and other clergymen. The fact that the editor was a confirmed bachelor could also have been material for innuendo, mockery, or rumors, but Janin did not go there.[80] Nor did he imply that La Mésangère took voyeuristic pleasure in women and women's clothing or wear it himself. Instead, he desexualizes the former priest completely, disconnecting him from sensual or high-minded pleasures as well. Janin portrays La Mésangère as a monomaniac (although he does not use the word which would only be coined in 1838), subject to only one obsessive passion: being Monsieur la Mode until he died.

Janin's 1830 tirade against La Mésangère certainly did not help sales of *Journal des Dames et des Modes* or the editor's morale. He had already grown weary of the continual stress of running the periodical. There were other publishing projects he cared about more. Perhaps Janin's libelous article forced his hand, giving him a reason to distance himself from the magazine.[81] In spring 1830, La Mésangère decided to entrust the periodical to his longtime contributor, collaborator, and confidant, the thirty-five-year-old journalist Charles-Frédéric Herbinot de Mauchamps (1795–post-1850). Shortly thereafter, however, Herbinot was arrested for raping a servant girl and sentenced to eight months in prison.[82] As his employer, La Mésangère not only had to pay Herbinot's legal fines, he also feared what the scandal would do to his own reputation and that of his journal. Saddled once again with managing the magazine, the editor worked at a frenetic pace, complaining of deep exhaustion and despair.[83] It did not help that so many of his closest friends were dead or dying.[84] Soon after, however, something momentous occurred that made matters even worse for La Mésangère and his *Journal des Dames et des Modes.*

Over a period of just three days in late July, a second revolution brought about a seismic social and political upheaval in France that dethroned the Bourbon king, Charles X. Although a royalist, La Mésangère would have been pleased to see this unpopular monarch go, but he favored a legitimist successor, which is to say another Bourbon. Instead, the man crowned was Louis-Philippe, the heir apparent to the Orléans line. Like the rising middle classes that had helped put him on the throne, the new king disapproved of what he saw as the excess and decadence of previous reigns, including that of Napoleon's court.[85] In the name of moderation, the July Monarchy melded elements of the masculine, religious, and political "renunciations" of the past and dropped the old-fashioned urbanity that *Journal des Dames et des Modes* had long represented.[86] For La Mésangère and the press in general, this regime meant a new set of mores, masters, censors, modes of production and distribution, reading publics, and competitors.

Exhausted and discouraged, the man behind the Invisible Men whose sobriquets, "One Hundred Eyes" and "Argus," implied an ability to be anywhere and see everything, became a recluse. In his apartment on Boulevard Montmartre, it is said that he saw only his office clerk and his friend and confidant, Edmée Marguerite Dubois Miolle, a widow and the concierge of the building.[87] After a brief illness, on February 22, 1831, the son of a minor nobleman from rural Anjou, a teaching priest, then director of the *collège* in La Flèche, prolific author, publisher of thousands of engravings, and editor of the first major fashion magazine in Europe, surrounded by a dozen friends and colleagues, breathed his last. It was almost a year to the day since the publication of Janin's character assassination in *La Mode*.[88] La Mésangère was sixty-nine. By July 5, 1831, six months after La Mésangère's death, Baron Alfred Xavier de La Douespe Dufougerais (1804–1874), age twenty-six, a lawyer and, in his spare time, a man of letters, followed the takeover strategies of Sellèque and La Mésangère in the early days. An editor of *La Mode*, where Janin's two attacks on La Mésangère appeared, Dufougerais acquired *La Mode* and then La Mésangère's *Journal des Modes et des* Dames, and subsumed into it another fashion magazine rival, *La Vogue*. His reign did not last long. By May 1834, weakened by bad health, he sold his fashion press acquisitions.[89]

Despite Janin's hate-filled diatribe against him, La Mésangère's funeral was well attended. Eulogies and tributes to him offered an entirely different picture of the late editor than the one Janin was selling.[90] They praised in glowing terms La Mésangère's goodness, modesty, humility, generosity, and kindness—the very qualities that Janin scorned or ignored. On the other hand, none of them made any explicit move to defend the late La Mésangère against Janin's charges. Perhaps they knew nothing about them or believed a response was beneath their dignity or that of the late fashion editor.

That might be the end of La Mésangère's story. But it isn't. After his death, an unexpected chapter opened. As only insiders would have known, La Mésangère's apparent renunciation of material goods was not what it seemed. He had secrets. They were not the open secret to which Janin alluded in his article of 1830—La Mésangère had a passion for fashion—nor were they particularly scurrilous—just astonishing. The apartment of the parsimonious old editor in his cornflower blue suit of yesteryear held a shocking quantity of rare and valuable objects, including, according to one contemporary, jaw-dropping amounts of clothing. What kind of renunciation was this?

Something similar could be said of Napoleon's iconic two-cornered hat. Usually understood as part of his own version of modern masculinity as renunciation, his bicorn was far from the unique, unchanging object it seemed to be. By the end of their lives, neither Napoleon nor La Mésangère openly opted for splendor or fashionableness. After their deaths, however, Napoleon's hat and the contents of La Mésangère's "closet" had surprising afterlives. Public reactions to them gave new meanings to these objects that underscore the differences in the two men's versions of masculine renunciation and suggest their larger implications for masculinity during this period and our own.

Chapter Six

AFTERLIVES

My hat it has three corners,
Three corners has my hat,
And had it not three corners,
It would not be my hat.

—Children's song, date unknown

"But he doesn't have anything on!"

—Hans Christian Andersen, "The Emperor's New Clothes" (1837)

FOR MANY, La Mésangère was supposed to be the "emperor" of fashion, yet his version of the Great Masculine Renunciation of fashion was extreme and idiosyncratic. For his three decades as fashion editor, he appears not to have changed his personal style since the 1790s, but being faithful to his superannuated look may have had one possibly desirable effect for La Mésangère: It concealed from the public what appears to have been his passion for shopping, collecting, and acquisition.[1]

After the editor's death in 1831, it took court officials four months to conduct a complete probate of the editor's possessions—so vast were the number of antiques, books, and art works. Organizing the public auction took several more months.[2] La Mésangère's twentieth-century biographer, Annemarie Kleinert, writes that in his apartment at 1, Boulevard Montmartre, the authorities "found several bunches of keys to cupboards, chests of drawers, and consoles full of papers and precious objects."[3] These included "carved and chiseled combs, clocks, precious candlesticks, ebony boxes, goblets covered in wicker, agate salt cellars, [and] pearl-embroidered purses."[4] The most valuable rooms were "the vast library containing thousands of books" and a cabinet of curiosities "called a *cabinet noir*, which held a great number of precious objects."[5] In addition to thousands of old and rare books, there were also thousands of drawings, watercolors, and oil paintings. The latter included "1,500 miniatures of famous men and women from the fourteenth century on."[6]

If gossip and rumor had not already leaked La Mésangère's "secret," publishing the inventory for the upcoming series of auctions months later officially "outed" La Mésangère as a wealthy man and avid collector. Even if many of the objects listed had been gifts to curry favor with him, the total amounts are astonishing: dozens and even hundreds of objects in each category. As a member of the Royal Antiquarian Society of France for almost twenty years, this would hardly be surprising. He treated his acquisitions with care and made them his own by storing them in pieces of furniture made for this purpose and keeping them under lock and key. Kleinert reports that the total value of items from his estate at auction was 55,000 francs—the equivalent [in 2001] of "hundreds of millions of francs," a considerable fortune.[7] The amounts and total value are so staggering that they make the most well-to-do men's various compromises with "true" masculine renunciation during that period seem positively monkish. These purported facts about La Mésangère's fortune put paid to Janin's 1830 article, which damns the editor's life as parsimonious and shabby. The editor might have looked like a fuddy-duddy on the street, but what he had at home was apparently another matter entirely.

For this avid collector, his several-room apartment just above the magazine's first-floor office served as a retreat, a closet, and a display case. It was a safe place to hide, store, protect, preserve, and admire the cherished objects in his collection. The locks on his cupboards, consoles, and display cabinets indicate that La Mésangère made sure that he would be the one to decide whether, when, and how others would be able to see his extraordinary assemblage. After his death, however, his collections, auctioned off in pieces, would never again be seen all together.

La Mésangère had been of central importance to the fashion press, but in the two decades after his 1831 death notice, which declared him a secular saint, appeared in *Journal des Dames et des Modes*, only six articles about his life and career appeared in print. In each, a different La Mésangère emerged. For all these publications, the question was whether the deceased editor deserved to pass into the ultimate men's club: immortality. This judgment depended on the criteria and scales by which the authors measured proper masculinity but also what they chose to convey and conceal about the deceased editor and, by extension, themselves. The six writers disagree about whether La Mésangère's collecting was admirable or suspect, and for what reasons. To understand what was at stake in these contestations of masculinity, historian Leora

Auslander, writing about how consumer practices in nineteenth-century France were gendered, argues that collecting was an invention of the 1830s and, in the beginning, a predominantly male avocation. The fact that La Mésangère had started amassing his substantial collection probably long before then makes him a forerunner and typical of changing ideas about what activities counted as masculine.

When, as Auslander explains, collecting "was productive of self and of a durable legacy beyond the self," i.e., it was considered both an investment and knowledge-producing, it was deemed "appropriately masculine." However, "when collectors went too far and sought their individuation, emotional satisfaction, and immortality *exclusively* through their collections, they were calumniated by critics and incorporated in the category 'dandy,'"—the term applied to many others, including Emile de Girardin and Charles Lautour-Mézeray, the editors of *La Mode* and one of its contributors, the critic Janin (see chapter 5).

Auslander defines "dandy" as an effeminate male who "lived elegantly," "dressed carefully, expensively, and distinctively." As she explains, at that time, the dandy embodied the "inappropriately narcissistic man, or perhaps more accurately, the model of a man who commodified himself as an object for the consumption of others. . . . Some dandies were heterosexual, some were homosexual. A few married, most did not." Dandies were often considered problematic if they did not have traditional families. Even when they had to support their sartorial and social habits with paid employment, they took pains to appear unproductive in that sense too. "Normative collecting," by contrast, "allowed domestic consumption, normally encoded as feminine, to be recoded as masculine and manly."[8] The published comments about La Mésangère, his attire, and his collections highlight the anxieties around this question in the 1830s and 1840s, during the early afterlife of the fashion editor and business entrepreneur who had come so far but ended in penury.

MANLY COLLECTOR OR DANDY?

A tribute to a deceased member of the Royal Antiquarian Society in its annals had to be respectful, and this is true of the one written by François Mongin de Montrol (1799–1862), published in 1834. The society was, after all, a club in which men of some distinction if not necessarily breeding socialized and preserved the country's artistic and cultural heritage. However, de Montrol's praise is often faint. He notes that La Mésangère's collection reflected his historical research and knowledge but in such bland terms they convey that this is not so uncommon. His prose about La Mésangère's antiques, rare books, and many art works also sounds boilerplate: They "were as interesting to reflect upon as they were curious to see," he writes, and they fetched "a high price."[9] For avid and well-heeled antiquarians, more was more and better was much better, but this collection, according to de Montrol, did not meet that higher bar.

The article does mention that La Mésangère edited a fashion periodical. However, after giving the full title, de Montrol's later remarks leave out "les dames," making it *Fashion Journal* rather than *Ladies' Fashion Journal.* Was this deletion a way to "save" the periodical and its editor from derision? De Montrol acknowledges that such a journal might seem frivolous, but he declares that readers of the future will find it "the most interesting and picturesque archives of the first days of the Republic and after." De Montrol also deems the periodical to be highly moral: "In this journal, nary a line might be disavowed by a man of good taste and respectable mores." He adds that it contained "articles by some of our wittiest writers. No article in it ever offended anyone—a rare enough phenomenon in journalism,"—a swipe at the press of the mid-1830s. All in all, in de Montrol's short article, La Mésangère sounds like a good, if not first-rate, collector, a valuable cultural historian, and an honorable man.

Through de Montrol and their shared gentlemen's club, La Mésangère thus lives on as a man's man, secular through and through.[10] As if to seal the deal, de Montrol concludes, "the success of the *Journal des Modes* [*sic*] made La Mésangère's fortune." It gave this "good and amiable man [who will be] sadly missed by all those who knew him . . . a comfortable life, peaceful and beneficent"—a just reward for a respectable man who apparently never stepped outside the lines of moral or normal.[11] Nowhere does de Montrol mention La Mésangère's oddities, from his previous career as a teaching priest to his archaic dress as a fashion editor. His job was to make La Mésangère appear as upright as possible—a task that involved some degree of cover-up.

That same year, 1834, La Mésangère's *Journal des Dames et des Modes*, which had been bought out by a joint-stock company, published an anonymous article about the late editor in the November 15 issue. The text does not bring up the famous editor's impressive collections nor his popular and academic works. However, it raises La Mésangère social status by restoring the nobiliary particle *de* to his name, which La Mésangère had dropped decades before.[12] This article, like de Montrol's, refrains from commenting on the former priest's idiosyncrasies of dress and old-fashioned lifestyle. Instead, the remarks transform the mild-mannered but canny entrepreneur into a model of virility and conquest comparable to none other than the late emperor Napoleon.

The article goes even further, stating that the two emperors "shared power": Napoleon "conquered masculine Europe; feminine Europe fell to" La Mésangère.[13] Appropriating the simplifying and inaccurate myth of gender complementarity, the statement gives the impression that the two genders, like their two domains of influence (public and private), were separate and coequal.[14] In fact, they were interdependent and Napoleon and the male sphere ruled decidedly over both.

The anonymous author goes one step further, overturning the usual male hierarchy that holds the military as the ultimate expression of admirable manliness. The article claims that La Mésangère's legacy had endured and would endure far longer than that of the "real" emperor: "Napoleon lost his conquests, but we still have those of M. de La Mésangère."[15] In this ironic passage, "we"—the current editor and the presumably male stockholders but also perhaps men in general—were the ultimate winners, ready to enjoy their "emperor state" over women. (Two years later, the magazine made the same claim verbatim.)

Apparently annoyed by this grandiose claim in *Journal des Dames et des Modes*, Janin, the author of the editor's character assassination of 1830, decided some years later to update his attack. By then, La Mésangère's trove of books, art, and antiquities would have been a matter of common knowledge in journalistic circles. Janin could have expounded on this information to reassess his churlish assessment of La Mésangère.[16]

Instead, Janin returns to lambasting, albeit with far more precision if not necessarily more accuracy, the editor's clothing. According to Janin, at the end of La Mésangère's life, he was still wearing the costume of the counterrevolutionary *Incroyables* of the late 1790s, more than three decades before. The critic alleges that La Mésangère carried a gold snuffbox, wore jewels, earrings, and a "pigeon wing" wig with long forelocks, the rest of the *perruque* pulled together in a ponytail in back. But he also asserts that La Mésangère wore far more antiquated attire, perhaps from as late as the 1500s: a ruffle at the neck and sleeve cuffs. His legs "squeezed into silk stockings" borne up by his "pretty feet" in "gold-buckled patent leather shoes, an ornate cane, and a waistcoat that went down to the middle of his belly."[17]

Taking Janin at his word is rarely a good idea. But these specific denigrating comments in combination with Gavarni's purported remarks about La Mésangère as the quintessence of an earlier kind of elegance suggests that the former priest and famous fashion editor's attire may have been a form of resistance to chrononormativity. In *Time Binds*, queer theorist Elizabeth Freeman defines this term as "the use of time to organize individual human bodies toward maximum productivity," including procreation. In other words, "people are bound to one another, engrouped, made to feel coherently collective, through particular orchestrations of time." When there is resistance to this collective time-sharing, as is the case with anachronistic style, this "stubborn lingering of pastness . . . is a hallmark of queer affect: a 'revolution' in the old sense of the word, as a turning back."[18]

Seen in this light, La Mésangère's attachment to the past in his attire and aesthetic preferences included personal and political nostalgia for a time long past, but Freeman's reference to Heather Love's *Feeling Backward* is especially suggestive. As Freeman writes, Love, discussing a later historical period, "astutely diagnoses the 'backwards' emotions elaborated by artists for whom the birth of the modern homosexual identity-form was constraining rather than liberating: shame, passivity, melancholy, and recoil, to name but a few, were ways of refusing the progressive logic by which becoming ever more visible was correlated with achieving ever more freedom." Yet one could argue that during a much earlier period, La Mésangère, by contrast, would have been quite conspicuous in his old-fashioned dress and yet, at the same time, effectively invisible—i.e., considered of no social consequence.[19] Alternatively, his eccentric attire might have suggested to others equally "regressive" that he was one of them—whatever category or jumble of categories and values that might imply.

In short, it appears that La Mésangère's clothing was wildly anachronistic for all five political regimes that followed the Revolution—the Consulate, the Directory, the Empire, the Restoration, and the July Monarchy. But it could also be read as a confusing mix of youthful rebellion against revolutionary mores with an insistence on Old Regime elegance. Janin concludes ironically: La Mésangère was "dressed for time immemorial."[20]

Rather than cut down La Mésangère as a poor excuse for a man, as he had done in his 1830 article, Janin takes the opposite tack: overblown satirical praise. By founding "the only enduring journal, the only eternal journal, the only journal that escaped censure and condemnation," Janin's article declares, La Mésangère was "the dominator."[21] Janin calls him "a hero of étiquette [taste, decorum]" but also "a fashion tyrant."[22]

The critic's mock-heroic encomium seems to have less to do with the real man than a macho game of one-upmanship in celebrity, visibility, and power. In this second article, Janin picks up on the idea of La Mésangère as "emperor" in the November 15, 1834 article from *Journal des Dames et des Modes* only to scorn the idea. Although La Mésangère was emperor of the feminine world, he argues, this consisted of nothing but frivolous trifles.[23]

In diminishing La Mésangère's status as "tyrant," Janin takes to heart the false assumption characteristic of the Great Masculine Renunciation that *la mode* lines up with the feminine. Thus, fashion magazines are assumed to cater exclusively to women's interests, never to men's clothing, male editors, or male readers, such as themselves. *La mode*, in Janin's examples in this article, is never about the color of men's silk stockings or the latest in male walking stick styles. It is instead an all-female, all-feminine, thoroughly trivial world: "[La Mésangère] was the supreme arbiter of changes in gauze and revolutions in satin," feathers on ladies' hats, and "the most beautifully colored ribbons."[24] Janin continues with his exaggerated lampoon: "Never had such a task been assigned to a mortal of our sex and never was such a task so well accomplished."[25] Going further overboard, he declares that La Mésangère was "a thousand times more absolute and more in command in his domains than the Emperor Napoleon in his realms." This statement cuts both "great" men down to size, belittling their reigns, even as Janin present himself as a "greater" man able to call out the failings of both.[26]

These three contemporaries of La Mésangère—de Montrol writing for the antiquarian society annals, the anonymous author of the "two emperors" comparison in *Journal des Dames et des Modes*, and the poison-pen critic Janin—remake the late La Mésangère each in his own way: as an upstanding and conventional man; as a "conqueror" of the female sex; and, finally, as a foolish old man who reigns over mere "satin and ribbons." The first and second of these makeovers underplay, or sideline entirely, La Mésangère's many idiosyncrasies and "unmanly" characteristics. The third, by Janin, highlights his peculiarities as if this were flattery when in fact it was a supreme takedown.

Eight years later, in 1842, La Mésangère began appearing in French biographical dictionaries. These entries generally consist of a longish paragraph on the fashion editor's life followed by another that lists his published works and other professional activities. Louis Gabriel Michaud's (1773–1858) prestigious *Biographie Universelle ancienne et moderne* sets the tone. The entry, attributed to "Michaud jeune" [presumably Michaud's son], gives standard background information on the late editor's birthplace, early studies, first teaching job, prejudices against him as a former priest during the French Revolution, and explains that he and Sellèque were responsible for *Journal des Dames et des Modes.* The article takes for granted La Mésangère's masculinity, neither playing it up, as de Montrol, Dufougerais, and Janin all did, nor down—albeit with two notable exceptions.

Michaud jeune calls La Mésangère a priest even though he had resigned from the Church in the 1790s, and is the first to underscore the incongruity: "It was *assez piquant*" [somewhat curious, intriguing, amusing, titillating] "to see a very serious clergyman (*ecclésiastique*) of austere morals" "keep the accounts, do the writing, go to public spectacles and public spaces to observe what [fashionable] ladies were wearing." This last comment suggests that *piquant* here is not positive but negative: naughty, shady, suspect—a degree of deviation from social and moral norms that is far more than a faux pas. A priest-turned-fashion-editor was improper, unseemly, indecorous—queer in that sense. In the end, however, mention of those aspersions in the article disappear. No "stain" remains on his character: the fashion magazine "business prospered. La Mésangère earned an honest fortune, which sufficed for his simple tastes."[27]

In this remark, Michaud jeune aligns La Mésangère with upright bourgeois morality by associating him with renunciation and a probity uncorrupted by either *le beau monde* or the working poor. The article also refers to an encomium to women that was published in *Journal des Dames et des Modes* after the editor's death.[28] In sum, the entry suggests impropriety but ends, rather like de Montrol's obituary had, by saving La Mésangère's reputation as an upstanding citizen—or does it?

What is most striking about this biographical entry is a four-sentence footnote attributed to "F—lle," which is likely a reference to François-Joseph-Marie Fayolle (1774–1852), a mathematician who wrote about music and contributed articles to reference works, including the *Biographie Universelle.* The note reads like "insider" information and makes several stunning claims about La Mésangère's character, habits, and personality that no one had ever made in print.[29] At first glance, Fayolle's comments seem matter of fact, but there is also something a bit too *piquant* about them.[30]

LA MÉSANGÈRE *AU FÉMININ*?

Born in 1774, Fayolle was eleven years younger than La Mésangère, but by the 1800s, they were both men of letters living in Paris. Although they may not have known each other personally, they certainly knew of each other professionally. La Mésangère occasionally published Fayolle's poetry in *Journal des Dames et des Modes* and for three years, Fayolle edited *Petit Magasin des Dames* [Ladies' Little Magazine] (1804–1806), a literary periodical presumably for women readers that steered entirely clear of La Mésangère's bailiwick and the superficial femininity represented by *la mode.*

Although Fayolle never published anything about La Mésangère, his alleged remarks cited in Michaud's *Biographie Universelle* of 1842 and, later, in Ferdinand Hoefer's *Nouvelle Biographie Générale* of 1859 changed all that.[31] For Fayolle, La Mésangère's death, eleven years before had made the famous editor and quasi-saintly man if not a perfect target, an easy one. He claims that La Mésangère's habits were not only immoderate but nonsensical: "[He] would go out without an umbrella. If it started to rain, he would buy one. He often forgot his snuffbox so he would buy another. Every time he went out, he would buy something: a pair of silk stockings, a pair of shoes, a frock coat, or a hat."[32] These tidbits of information appear to push La Mésangère from the *piquant* but harmless priest-turned-fashion editor to a chronically absentminded and compulsive spendthrift.[33]

It is, however, the final sentence of Fayolle's remark that makes the editor appear extravagant to the max. Fayolle is quoted as claiming that in addition to the thousands of antiques, pieces of furniture, books, and art works, a total of 3,302 personal items were found in La Mésangère's apartment after he died, to wit: "one thousand silk stockings, two thousand shoes, six dozen blue frock coats, one hundred bowler hats, forty umbrellas, and ninety snuffboxes along with ten thousand francs in 15 and 30 sous coins."[34] Any of these amounts would have been staggering for a private citizen in Europe in his time, and perhaps even ours.[35] Far from making him a man to admire, as others had done, albeit by sardonic exaggeration in the case of Janin, Fayolle alleges that La Mésangère was frivolous and fallible, more feminine than masculine: the opposite of male simplicity, austerity, control, and even heroism that others, such as the new editors of *Journal des Dames et des Modes*, were "selling" as the "real" La Mésangère.

If Fayolle's statement is true, it means that La Mésangère, who appeared to embody both the Great Masculine and

Clerical Renunciations, highlights a principal paradox of both. Renunciation is never absolute. It is always mixed. As Fayolle portrays it, La Mésangère's self-presentation was merely a social performance of rational and manly restraint. Although La Mésangère appears to have consistently said "no" to the latest *modes*, this "renunciation" camouflaged for the public his extravagant acquisitiveness. His fellow antiquarians, the shopkeepers he bought from, and his intimates would have known better.

■ ■ ■

Since Michaud's 1842 publication of *Biographie Universelle*, any entry of any substance on La Mésangère in nineteenth-century French biographical dictionaries repeats Fayolle's statement without preamble, context, comment, or critique.[36] In the 2025 French Wikipedia article on La Mésangère, his remarks take up more than half the short entry. It is as if, post mortem, Fayolle continues to belittle La Mésangère—quite literally, by taking over the space that La Mésangère would rightly occupy in reference works. Today, as a result, if the general public knows the fashion press impresario at all it might be primarily for his overflowing "closet."

Although Fayolle's claim is widely cited, few critics, scholars, historians, reference work writers, or commentators appear to have questioned its veracity or its politics.[37] A couple authors give some context; Kleinert provides quite a bit, but no one notes faulty reasoning, inconsistencies, blind spots, or mixed motivations.

GETTING THE LAST WORD

The numbers cited in Fayolle's incantatory recitation (1,000, 2,000, six dozen, 100, 40, 90, 10,000) are so tidily rounded that they cannot be taken as facts but only as very rough approximations and, probably, exaggerations. Putting aside the problem of their implausibility for a moment, what exactly were these numbers and categories of clothing and accessories (shoes, blue frock coats, bowler hats, umbrellas, snuffboxes, and small change) meant to imply about the man who had them in his possession? To know, we would need information that is not supplied in reference works. Specifying that the seventy-two frock coats were blue clearly indicates that they were for La Mésangère himself, but were they all one size? Snuffboxes were also typically for men.[38] The other items—shoes and umbrellas—could be for women or men. Other questions remain: Were these new or used, the latest fashion or La Mésangère-style old-fashioned? Were they all treated with care as part of a valuable, even historic collection as La Mésangère did with his antiquities, or were they crammed together in trunks and wardrobes or dressers and other such furniture?

Fayolle offers explanations for the editor's astonishing cache, but they are illogical and lame. First, forgetfulness could not possibly account for such astronomical numbers for one person; other factors would have to have been at play. Second, some men certainly indulged in compulsive shopping during this period, but Fayolle's claim puts La Mésangère far outside gender norms of the time. Disjointed and irrational, Fayolle's statement may reveal his own mixed feelings about his late colleague and rival. Spiteful or not, his comments certainly cast doubt on La Mésangère's fame as an unprepossessing saint—a common theme in the statements about him in *Journal des Dames et des Modes* (1831), de Montrol (1834), and Michaud jeune (1842). In contrast, Fayolle demeans La Mésangère as a peculiar oddball, decidedly outside the protective cover of the standard Great Masculine Renunciation.[39] He exposes La Mésangère as a man with feminine proclivities (extravagance, a weakness for fashion) and fallibilities (forgetfulness, obsessive behaviors). Pointing to these foibles lets Fayolle play the more serious, manly, and godly author and editor. It is his comments that have endured for almost two centuries.

Even Kleinert, the foremost expert on La Mésangère, appears to buy Fayolle's claims about La Mésangère's overstuffed "closet" But she offers a different reason. Kleinert states that the clothing items, which number in the dozens, hundreds, and thousands "must have been (*devaient être)* gifts from merchants who wanted La Mésangère to talk up their wares in his magazine."[40] In nineteenth-century France, this was, indeed, common practice. Yet the expression "must have been" is based on a supposition that the editor would have always been in strict control of himself, which means he could *not* have been as absentminded or compulsive as Fayolle suggests. Kleinert offers a final argument in La Mésangère's defense as if it clinched the case: He "was not a pretentious man who was always changing his clothes."[41]

Kleinert's apparently simple and objective defense, I argue, is one of the legacies of the Great Masculine Renunciation: the myth that "real" men, especially admirable ones don't and should not care about clothing. In her view, all those clothes and accessories were merely a function of La Mésangère's job. Kleinert thus "saves" his reputation by refusing to admit that he had a closet, let alone anything like such an excessive one.

Her remark safeguards La Mésangère's normative masculinity. At the same time, this kind of reasoning would have forestalled my questions here: What we can learn about "normal" when we "queer," or turn inside out, our assumptions? This same method yields fresh insights into the afterlife of Napoleon. Just as La Mésangère has "become" his overstuffed closet, Napoleon has "become" his two-cornered hat.

NAPOLEON = BICORN

In the decades after the former emperor's death in 1821, the public could not seem to get enough of Napoleon's likeness, which was also to say his fame and mystique. Artists, publishers, and manufacturers obliged, meeting that demand and further stoking it, as they still do today: with paintings, prints, illustrations, statuettes, and souvenirs, from spoons and plates to figurines, and from letter openers to canes and snuffboxes. Representations of him in his imperial gold laurel crown and his crimson velvet, ermine-lined mantle began to lose some of their appeal. Perhaps all that opulence dated him as a figure of legendary wealth and power from the past rather than a modern version of a Great Man in his uniform, which is what artists and consumers seem to have preferred.[42] These visual depictions of Napoleon, from the 1820s on, usually took two forms—his officer's uniform, at or below his eventually lofty rank, or manly but homely civilian attire. In both these understated modes, Napoleon almost always wears his plain, black, bicorn as he habitually styled it: sideways over his ears with a simple cockade held in place by a single black braid.[43]

Early on, however, some artists did more than picture him in his hat. They started representing Napoleon as if he *were* his hat. Most famously, in 1826, five years after Napoleon's death, history painter Carl von Steuben (1788–1856), an admirer, paid him homage in just this way (see figure 6.1). Van Steuben offers a chronological set of images from Napoleon's career in a painting titled *Les Huit époques de Napoléon* [The Eight Ages of Napoleon]. Given Napoleon's fame, the title is probably as superfluous now as it was in 1826: When a plain black bicorn handily dominates vast landscapes, who else could "be" that hat?[44]

No human figures appear, but the hat is impossible to miss, and the hat *is* Napoleon. Larger than life, it dominates the foreground of every scene and makes everything else seem insignificant, a mere backdrop to the main event. In each scene, the hat looks entirely autonomous, reinforcing an essential part of the myth of the Great Man: He was dependent only on himself, his genius, and his lucky star. (The latter appears in the middle image on the top row, shining brightly above Notre Dame Cathedral.) The background of each carefully curated vignette represents a moment in the emperor's career: the barrage of cannon fire that Artillery Commander Bonaparte aimed at the royalists threatening a coup against the National Convention in 1795; Emperor Napoleon I's 1804 coronation in Notre Dame Cathedral; the Italian and

Egyptian campaigns; peace treaties in Europe; the devastating rout Napoleon and his troops suffered in Moscow; his one-hundred-day return to power; his stunning defeat at Waterloo; and his death in exile on Saint Helena.[45]

Unlike so many of the representations of Napoleon, von Steuben's work celebrates the emperor's legendary status. Yet it also bares the fundamental volatility of fame by introducing the element of time and death. Even the scenes of triumph are somber, dominated by browns, yellows, and greys. Every landscape appears to be a no-man's-land in which the only "man" standing is Napoleon's hat. The diverse and highly expressive positions it takes up suggest a range of emotions. Initially, it stands straight and resolute, its back to us. Then the bicorn faces other directions and strikes other attitudes until the last vignette. There, it is lying down, its underside exposed, facing a faraway landmass planted with a French flag.

As his hat, Napoleon appears in von Steuben's work as a quintessential example of the Great Masculine Renunciation as a matter of virility. Napoleon's hat is a recognizably modern, manly compromise with the dictates of fashion: Follow them, but from a safe distance and not to excess. The implication was that he had other, far more important things to worry about and that taking a critical distance from "feminine" frivolity was only natural. The unchanging hat is always "in uniform"—sempiternal, unique, undiminished by effeminate vanity and excrescences. In these ways, von Steuben's painting and other depictions of the emperor in, or as, his bicorn have helped make Napoleon the poster boy for the modern manly man.[46] Nevertheless, as this book has shown, neither the man nor

FIGURE 6.1 "Napoleon as His Hat." Etching: by Charles-Auguste Bouvier, "Napoleon, by a history painter" (1837) after a painting by Karl Von Steuben, *The Eight Ages of Napoleon* (1826).
Source: Copyright British Museum

these cultural codes refer to a single, obvious, natural, and unchanging set of ideas and behaviors.

Typical of the "manly" version of Napoleonic lore, the hat in Von Steuben's work appears to have sprung fully formed during the French Revolution as if Napoleon were an unchanging essence. His depiction reinforces the myth of the former emperor's singularity, takes for granted his masculinity, and presents him, in effect, as destined for greatness. Although the image offers a mixture of scenes of triumph and defeat, the hat appears always the same, completely untouched by changes in *la mode*—a clear refusal of woman's putative taste for ever-changing fashionable self-display. Similarly, the image completely leaves out the splendiferous side of Napoleon's closet with which he wielded so much power as emperor.

The renunciation side of Napoleon's closet rests on a palimpsest of mutually reinforcing dicta. Provincial and bourgeois admonitions against "feminine" and aristocratic excess were consonant with the Church's hostility toward fashion and vanity at least for its rank-and-file clergymen. Meanwhile, schoolboy and military uniforms shared the slow pace of change that Englishmen's fashions had taken. While these styles were initially mocked by the fashion press in France, the Revolution redefined them as mandatory male patriotism. Uniform attire was in turn reinforced by other "manly" standards of dress associated with the Great Masculine Renunciation—a style that pretended to renounce fashion although it was itself a fashion.

NOT "ONE"

In the same way that von Steuben's painting equates Napoleon with a single hat, the bicorn itself appears to be one, unvarying, unique. But this was never the case. Even before Napoleon reigned as emperor, tens of thousands of military men wore the same head covering. They wore it the way he did, sideways, *en bataille*, as part of their uniform, although many preferred making the two-cocked hat run front to back. Vast numbers of male civilians did the same. Although the hat was traditionally black, its sleek, potentially exaggerated shape and pointy projections made it especially eye-catching.[47]

Making what appears to be the same bicorn stand in for Napoleon in all eight vignettes, which depict events that took place over three decades, obscures the fact that it was not his only head cover. He wore the gold laurel crown at his coronation, "velvet bonnets for traveling, and a round [bowler] hat" for "his civilian dress."[48] Even Napoleon's bicorn was not a single style. In the military, it changed according to army dictates. When he was emperor, its front and back "rose higher to follow the fashion."[49] This was not a renunciation of *la mode*—just a tempered distance from it.

Nor was there a single bicorn. Poupard, the hatmaker to Napoleon, "seems to have supplied thirty-eight beaver-felt bicorns to the emperor" between 1811 and 1815, an "average of eight per year."[50] Why so many? Did his valet throw them away when they started looking scruffy, smelled of sweat, or fell out of fashion? Did he stockpile them, choosing the one he thought would most strike His Imperial Highness's fancy or least irritate him? In any case, during his reign not to mention beforehand, Napoleon I probably wore at least a hundred different bicorns—not to mention dozens of others before and after. In these ways, under the aegis of the Great Masculine Renunciation, the appearance of singularity and sameness helped camouflage the affinities of conventional male norms with "unmanly" excess that might otherwise raise eyebrows, as it did with Fayolle's purported reactions to La Mésangère's "closet": the sheer enormity of his collection of clothing and accessories, on the one hand, and his obsessive shopping habits, on the other hand.

By contrast, Van Steuben's depiction of Napoleon as his hat appears to confirm him as the quintessence of this period's mainstream, masculine norms of virility and dress: simplicity, stability, and continuity. Yet, the bicorn, tipped, tilted, and overturned, also underscores the precarity not only of the symbol but also of the man and, for that matter, masculinity or any other gender configuration.

Both the understated and ostentatious sides of Napoleon's closet have always been contradictory and plural in the meanings attributed to them: absolute authority and illegitimate rule, phallic plenitude and castrated lack, spectacular triumph and melancholic isolation—all of them inseparable, interdependent. The same goes for La Mésangère, the former priest and famous fashion editor—although not nearly to such extremes.

■ ■ ■

In its unorthodox approach to fashion history and masculinity, this book uses a queer lens to examine heteronormativity and eccentricity in the life and times of Napoleon Bonaparte, the Emperor of the French, and Pierre La Mésangère, the "emperor" of fashion.

When I started this project, I wanted to find out why traditional men in the West still wear a far narrower range of clothing than most women. The discovery of La Mésangère and his closet was a revelation; so was pairing him with Napoleon. Both men had a convoluted relationship to the clothing they wore that sometimes turned inside out the elite masculine norms I thought I would be studying. The lives of my two subjects also alerted me to the essential roles that schooling, the state, the army, and the Church played in constructions of modern masculinity. Although all these institutions required uniforms, many men took liberties, opted out, or redefined the norm—and that was true for fashionable men as well.

My research on elite men during this period explores the ways in which the Great Masculine Renunciation of fashion, whose hegemony continues, is not monolithic: It is rife with paradoxes, exceptions, reversals, and contradictions. The same is true of the Great Political Renunciation and the Great Religious Renunciation whose histories I have traced here. The ways they were instituted and reactions to them differ in important respects as well.

The Great Religious Renunciation of fashion, begun in the sixteenth century, was a slow, gradual, institutionalized imposition of sartorial and behavioral standards on clergymen who ended up adopting them as if these were a given. The French Revolution and its call for a Great Political Renunciation was, by contrast, sudden, and dramatic with its highly persuasive disincentives: fines, imprisonment, and the guillotine. The Great Masculine Renunciation, by contrast, was secular, incremental, and often voluntary. By the time it was generally accepted, the supposition was that no "normal" man would want to be seen as feminine. Originally aimed at the elite who had something to renounce, it became a hetero-masculine style that incorporated elements of middle-class attire, which in turn took cues from those higher up. As I have shown, the male attire and behavior expected in all three patriarchal categories, masculine, political, and religious, still pertain today.

For men in traditional positions of power, such as those in the government of the United States, we are still seeing the Great Masculine Renunciation in male attire. But since 2024, this three-hundred-year-old gender paradigm has been matched with its opposite, not so much for clothing but for everything else. I call it the Great Display of Ostentation: bigger is better, whether it is a house, a monument, ambition, predatoriness, or lots of gold—a perennial favorite.

Both the Great Masculine Renunciation and the Great Display of Ostentation are powered in part by a fear of women and male effeminacy. Bringing together the sixteenth- and seventeenth-century Great Religious Renunciation, the Great Political Renunciation occasioned by the decade after the fall of the Bastille in 1789, and the enduring Great Masculine Renunciation reveals the tenacity and nimbleness of masculine privilege and power in manufacturing consent even from those who suffer most from it.[51] But these three intertwined histories also remind us that the hierarchies and myths of gender and heteronormativity only seem permanent and absolute. Change is in our power.

NOTES

PREFACE: FATHER MCCRORY'S BELLY BUTTON

1. The idea of being in or out of the closet is still problematic today because it simplifies a highly complicated dynamic. For example, "Many LGBTQ people have been neither 'inside' nor 'outside' the closet, but have rather revealed or concealed their sexuality, more or less overtly or discreetly, according to the situation." *A Queer History of Fashion: From the Closet to the Catwalk* (Fashion Institute of Technology, 2013), 11.
2. For a reader-friendly, highly useful explanation of common misconceptions about gender, sexuality, and heterosexuality in particular, see Hanne Blank, *Straight: The Surprisingly Short History of Heterosexuality* (Beacon Press, 2012).

INTRODUCTION: THE EMPEROR, THE PRIEST, AND THE CLOSET

1. *Journal des Dames et des Modes*, November 15, 1834, repeated on February 20, 1836. Quoted in Annemarie Kleinert, *Le "Journal des Dames et des Modes" ou la Conquête de l'Europe féminine (1797–1839)* (Jan Thorbecke, 2001), 1. For further analysis of this remark, see chapter 6.
2. Simone de Beauvoir, *The Second Sex* (Vintage, 1973), 301; Judith Butler unpacks this famous quote in "Sex and Gender in Simone de Beauvoir's

Second Sex," *Yale French Studies* 72 (1986): 35–49. On the controversies about the indefinite article "a" before "woman" in the English translation, see *On ne naît pas femme: on le devient: The Life of a Sentence*, ed. Bonnie Mann and Martina Ferrari (Oxford University Press, 2017).

3. The historical record indicates, for example, that some of the men close to Napoleon had sexual relations with men, most famously Jean-Jacques-Régis de Cambacérès, duke de Parme (1753–1824), whom Napoleon picked as Second Consul (see chapter 4). Some claim that Napoleon himself was homosexual or bisexual. See Frank M. Richardson, *Napoleon: Bisexual Emperor* (Horizon Press, 1972). I am less interested in labels than in noting the permeable boundaries between male homosociality (social bonds between men that are presumably not homosexual) and homosexuality. See also Brian Martin, *Napoleonic Friendship: Military Fraternity, Intimacy, and Sexuality in Nineteenth-Century France* (University of New Hampshire Press, 2011).
4. See Annemarie Kleinert, "Un Prêtre fléchois devenu auteur, éditeur et journaliste: Pierre La Mésangère (1761–1831)," *Cahier Fléchois* 19 (1998): 28–53, 38.
5. David Kuchta, a prominent early scholar on fashion history and masculinity in England dates the move toward simplicity in male dress to the inception of the three-piece male suit in 1666. He argues that it brought about "the fashioning of a new masculinity, a new ideology about the morality, politics, and economics of elite men's consumer practices, an ideology still present today." *The Three-Piece Suit and Modern Masculinity: England, 1550–1850* (University of California Press, 2002), 2.
6. On the French reputation for frivolity and changes in the meaning of luxury (from excess to pleasure), which is to say the production and consumption of "frivolous" goods associated with Paris shops newly considered "an economic imperative for the nation," see Rebecca L. Spang, "The Frivolous French: 'Liberty of Pleasure' and the End of Luxury," in *Taking Liberties: Problems of a New Order from the French Revolution to Napoleon*, ed. Howard G. Brown and Judith A. Miller (Manchester University Press, 2002), 122.
7. See Jennifer Jones, *Sexing la Mode: Gender, Fashion, and Commercial Culture in Old Regime France* (Berg, 2004) and "Repackaging Rousseau: Femininity and Fashion in Old Regime France," *French Historical Studies* 18, no. 4 (1994): 939–67. For other feminist analyses of Rousseau, see her n. 3.

8. Peter McNeil, "Conspicuous Waist: Queer Dress in the 'Long Eighteenth Century,'" in Valerie Steele, ed., *A Queer History of Fashion: From the Closet to the Catwalk* (Yale University Press, 2013), 94.
9. For excellent, highly detailed information about the *Incroyable* look and much of the other male attire discussed in this book, see Lydia Edwards, *How to Read a Suit: A Guide to Changing Men's Fashion from the 17th to the 20th Century* (Bloomsbury, 2020). For more on a slightly earlier male type and his female counterpart, see Ewa Lajer-Burcharth, "The *Muscadins* and the *Merveilleuses*: Body and Fashion in Public Space under the Directory, 1795–1799," in *Repression and Expression: Literary and Social Coding in Nineteenth-Century France*, ed. Carrol F. Coates (Peter Lang, 1996), 137–46.
10. Chloe Chapin explores the Great Masculine Renunciation's "profound, lasting impact not just on men, but on broader understandings of gender, class, and nationality." "Masculine Renunciation or Rejection of the Feminine? Revisiting J. C. Flügel's *Psychology of Clothes*," *Fashion Theory* 26, no. 7 (2021): 983–1008. See also Joanna Bourke, "The Great Male Renunciation: Men's Dress Reform in Inter-war Britain," *Journal of Design History* 9, no. 1 (1996): 23. Others who contest some of the claims about the Great Masculine Renunciation include Ewa Lajer-Burcharth who argues that, far from renouncing flashy attire, during the Directory (1795–1799), flamboyance was all the rage especially for counterrevolutionary men, as we shall see. *Necklines: The Art of Jacques-Louis David After the Terror* (Yale University Press, 1999). David Kuchta's study of men's inconspicuous consumption in England (1550–1850), unpacks a host of factors that complicate Flügel's insightful but sweeping statements. See Kuchta, *The Three-Piece Suit,* particularly 163–72. Daniel L. Purdy points out that, for a time, women too gave up much of the color and elaborate ornamentation that had been de rigueur (see the woman on the left in figure 0.1). *The Rise of Fashion: A Reader* (University of Minnesota Press, 2004). On masculinity, clothing, materialism, and fashion magazines in eighteenth-century Germany, see also Purdy, *The Tyranny of Elegance: Consumer Cosmopolitanism in the Age of Goethe* (Johns Hopkins University Press, 1998); Christopher Breward, investigating the continuing masculine "renunciation" in England in the 1860s, observes that British men's sense of self nevertheless depended heavily on shopping and attire. *The Hidden Consumer: Masculinities, Fashion, and City Life, 1860–1914* (Manchester University Press, 1999).

11. J. C. Flügel, *The Psychology of Clothes* (Hogarth Press, 1930), 111. In this book, I use Flügel's work solely for his insights into the Great Masculine Renunciation. I disagree with most of his dated remarks on other matters. For an extended discussion of Flügel on male and female subjectivity, see Kaja Silverman, "Fragments of a Fashionable Discourse," in *Studies in Entertainment Critical Approaches to Mass Culture*, ed. Tania Modleski (Indiana University Press, 1986), 139–51; and Christopher M. Rudeen and Elizabeth Lunbeck, "The Analyst's New Clothes: Reading J.C. Flügel into Fashioning Masculinities," in "Review of *On Fashioning Masculinities: The Art of Menswear*, Victoria and Albert Museum," *Psychoanalysis and History* 25, no. 1, n.p; they cite the same passage in Flügel.
12. Steele writes that the Great Masculine Renunciation was a backlash against the emergence and visibility of "queer" men in eighteenth-century Europe: mollies, macaronis, and the "man milliner" who "transgressed sex and gender norms." These men "de-legitimized what had previously been considered ideally 'masculine' and aristocratic styles, which were now beginning to be perceived as 'effeminate,' . . . especially when men of the popular classes imitated aristocratic beaux." Steele, *A Queer History of Fashion*, 16–17. See also McNeil, "Conspicuous Waist."
13. For the first millennium and beyond, "priestliness" was not a world unto itself. In contrast with monks living in monasteries and hermits living in isolation, a priest's job was to be in the world although not of it. For excellent perspective on priests' absence from the scholarly conversation, see Paul Airiau, "Le Prêtre catholique; masculin, neutre, autre? Des débuts du XIXe siècle au milieu du XXe siècle," in *Hommes et masculinités de 1789 à nos jours, ed. Régis Revenin* (Autrement, 2007), 191–207; John Harvey's landmark study, *Men in Black* (Reaktion Books, 1995), has a great deal to say about French dress, black and colored, military uniforms, and bright-colored women's dress in relationship to masculinity, but it mentions clergymen on only a few occasions.
14. On queer disidentification, see José Muñoz, *Disidentifications: Queers of Color and the Performance of Politics* (University of Minnesota Press, 1999).
15. David Marshall Martin, *Ecclesiastical Dress and Vestments of the Roman Catholic Church from the Eleventh Century to the Present: A Handbook of Patterns, Construction, and Vesting Procedures for Use in the Theatre* (University Microfilms International, 1983), 24–25. See also Jean Gaudemet, "Préface,"

in Louis Trichet, *Le Costume du clergé: Ses Origines et son évolution en France d'après les règlements de l'Eglise* (Editions du Cerf, 1986), 10. For a detailed, fully illustrated history of men's dress from the 1600s to 2000 and explanations of its many components, see Edwards, *How to Read a Suit.*

16. According to Trichet, *Le Costume du clergé*, there was much less concern about nuns' dress and much less resistance on their part to the imposition of restrictions.
17. For the word's fascinating and far longer history in England, see Danielle Bobker, *The Closet: The Eighteenth-Century Architecture of Intimacy* (Princeton University Press, 2020). For a brilliant, early think piece about physical closets and homosexual identity, see Henry Urbach, "Closets, Clothes, Disclosure," *Assemblage* 30 (1996): 62–73.
18. "Despite the increased specialization of rooms, the majority of Parisians, on the eve of the revolution [of 1789] had neither dining room, nor salon, nor antechamber, nor *cabinet de toilette*." Annik Pardailhé-Galabrun, *La Naissance de l'intime: 3.000 foyers parisiens, XVII–XVIII siècles* (Presses Universitaires de France, 1988), 267.
19. On the placement of rooms and their furnishings in Paris during this period, see Pardailhé-Galabrun, *La Naissance de l'intime*, 316–22.
20. Louis XVI initially banned the play in France for its pointed critique of the aristocracy. On the slipperiness of Chérubin's gender identification, see Elizabeth J. MacArthur, "Embodying the Public Sphere: Censorship and the Reading Subject in Beaumarchais's *Mariage de Figaro*," *Representations* 61 (Winter 1998): 60–62.
21. Michel Foucault famously dates the invention of homosexuality to the publication of a text by a German psychiatrist in 1870. He writes, "Homosexuality appeared . . . when it was transposed from the practice of sodomy onto a kind of interior androgyny, a hermaphrodism of the soul. The sodomite had been a temporary aberration; the homosexual was now a species." *The History of Sexuality*, 4 vols., trans. Robert Hurley (Random House, 1978), 1:43. See also Jonathan Ned Katz, *The Invention of Heterosexuality* (University of Chicago Press, 2007) and David M. Halperin, *One Hundred Years of Homosexuality and Other Essays on Greek Love* (Routledge, 1990).
22. On gender, sexuality, and dress from the Renaissance to the 1760s, see McNeil, "Conspicuous Waist," 79–99.
23. Valerie Steele, "A Queer History of Fashion: From the Closet to the Catwalk," in *A Queer History of Fashion*, 12–13.

24. For male homosexuality during the Napoleonic period, see, for example, Michael Sibalis, "The Regulation of Male Homosexuality in Revolutionary and Napoleonic France, 1789–1815," in *Homosexuality in Modern France*, ed. Jeffrey Merrick and Michael Sibalis (Oxford University Press, 1996), 80–101 and Michael Sibalis, "Une subculture d'efféminés? L'homosexualité masculine sous Napoléon Ier," in *Hommes et masculinités de 1789 à nos jours, contributions à l'histoire du genre et de la sexualité en France*, ed. Régis Revenin (Autrement, 2007), 75–95. For caveats on some of these findings, see Jeffrey Merrick, *Sodomy in Eighteenth-Century France* (Cambridge Scholars Publishing, 2020), which offers detailed corrections of previous research and a report on twentieth and twenty-first-century research. For examples around the world during this period, see Bryant T. Ragan Jr. and Jeffrey Merrick, *Eighteenth-Century Homosexuality in Global Perspective*, special issue of *Historical Reflections* 33, no. 1 (Spring 2007).
25. Randolph Trumbach analyzes the so-called mollies (effeminate sodomites of the popular classes), macaronis (highly foppish men), and the "man milliners" (men who sold women's clothing) in London. They "did not turn themselves into women but instead combined into a third gender selected aspects of the behavior of the majority of men and women." Trumbach, *Sex and the Gender Revolution, vol 1: Heterosexuality and the Third Gender in Enlightenment London* (University of Chicago Press, 1998), 3; McNeil notes that "in England, in the eighteenth century two genders—male and female—and three sexes—man, woman, and hermaphrodite were recognized. . . . Men who had sex with men were not at that early date assigned to a third gender—both sexes were considered capable of having sex with either sex." McNeil, "Conspicuous Waist," 81; Steele notes, "not every fop or macaroni was queer, but as soon as a sense of gay identity began to emerge in public, it was expressed in fashion." Steele, *A Queer History of Fashion*, 15.
26. McNeil, "Conspicuous Waist," 85. For highly detailed analyses of "queer" clothing during this period, including earlier centuries, see the entire article.
27. In its examination of fashion from the late eighteenth century to the present, Valerie Steele's edited volume, *A Queer History of Fashion*, focuses on "queer" and fashion from a wide variety of angles; *Fashioning Masculinities: The Art of Menswear*, ed. Rosalind McKever and Claire Wilcox, with Marta Fraceschini (V&A Publishing, 2022), takes a wider,

more global angle on the question of gender and male fashion but soft-pedals the queer question.

28. In this respect, *Napoleon's Closet* shares Annamarie Jagose's counterintuitive queer approach in *Orgasmology* (Duke University Press, 2012), which uses "unqueer figures" to unsettle the usual opposition between the queer and the heteronormative.
29. Eve Sedgwick, *Tendencies* (Duke University Press, 1993), 8.
30. Siobhan B. Somerville explains the two principal meanings of the word: "an umbrella term that refers to a range of sexual identities that are 'not straight'" or, more relevant for this study, a term to "call into question the stability of any such categories of identity based on sexual orientation. In this second sense . . . to 'queer' becomes a way to denaturalize categories such as 'lesbian' and 'gay' (not to mention 'straight' and 'heterosexual'), revealing them as socially and historically constructed identities that have often worked to establish and police the line between the 'normal' and the 'abnormal.'" "Queer," in *Keywords for American Culture Studies,* 3rd ed., ed. Bruce Burgett and Glenn Handler (NYU Press, 2020), 198–202.
31. Carla Freccero, *Queer, Early, Modern* (Duke University Press, 2006), 4.
32. Judith Butler, "Critically Queer," *GLQ: A Journal of Lesbian and Gay Studies* 1, no. 1 (1993): 22.
33. François-Yves Besnard, *Un Prêtre en révolution: Souvenirs d'un nonagénaire*, ed. Martine Taroni (Presses Universitaires de Rennes, 2011), 91.
34. In *Napoleon: A Life* (Penguin, 2014), Andrew Roberts summarizes these considerable difficulties and the history of myths, inaccuracies, and pointedly hostile or glorifying biographies about Napoleon, and the ways our view of him have changed since the publication, beginning in 2004, of the 33,000 letters verified to be his (34–45).
35. Patrice Gueniffey, *Bonaparte: 1769–1802*, trans. Steven Rendall (Harvard University Press, 2015), 84.

1. BOYS, *CULOTTES*, AND CASSOCKS

1. For an illustrated history of children's clothing in France, see Marie Simon, *La Mode enfantine* (Editions du Chêne, 1999). The use of pink and blue did not begin until the nineteenth century and was not widespread until the 1930s.

2. When talking about my subjects as infants and schoolboys, I call them by their first names, Napoleon and Pierre. Once they start training for their careers, I use their last names: Bonaparte and La Mésangère. When La Mésangère is ordained a priest, I give him the honorific title "Father." When Bonaparte became emperor, he claimed his first name, Napoleon, to go with his new title, and that is how I refer to him during his reign and after.
3. Linda A. Pollock, *Forgotten Children: Parent-Child Relations from 1500 to 1900* (Cambridge University Press, 1983), 24. See also Philippe Ariès, *Centuries of Childhood: A Social History of Family Life,* trans. Robert Baldick (Vintage, 1962), 365. For François-Yves Besnard's description of his childhood dress and that of others in the region, see *Un Prêtre en révolution: Souvenirs d'un nonagénaire,* ed. Martine Taroni (Presses Universitaires de Rennes, 2011), 29.
4. Ariès, *Centuries of Childhood,* 365. One estimate for the literacy rate in France between 1701 and 1800, based on consumption, is 29 percent. Etjlo Buringh and Jan Luiten Van Zanden, "Charting the 'Rise of the West,'" *The Journal of Economic History* 69, no. 2 (2009): 434.
5. See Besnard, *Un Prêtre en revolution*; Ariès, *Centuries of Childhood*; and Pollock, *Forgotten Children.*
6. Sometimes, to economize, this literally meant wearing the pants of the family, a father or older brother's castoff, which was "taken apart and resized to fit." Besnard, *Un Prêtre en révolution*, 90.
7. On dyes, see Philippe Haudrère, "Le Cadre de la vie quotidienne des nobles à Angers au XVIIIe siècle," *Annales de Bretagne et des pays de l'Ouest* 106, no. 3 (1999): 101.
8. Why this was true is a matter of debate. What is more important for this argument is the adamancy with which people held the view that nothing else was normal.
9. Jacques Ruppert et al., *Le Costume français* (Flammarion, 1996), 180.
10. For corsets used by military men and dandies, see Valerie Steele, *The Corset: A Cultural History* (Yale University Press, 2001), 36; On stocking padding, see Denis Bruna, *Fashioning the Body: An Intimate History of the Silhouette* (Yale University Press, 2015).
11. Dorothy Carrington, *Napoleon and His Parents on the Threshold of History* (Dutton, 1990), 129. Carrington generally takes issue with the common idea of Carlo Buonaparte as extravagant and irresponsible, but she makes clear his appreciation for and indulgence in fine clothing.

12. See Carrington, *Napoleon and His Parents*, 129.
13. On makeup for men as well as women, see Morag Martin, *Selling Beauty: Cosmetics, Commerce, and French Society, 1750–1830* (Johns Hopkins University Press, 2009).
14. Baron Hippolyte Larrey, "Souvenirs dictés par Madame Mère," in *Madame mère (Napoleonis mater): Essai historique*, 2 vols. (Paris, 1892), 2:530.
15. Annemarie Kleinert, *Le "Journal des dames et des modes" ou La Conquête de l'Europe féminine (1797–1839)* (Jan Thorbecke, 2001), 58.
16. Besnard, *Un Prêtre en révolution*, 91.
17. Besnard, *Un Prêtre en révolution*, 91.
18. Besnard, *Un Prêtre en révolution*, 94–95. After getting caught up in the excitement of revolutionary idealism, Besnard played a role in regional and national republican politics for which he was much maligned. Martine Taroni, "Introduction," in Besnard, *Un Prêtre en révolution*, 19. Disillusioned, he tried his hand at commercial ventures and then headed back to the Angers region to run an orchard.
19. Haudrère, "Le Cadre de la vie quotidienne," 101.
20. Haudrère, "Le Cadre de la vie quotidienne," 101. In western France, silk, which had to be imported all the way across the country from Lyon, was a luxury. Yet when it came to the expensive, fine wool that came from the area, regional loyalties, pride, and perhaps self-interest may have trumped moderation.
21. Haudrère, "Le Cadre de la vie quotidienne," 101.
22. Besnard, *Un Prêtre en révolution*, 40.
23. Ernest Glasson, "Les Origines du costume de la magistrature," in *Nouvelle Revue historique de droit français et étranger* (1884), 109–37. As late as the 1780s at the Academy of Science, "older colleagues and all physicians wore the black costumes and ponderous wigs proper to a learned profession in earlier, stiffer times." Charles Gillispie, *Science and Polity in France: The End of the Old Regime* (Princeton University Press, 1980), 93. The Society of Medicine had stricter rules: "whoever did not wear the official fur and the scholastic gown was to be held incapable of making any discovery" (198).
24. Kleinert, *Le "Journal des Dames et des Modes,"* 59.
25. Gillispie, *Science and Polity*, 118, 123.
26. Jean de Viguerie, *L'Institution des enfants: L'Éducation en France XVI*[e]*–XVIII*[e] *siècle* (Calmann-Lévy, 1978), 289. Like the tie in modern men's

traditional business dress, even if everything else was sober in form and pattern, one place allowed for vanity and some singularity.

27. Besnard, *Un Prêtre en révolution*, 60.
28. When helping officiate at Mass, they wore miniature versions of the priest's costume: a full-length cassock, surplice (a loose, wide-sleeved robe), and a square bonnet. Besnard, *Un Prêtre en révolution*, 60.
29. On the Oratorians, see John McManners, *French Ecclesiastical Society under the Ancien Régime: A Study of Angers in The Eighteenth Century* (Manchester University Press, 1960) and Jacques Maillard, *L'Oratoire à Angers aux XVIIe et XVIIIe siècles* (Klinksieck, 1975); Kleinert claims that La Mésangère may have attended either the Oratorian school mentioned here or the military school at La Flèche, where, under its new guise as an elite middle school run by the Fathers of Christian Doctrine, he would later teach. Elsewhere, however, she says that if he went to La Flèche as a middle school, it was only temporary, making his attendance at the Oratorian school more probable and of longer duration. I believe that this latter conclusion makes the most sense given the timing of his later studies at the seminary and his ordination. Kleinert, *Le "Journal des Dames et des Modes,"* 332, 59.
30. Besnard, *Un Prêtre en révolution*, 78. What makes this conspicuous consumption especially notable is that the Oratorians in Angers had very low salaries: "80 livres per year—hardly enough to make others envious. The bursar, the cook and even the gardener earned more." André Bendjebbar, *La Vie quotidienne en Anjou au XVIII*[e] *siècle* (Hachette, 1983), 159.
31. Besnard, *Un Prêtre en révolution*, 78.
32. Besnard, *Un Prêtre en révolution*, 78.
33. The myths and fears about the dangers of feminine contagion and influence were alive and well, as demonstrated in *Manon Lescaut*, the best-selling novel by François Antoine, abbé Prévost (1697–1763), who was educated at La Flèche, where La Mésangère would later teach, when it was run by Jesuits. The novel follows Des Grieux, a young gentleman headed for the seminary who meets a young *femme fatale* on her way to a convent school, plunging him into a life of decadence and criminality. Thanks to the young woman's ignominious death and to Tiberge, a fellow seminarian-turned-priest and Des Grieux's forever jilted but pathologically loyal friend, the homosocial bond ultimately trumps the heterosexual plot. Des Grieux is welcomed back to the bosom of his family and his aristocratic privileges.

34. His mother, still living in Corsica, never visited. Napoleon's father Carlo, short on funds, only made it to Brienne once, and that was during his son's last year. Arthur Chuquet, *La Jeunesse de Napoléon*, 3 vols. (Paris, 1897–1899), 1:86; For a more impressionistic account, see Guy Godlewski, "La Vie quotidienne de Napoléon à Brienne," *Revue du Souvenir Napoléonien* 265 (August 1972): 4–10.
35. Chuquet, *La Jeunesse de Napoléon*, 1:103.
36. The yearly cost, which the king bore for the fellowship boys, was seven hundred livres, more than six times the 110 livres Carlo paid for Napoleon's education in Autun. Chuquet, *La Jeunesse de Napoléon*, 1:83.
37. Chuquet, *La Jeunesse de Napoléon*, 1:103.
38. Chuquet, *La Jeunesse de Napoléon*, 1:103
39. Chuquet, *La Jeunesse de Napoléon*, 1:113.
40. Viguerie, *L'Institution des enfants*, 71–77, cited in Adrian O'Connor, *In Pursuit of Politics: Education and Revolution in Eighteenth-Century France* (Manchester University Press, 2017), 18.
41. Some scholars maintain that, given his identification with the poor, Christ probably wore a knee-length tunic that showed his legs rather than a long flowing robe. The cloth would have been cheap and, if dyed at all, probably light red, green, or orange, the least expensive options at the time. Joan E. Taylor, *What Did Jesus Look Like?* (Bloomsbury, 2018), 186.
42. Godlewski, "La Vie quotidienne," 4.
43. Chuquet, *La Jeunesse de Napoléon*, 1:119.
44. Quoted in Alan Schom, *Napoleon Bonaparte* (Harper Collins, 1997), 4.
45. Schom, *Napoleon Bonaparte*, 5.
46. "Characteristic Traits of Bonaparte in His Youth and a Refutation of Diverse Anecdotes Published on this Subject" is an anonymous forty-five-page pamphlet, published in London in 1797 and translated that same year into French, signed "C.H." The document was presumed to have been written by a foreign student who was at Brienne with Napoleon. Godlewski, "La Vie quotidienne," 8.
47. On the tangle of difficulties determining which of Napoleon's letters are authentic, see Jacques-Olivier Boudon, "Introduction générale," and Thierry Lentz, "Introduction: Les apprentissages de Bonaparte," in *Correspondance générale de Napoléon Bonaparte*, 15 vols, ed. Fondation Napoléon (Editions Fayard, 2004), 1:19–37. In one of the counterfeit letters, Napoleon complains bitterly to his father that his indigence makes

him a laughingstock of those "popinjays" who are all glibness, conceit, and foppishness. Quoted in Captain D. A. Bingham, *A Selection from the Letters and Despatches of the First Napoleon with Explanatory Notes*, 3 vols. (1884), 1:7.

48. Bonaparte, "Brienne, [25 June] 1784," *Correspondance générale*, 1:43–44.
49. Chuquet, *La Jeunesse de Napoléon*, 1:130.
50. Godlewski, "La Vie quotidienne," 4.
51. Chuquet, *La Jeunesse de Napoléon*, 1:407.
52. Chuquet, *La Jeunesse de Napoléon*, 1:383.
53. Quoted in Chuquet, *La Jeunesse de Napoléon*, 1:406.
54. Quoted in Chuquet, *La Jeunesse de Napoléon*, 1:406. Some biographers apply the latter term to Pierre-François Laugier de Bellecour, son of an impoverished baron and one of Napoleon's few friends at Brienne, who will make an appearance in chapter 3.
55. Kleinert, *Le "Journal des Dames et des Modes,"* 59.
56. McManners states that in the 1770s "in Angers, the thrusts of anticlericalism were as effective as swordplay against a feather-bed." *French Ecclesiastical Society*, 44. Other historians claim that it was more pervasive and pernicious. See Alec Mellor, *Histoire de l'anticléricalisme français* (Mame, 1969) and Jean Réveille, "Anticlericalism in France," *The American Journal of Theology* 9 (1905): 605–20.
57. Besnard, *Un Prêtre en révolution*, 81. Much later, Pierre-Jean de Béranger (1780–1857), the popular and prolific French songwriter, would deride priests in similar terms.
58. François Marie Arouet de Voltaire, "Philosophical Dictionary," in *Homosexuality in Early Modern France: A Documentary Collection*, ed. Jeffrey Merrick and Bryant T. Ragan Jr. (Oxford University Press, 2001), 156.
59. Dominique Julia, "L'éducation des ecclésiastiques aux XVIIe et XVIIIe siècles," in *Problèmes de l'histoire de l'éducation: Actes des séminaires organisés par l'École française de Rome et l'Università di Roma—la Sapienza (janvier–mai 1985)*, Collection de l'École Française de Rome 104 (Publications de l'Ecole Française de Rome, 1988), 153–54.
60. Julia, "L'éducation," 153.
61. Besnard, *Un Prêtre en révolution*, 102.
62. Besnard, *Un Prêtre en révolution*, 108. Gary Ferguson points out that we have a long way to go in our understandings of gender and sexuality vis-à-vis the confessional. While the confessional has been recognized "as a privileged site for the evolution of the modern, introspective, sexual subject,"

with the potential to "awaken and teach desire as well as shame and discipline it," unfortunately "the potentially highly sexually-charged nature of such interchanges" has "generally not retained scholars' attention." "Masculinity, Confession, Modernity: François de Sales and the Penitent Gentleman," *L'Esprit Créateur* 43, no. 3 (2003): 16–25; See also Richard Rambuss, *Closet Devotions* (University of North Carolina Press, 1998), which connects prayer closets in domestic spaces with the internalization of sexuality.

63. Besnard, *Un Prêtre en révolution*, 108.
64. Besnard, *Un Prêtre en révolution*, 108. The fact that other seminarians knew of their close relations to the priests would have made the *mystiqueurs* of limited use as undercover spies on the other boys.
65. Besnard, *Un Prêtre en révolution*, 108; For later use of the term, see Albert Houtin, *Une Vie de Prêtre: Mon Expérience, 1867–1912* (F. Reider, 1926), 101.
66. Gary Ferguson, *Queer (Re)Readings in the French Renaissance: Homosexuality, Gender, Culture* (Ashgate, 2008), 185. "Descriptions of homosexual men as cliques, cabals, or sects was a common tool in contemporary satire." But whereas the *mignons* were known for their fastidiously elegant finery and hairstyles, nothing appears to have distinguished the *mystiqueurs* from their fellow seminarians. In this sense, uniform attire protected them from detection by outsiders. On *les mignons,* see Pierre de L'Éstoile, *Mémoires-Journaux*, 11 vols., ed. G. Brunet et al. (Paris, 1888), 1:142–43; Joseph Cady, "The 'Masculine Love' of the 'Princes of Sodom': 'Practicing the Art of Ganymede' at Henri III's Court," in Jacqueline Murray and Konrad Eisenbichler, eds., *Desire and Discipline: Sex and Sexuality in the Premodern West* (University of Toronto Press, 1996), 123–54; and Nicolas Le Roux, *La faveur du roi: Mignons et courtesans au temps des derniers Valois* (Champ Vallon, 2001).
67. Besnard, *Un Prêtre en révolution*, 108.
68. Julia uses the same term to discuss the fear of homosexual relations in the seminary. "L'éducation," 153–54.
69. Besnard, *Un Prêtre en révolution*, 108.

2. BOYS TO MEN: TRAINING AND CLOTHING THE ELITE

1. Thomas Cauvin, *La Flèche et ses environs* (Res Universis, 1990), 116.
2. Charles Boucher, *La Flèche sous la Révolution, 1789–1805: Mémoires inédits du chirurgien Charles Boucher, publication intégrale et critique par Alain de Dieuleveult* (A. de Dieuleveult, 1982), 120. For a similarly impressionistic

and largely undocumented account with a distinctly Bonapartist bent, see François-Roger-Fidel Marchant de Burbure, *Essais historiques sur la ville et le collège de La Flèche* (Pavie, 1803).

3. In the early years, the school, known as the Collège Royal de La Flèche, counted among its former students not only the novelist, François Antoine, abbé Prévost (1697–1763), but also the philosopher René Descartes (1596–1650). On the school's history, see Bernard Beaupère, *Histoire du Prytanée* (Lavauzelle, 1985), and *La Flèche: Quatre siècles d'éducation sous le regard de l'Etat* (Prytanée national militaire, 2006).
4. Beaupère, *Histoire du Prytanée*, 17; "1,500 livres salary [paid] to the principal . . . 1,100 to the professors of philosophy and rhetoric," and a still princely nine hundred livres to those who taught the youngest children, these were significantly higher than the salaries paid to teachers when La Flèche had been a military academy. André Bendjebbar, *La Vie quotidienne en Anjou au XVIIIe siècle* (Hachette, 1983), 159.
5. Burbure, *Essais historiques*, 320.
6. Benjamin Bois, *La Vie scolaire et les créations intellectuelles en Anjou pendant la Révolution, 1789–1799* (Félix Alcan, 1929), 11–12. Quoted in Bendjebbar, *La Vie quotidienne*, 159.
7. Bendjebbar, *La Vie quotidienne*, 159.
8. Beaupère, *Histoire du Prytanée*, 14.
9. Beaupère, *Histoire du Prytanée*, 17, 14.
10. Jean de Viguerie, *Une Œuvre d'éducation sous l'Ancien Régime: Les Pères de la doctrine chrétienne en France et en Italie: 1592–1792* (Éditions de la Nouvelle Aurore, 1976), 579.
11. Viguerie, *Une Œuvre d'éducation*, 579.
12. See Beaupère, *La Flèche: Quatre siècles d'éducation*, 77, images, bottom.
13. Shame could go both ways. Louis Marie de La Revellière-Lépeaux (1753–1824) was a contemporary of Besnard and La Mésangère and, like them, from the Anjou region. In 1795, he became one of the five leaders during the Directory. Born to a bourgeois family, he reported that the best student in his school, Gendry, a baker's son, "was always clothed in indigence." On prize day, he did not show up because "his parents could not afford to buy him decent clothes." As a result, La Revellière-Lépeaux quips, this low-class boy's brilliance did not have any "embarrassing consequences" for the more privileged but less accomplished boys and parents in attendance. *Mémoires de Revellière-Lépeaux: Membre exécutif de la République Française et de l'Institut National*, 3 vols. (Paris, 1895), 1:15.

14. It took three hundred years for the school, now called the National Military Prytanée, to accept female students.
15. Bendjebbar, *La Vie quotidienne en Anjou*, 163.
16. Bendjebbar, *La Vie quotidienne en Anjou*, 164.
17. Bendjebbar, *La Vie quotidienne en Anjou*, 164.
18. The same is true of the concept of the social and psychological closet today.
19. Bendjebbar, *La Vie quotidienne en Anjou*, 163–64.
20. On this principle, as seen in the prison designs by the Englishman Jeremy Bentham (1748–1832), and its larger meanings for social and self-surveillance, see Michel Foucault, *Discipline and Punish: The Birth of the Prison*, trans. Alan Sheridan (Pantheon, 1977).
21. On gender roles at La Flèche under the Jesuits, see Sylvie Granger, "Terpsichore au collège: La danse dans l'enseignement jésuite," in *La Flèche: Quatre siècles d'éducation*, 209–40.
22. See a photograph of this practice in the late nineteenth century by which time La Flèche had once again become a military school. Daniel Potron, *Le Prytanée militaire de La Flèche à travers la carte postale* (Coconnier, 1989), 72.
23. Granger, "Terpsichore au collège," 229. Costumes for the male students at La Flèche cast as women in classical Greek plays may well have preceded by decades the craze for antiquity in women's fashions from the Directory through the Empire—an insight that might explode conventional understandings of neoclassical fashion. However, the schoolboys' costumes were not likely to have been transparent, as some of the most titillating female versions of these fashions were alleged to have been.
24. Viguerie, *Une Œuvre d'éducation*, 289.
25. A dwindling number of Doctrinarians were choosing to be ordained, which required a much more solemn vow to lead not just a modest but a chaste life. John McManners, "Religious Vocation," in *Church and Society in Eighteenth-Century France*, 2 vols. (Clarendon Press, 1998), 1:518.
26. Viguerie, *Une Œuvre d'éducation*, 288.
27. Viguerie, *Une Œuvre d'éducation*, 286. In the latter half of the century, a *vestiaire* (clothing allowance) was "paid by each house to its members in proportion to its revenues according to the decision of the community's chapter." Viguerie, *Une Oeuvre d'éducation*, 289.
28. McManners, *Church and Society*, 1:518. After the French Revolution, in 1790, four years after La Mésangère was ordained, "a Doctrinarian's

status is completely secular." They are "mere teachers and their novices are apprentice-teachers. Teaching at the middle school level does not require a special spiritual calling." Viguerie, *Une Œuvre d'éducation*, 249.

29. Viguerie, *Une Œuvre d'éducation*, 301.
30. This did not mean they refrained from monitoring and punishing bedtime intimacies.
31. McManners, *Church and Society*, 1:518.
32. Viguerie, *Une Oeuvre d'éducation*, 289.
33. This liberalization was a nonviolent, deliberative, and relatively democratic process made in response to the desire of many in the rank and file for a somewhat more secular masculine look and life. Viguerie speculates that the relaxation of rules may have come about so that Doctrinarians could "spare themselves the trials of temptation." *Une Œuvre d'éducation*, 302. It also spared the religious fraternity ever more fruitless attempts at regulation and the bad taste of conflict among the brethren.
34. Viguerie, *Une Œuvre d'éducation*, 287.
35. Viguerie, *Une Oeuvre d'éducation*, 287.
36. September 13, 1763, Archives Château Requista, cited in Viguerie, *Une Œuvre d'éducation*, 289.
37. McManners, *Church and Society*, 1:518. Viguerie, *Une Œuvre d'éducation*, 289.
38. Viguerie, *Une Œuvre d'éducation*, 289.
39. Viguerie, *Une Œuvre d'éducation*, 287.
40. Annemarie Kleinert notes that the publication date may have been 1789 or 1790. The second edition, published in 1797, *did* identify the author as La Mésangère.
41. Pierre de L'Éstoile, *Mémoires-Journaux*, 11 vols., ed. G. Brunet et al. (Paris, 1888), 1:142–43. Cited in Katherine B. Crawford, "Love, Sodomy, and Scandal: Controlling the Sexual Reputation of Henry III," *Journal of the History of Sexuality* 12, no. 4 (October 2003): 524. In his memoirs, Besnard called the Angers seminarian priests' favorites, including the handsome and soulfully flirtatious young Craon, *les mystiqueurs* but also *les mignons*—a reference to Henri III's male "court."
42. Pierre de La Mésangère, *Le Voyageur à Paris: Tableau pittoresque et moral de cette capitale*, 3 vols. (1797), 1:90.
43. The scholarship on gender and fops in English literature is ably summarized in Emma Katherine Atwood, "Fashionably Late: Queer Temporality and the Restoration Fop," *Comparative Drama* 47, no. 1 (Spring 2013): 23n4.

44. La Mésangère, *Le Voyageur à Paris*, 1:90.
45. Arthur Chuquet, *La Jeunesse de Napoléon*, 3 vols. (Paris, 1897–1899), 1:192–93.
46. Chuquet, *La Jeunesse de Napoléon*, 1:197. Although twentieth- and twenty-first-century biographers often depend on Chuquet, sometimes they choose to convey only one side or the other of the bifurcation between strict military discipline and sumptuous facilities and décor. For example, Vincent Cronin's *Bonaparte: An Intimate Biography* (Morrow, 1972) makes room primarily for the "feminine," luxurious side of the Ecole Royale Militaire, such as details about the decorations. Alan Schom underscores only soldierly austerity although he does point out the glamour of the uniform Bonaparte wore after graduating. *Bonaparte: A Life* (Harper Collins, 1997), 7.
47. Chuquet, *La Jeunesse de Napoléon*, 1:184.
48. Chuquet, *La Jeunesse de Napoléon*, 1:190.
49. Just two years after Bonaparte's departure from the Ecole in 1785, the new minister of war who replaced Ségur shut it down for precisely these reasons. Chuquet, *La Jeunesse de Napoléon*, 1:207.
50. For intellectual and cultural histories of the luxury debates in general and within the military during this period, see Maxine Berg and Elizabeth Eger, eds. *Luxury and Pleasure in the Eighteenth Century* (Palgrave MacMillan, 2003); Christy Pichichero, *The Military Enlightenment: War and Culture in the French Empire from Louis XIV to Bonaparte* (Cornell University Press, 2017); David Bell, *The First Total War: Bonaparte's Europe and the Birth of Warfare as We Know It* (Mariner, 2008); and David Bell, "The Unbearable Lightness of Being French: Law, Republicanism and National Identity at the End of the Old Regime," *The American Historical Review* 106, no. 4 (2001): 1215–35.
51. See Chuquet, *La Jeunesse de Napoléon*, 1:207–9. Later on, reflecting on his days at the Ecole Militaire, Bonaparte appears to have agreed on this last point. See Chuquet, *La Jeunesse de Napoléon*, 1:210, who quotes, without citing it, Emmanual de Las Cases's *Mémorial de Saint-Hélène*. The *Mémorial* famously reports conversations between an exiled Bonaparte and de Las Cases. However, it is "almost impossible to determine precisely what . . . are Bonaparte's own words and what are extrapolations, or—why not?—inventions." Thierry Lentz et al., eds., *Le Mémorial de Sainte-Hélène: Le manuscrit original retrouvé* (Perrin, 2017).
52. Chuquet, *La Jeunesse de Napoléon*, 1:261.

53. Chuquet, *La Jeunesse de Napoléon*, 1:261.
54. Even so, religion still played a prominent role. In addition to confession and prayers, these young officers-to-be had to attend Mass every day of the week—roughly six times the number required of Father La Mésangère and his teaching colleagues at La Flèche around the same time.
55. Chuquet, *La Jeunesse de Napoléon*, 1:261, 205.
56. Chuquet, *La Jeunesse de Napoléon*, 1:205.
57. Chuquet, *La Jeunesse de Napoléon*, 1:206.
58. Chuquet, *La Jeunesse de Napoléon*, 1:206.
59. Chuquet, *La Jeunesse de Napoléon*, 1:206.
60. On male honor and social class, see Robert A. Nye, *Masculinity and Male Codes of Honor in France* (Oxford University Press, 1993) and William M. Reddy, *The Invisible Code: Honor and Sentiment in Post-Revolutionary France, 1814–1848* (University of California Press, 1997).
61. Chuquet, *La Jeunesse de Napoléon*, 1:144.
62. Chuquet, *La Jeunesse de Napoléon*, 1:206.
63. Chuquet, *La Jeunesse de Napoléon*, 1:206.
64. Chuquet, *La Jeunesse de Napoléon*, 1:206.
65. Chuquet, *La Jeunesse de Napoléon*, 1:262.
66. Chuquet, *La Jeunesse de Napoléon*, 1:261–62.
67. Chuquet, *La Jeunesse de Napoléon*, 1:262.
68. There is a similar account, purported to be by Alexandre des Mazis (1768–1841) that, like Chuquet's, is problematic. Reading Chuquet's highly stylized version along with des Mazis's more sentimental rendition highlights the different kinds of mythmaking around Bonaparte's reputed intolerance for vice. The nominal author, des Mazis, was one of the five cadets, including Laugier de Bellecour and Bonaparte, who left Brienne for the Ecole in Paris. The text attributed to des Mazis represents Bonaparte as a force for good—albeit in far more tempered terms than Chuquet. It claims that Bonaparte generally bemoaned the Ecole students' "frivolousness, reigning vices (*désordres*), and the little care that was taken to monitor us and save us from corruption." Des Mazis's more nuanced text also gives both men more humanity and declines to take sides. It states that Laugier and Bonaparte were simply ill-matched: "[Laugier] was self-indulgent (*dissipé*) and his character was entirely different from Buonaparte's." For Des Mazis, the dramatic showdown was not just a moral but also a physical confrontation (pranks, bullying, and outright fighting), which took place before other Ecole Royale students.

Provoked by the name-calling, Bonaparte threw Laugier to the floor and claimed victory. "'I was insulted,' Bonaparte explained with the utmost self-possession, 'and I took my revenge.'" The Des Mazis text ends the scene not with a thundering renunciation but on a note of New Testament forgiveness: "From that time on, Laugier became more prudent. After military school, Buonaparte, regretting the loss of this friend who had such an aptitude for happiness, talked about him with a sincere feeling of affection." "Cahiers d'Alexandre des Mazis," cited in Paul Bartel, *La Jeunesse inédite de Napoléon d'après de nombreux documents* (Amiot-Dumont, 1954), Appendix II, 256–57.

69. Alan Schom, *Bonaparte: A Life* (HarperCollins, 1997), 7.
70. Schom, *Bonaparte*, 8.
71. Steven L. Kaplan, *La Fin des corporations*, trans. Béatrice Vierne (Fayard, 2001).
72. To understand how undermining the guilds' power affected shopping trips for clothing during this period, see Anne Higonnet, *Liberty, Equality, Fashion: The Women Who Styled the French Revolution* (W. W. Norton, 2024), 26–30.
73. Aileen Ribeiro, *Dress in Eighteenth-Century Europe, 1715–1789* (Holmes and Meier, 1984), 52. Illustration No. 20 shows a male doll made of beeswax from the 1780s.
74. Madeleine Ginsberg, "Fashion Plates," in *Encyclopedia of Costume and Fashion*, 3 vols., ed. Valerie Steele (Charles Scribner's Sons, 2005), 2:66.
75. Annemarie Kleinert, "La Naissance d'une presse de mode à la veille de la Révolution et l'essor du genre au XIXème siècle," in *Le Journalisme d'Ancien Régime*, ed. Pierre Rétat (Presses Universitaires de Lyon, 1982), 189.
76. Those who were lower on the social scale could get wind of new trends through cheap circulars called *avis* and *affiches*, which advertised the newest articles of clothing along with home furnishings and farm equipment. By the 1750s, monochrome fashion plates appeared in yearly almanacs. Popular caricatures did the opposite kind of work by offering negative examples, poking fun at individuals or types whose clothing miscues or excesses revealed their pretentions.
77. On the ways fashion became associated with femininity, women, and effeminacy in earlier fashion magazines illustrated only in black and white, see Reed Benhamou, "Fashion in the Mercure: From Human Foible to Female Failing," *Eighteenth-Century Studies* 31, no. 1 (Fall 1997): 27–43, https://www.jstor.org/stable/30053643.

78. Journalists were paid according to the number of lines of copy that made it into print. See Robert Darnton's landmark study, *The Literary Underground of the Old Regime* (Harvard University Press, 1982).
79. On the textile industry, see Kleinert, "Naissance," 190. Buisson engaged a M. Allemand (about whom almost nothing is known) as editor and de Montigny and Marie Jean Antoine Nicolas de Caritas, marquis de Condorcet (1743–1794) as consultants. See Annemarie Kleinert, *Die frühen Modejournale in Frankreich: Studien zur Literatur der Mode von den Anfängen bis 1848* (E. Schmidt, 1980), 67, 74. Condorcet was the most famous: A provincial nobleman come to Paris Condorcet was a mathematician, scientist, writer, secretary of the Legislative Assembly during the French Revolution, and inspector general of the Mint. Judged insufficiently radical during the Terror, he died in 1794 in prison. See Keith Michael Baker, "Condorcet," in *A Critical Dictionary of the French Revolution*, ed. François Furet and Mona Ozouf (Belknap, 1989), 204–13.
80. Annemarie Kleinert, *Le "Journal des Dames et des Modes," ou, La Conquête de l'Europe féminine (1797–1839)* (Thorbecke, 2001), 28–30.
81. Individual issues were not for sale separately although the engravings often were.
82. In French, masculine plural adjectives indicate that there is at least one male implied in a group. It does not necessarily indicate an all-male group. Any of these pronouns could imply one or more female journalists, but if so, she or they were well masked by the content.
83. See Margaret Waller, "Trouble in Argus City: Peacocking, Invisibility, and Masculinity," *Romanic Review* 107, no. 1–4 (2016): 25–46, http://ccl.idm.oclc.org/login?url=https://search-proquest-com.ccl.idm.oclc.org/docview/1953806892?accountid=10141 and "Disembodiment as a Masquerade: Fashion Journalists and Other 'Realist' Observers in Directory Paris," *Esprit Créateur* 37, no. 1 (Spring 1997): 44–54.
84. In the beginning, one-third of the illustrations featured men's wear. The percentage of male engravings went down somewhat after the first year, but for years this proportion, although lower, still held steady.
85. See "Cabinet" in *Dictionnaire de l'Académie Française*, 1694, 1762, 1798. See also the discussion of "cabinet" in the introduction to this book.
86. *Cabinet des Modes*, prospectus (October 4, 1785), 5.
87. *Cabinet des Modes*, prospectus, 5.
88. *Cabinet des Modes*, prospectus, 5.
89. *Cabinet des Modes*, June 15, 1786, 120.

90. *Cabinet des Modes*, September 1, 1786, 154.
91. *Cabinet des Modes*, November 15, 1785, 5. No mention was made of women doing the same with their female companions. As was typical of the period, the best and usually the only examples of Man with a capital *M* were men.
92. Bell, "The Unbearable Lightness of Being French," 1215–35.
93. The source of the motto is Antoine Houdar de La Motte, "Les Amis trop d'accord" [The Friends Who Agreed Too Much] (Paris, 1719), a verse fable. In the original, the line meant that a variety of opinion is the spice of life (or at least society). Yet *Magasin des Modes Nouvelles* generally shied away from differences of opinion. The motto would seem instead to point to the publication's heterogeneous contents and *la mode* itself. Both required and thrived on difference and change, albeit within the limits of good taste, as determined by the self-appointed fashion cabinet.
94. *Magasin des Modes Nouvelles,* May 30, 1787, 154.
95. From the 1740s on, many Englishmen's increasing concern was to avoid being seen as "too French," contaminated by this foreign influence. "As long as British patricians spoke French among themselves, the claim went, as long as they favoured French clothes, employed French hairdressers and valets, and haunted Parisian salons on the Grand Tour, as long as the taste for French cultural and luxury imports was allowed to put native artists, traders and manufacturers out of business, national distinction would be eroded and national fibre relaxed." Linda Colley, *Britons: Forging the Nation, 1707–1787* (Yale University Press, 1992), 88.
96. *Magasin des Modes Nouvelles*, May 20, 1787, 146.
97. *Magasin des Modes Nouvelles,* May 20, 1787, 146 (my emphasis). In the impassioned claim that *la mode* was women's work, the pronoun "we" distinguishes the journal's staff not just from women, as was usually the case, but from "they," men in general—another way in which the magazine occupied an in-between position on the gender of fashion.
98. *Magasin des Modes Nouvelles*, December 10, 1786, 22.
99. *Magasin des Modes Nouvelles*, November 20, 1787, 5.
100. *Cabinet des Modes*, November 1, 1786, 190.
101. *Cabinet des Modes*, November 1, 1786, 190.
102. *Magasin des Modes Nouvelles*, May 30, 1787, 153.
103. *Magasin des Modes Nouvelles*, July 11, 1789, 181.
104. This style, the magazine states, is an American import from more than a decade before when the French helped the American colonies and "we

were at war with the English." *Magasin des Modes Nouvelles*, July 11, 1789, 181.

105. *Magasin des Modes Nouvelles*, May 30, 1787, 156–57.
106. *Magasin des Modes Nouvelles*, May 20, 1787, 146. During the eighteenth and nineteenth centuries, Woman was said to be the ornamental sex whose natural and proper domain was the decorative and/or domestic detail. On the detail's feminization, see Naomi Schor, *Reading in Detail: Aesthetics and the Feminine* (Methuen, 1987). On its implications for fashion and popular culture, see 51–55.
107. Richard Wrigley, *The Politics of Appearances* (Berg, 2002), 61–62.
108. *Magasin des Modes Nouvelles*, June 1, 1789, 145.
109. Journals of this kind were often notoriously behind on their publication schedule. This issue may have gone to press *after* the fall of the Bastille on July 14, 1789. If so, this would make these comments *very* political indeed.
110. The second anecdote has a very similar historical setting, structure, and moral.
111. On wigs, see Michael Kwass, "Big Hair: A Wig History of Consumption in Eighteenth-Century France," *The American Historical Review* 111, no. 3 (June 2006): 631–59. See also Ina Baghdiantz McCabe, *A History of Global Consumption: 1500–1800* (Routledge, 2015), 229–69.

3. FASHIONING UNIFORM MEN FOR THE FRENCH REVOLUTION

1. There are hundreds of different accounts of this day. I rely primarily on Jacques Godechot's classic study, *The Taking of the Bastille, July 14th, 1789*, trans. Jean Stewart (Scribner's, 1970).
2. By most historians' estimations, it lasted until 1799, when Bonaparte, who had been promoted to general, overthrew the latest revolutionary government and established himself as First Consul.
3. For a gripping, detailed account of the Revolution from a fashion perspective with an emphasis on the royal family, see Caroline Weber, *Queen of Fashion: What Marie Antoinette Wore to the Revolution* (Henry Holt, 2006), which is the inspiration for this subheading.
4. Godechot, *Taking of the Bastille*, 243.
5. An inscription in Latin follows: "monstrum horrendum, informe, ingens, cui lumen ademptum" ("A horrible monster, deformed, huge, whose eye

had been taken,") Virgil, *Aeneid* 3.655–61, https://sententiaeantiquae.com/2017/03/05/humanizing-a-monster-the-saddest-scene-in-latin-literature/.

6. Godechot, *Taking of the Bastille*, 255. Étienne Alexandre Bardin, "Cocarde," in *Dictionnaire de l'armée de terre, ou Recherches historiques sur l'art et les usages militaires des anciens et des modernes*, 17 vols. (Paris, 1843), 5:1324.
7. For more on the cockade during this period, see Richard Wrigley, *The Politics of Appearances: Representations of Dress in Revolutionary France* (Berg, 2002), 96–134.
8. Seeing Louis XVI return to Versailles, cockaded hat in hand, Marie-Antoinette is said to have remarked, "I thought I had married a King of France, not a commoner." Weber, *Queen of Fashion*, 201.
9. Patrice Gueniffey, *Bonaparte: 1769–1802*, trans. Steven Rendall (Harvard University Press, 2015), 84.
10. Napoleon, *Correspondence générale*, no. 31 (July 22, 1789), 1:78–79. Quoted in Gueniffey, *Bonaparte*, 84.
11. The representatives were not the only ones being radicalized. In October, several thousand women, most from the lower, working classes, marched from Paris to Versailles to demand that the king provide more grain and return with his family and government to Paris. He did.
12. Alan Schom, *Napoleon Bonaparte* (HarperCollins, 1997), 15.
13. Schom, *Napoleon Bonaparte*, 12–16.
14. Gueniffey, *Bonaparte*, 91.
15. Gueniffey, *Bonaparte*, 96.
16. "In its beginnings, the revolution was not anticlerical." Louis Trichet, *Le Costume du clergé: Ses origines et son évolution en France d'après les règlements de l'Église* (Éditions du Cerf, 1986), 167. However, it quickly became so.
17. Lynn Hunt, *Politics, Culture, and Class in the French Revolution* (University of California Press, 1984), 53. See her excellent summary of the complicated politics of the gender/dress system during this period in Hunt, "Freedom of Dress in Revolutionary France," in *From the Royal to the Republican Body: Incorporating the Political in Seventeenth- and Eighteenth-Century France*, ed. Sara E. Melzer and Kathryn Norberg (University of California Press, 1998), 224–49. For more on the ups and downs and intricacies of this question to which I cannot do justice here, see Wrigley, *Politics of Appearances*.

18. The periodical avows that the styles in the fashion engravings were three weeks out of date, which was understandable, under the circumstances. In addition, several later issues never appeared at all, and there were multiple indications of editorial inattentiveness during this period.
19. *Magasin des Modes Nouvelles Françaises et Anglaises*, September 21, 1789, 227 and July 21, 1789, 185–86. However, the August 10, 1789 issue did not burn any bridges with royalist readers. It featured two fashion engravings of women in half-mourning for the dauphin, the seven-year-old son of Marie-Antoinette and Louis XVI, who had died of tuberculosis a little over two months earlier, on June 4.
20. *Magasin des Modes Nouvelles*, October 21, 1789, 242.
21. *Magasin des Modes Nouvelles*, September 21, 1789, 228.
22. On the controversy about the cost, see Wrigley, *Politics of Appearances*, 66. On the National Guard uniform, see Nicole Pellegrin, *Les Vêtements de la liberté: Abécédaire des pratiques vestimentaires françaises de 1780 à 1800* (Éditions Alinéa, 1989), 92–93.
23. *Magasin des Modes Nouvelles*, September 11, 1789, 217, 218.
24. *Magasin des Modes Nouvelles*, October 1, 1789, 241.
25. Dale L. Clifford, "Can the Uniform Make the Citizen? Paris, 1789–1791," *Eighteenth-Century Studies* 34, no. 3 (Spring 2001): 364.
26. Alexander Maxwell, *Patriots Against Fashion: Clothing and Nationalism in Europe's Age of Revolutions* (Palgrave Macmillan, 2014), 70.
27. In Paris, defining active citizenship as the ability to join the National Guard, the citizen militia, in effect made it male. The uniform, which was a civic right and duty, and citizenship "were therefore literally equivalent" or at least closely linked in "the popular conception of citizenship." Timothy Tackett, *The Coming of the Terror in the French Revolution* (Harvard University Press, 2015), 74.
28. Clifford, "Can the Uniform Make the Citizen?," 363–64.
29. *Magasin des Modes Nouvelles*, October 1, 1789, 235.
30. *Magasin des Modes Nouvelles*, October 1, 1789, 235.
31. *Magasin des Modes Nouvelles*, October 1, 1789, 235.
32. *Magasin des Modes Nouvelles*, October 1, 1789, 235–36.
33. *Magasin des Modes Nouvelles*, October 1, 1789, 237. Abbés per se would not necessarily have been class interlopers in the periodical. Often, they were men of breeding and education. Whatever their social status, they enjoyed more leeway in their clothing and coiffure than parish or teaching priests.

34. *Magasin des Modes Nouvelles*, October 21, 1789, 244. If, on the other hand, the 'a' was a typographical error, which was a highly common occurrence in the press of the time, what was shiny black was the *abbé*'s *culotte*.
35. *Magasin des Modes Nouvelles*, October 21, 1789, 244–45.
36. *Magasin des Modes Nouvelles*, October 21, 1789, 245.
37. Despite the snarky attitude, *Magasin des Modes Nouvelles* avows that "[*abbés*] of this kind" are among its readers. *Magasin des Modes Nouvelles*, October 21, 1789, 244–45.
38. Agathe Lhommede, "Le Brun-Tossa," in *Dictionnaire des journalistes (1600–1789)*, IHRIM UMR 5317/MSH-LSE USR 2005 (2019), https://dictionnaire-journalistes.gazettes18e.fr/journaliste/476-jean-brun-dit - Le Brun-tossa.
39. Le Brun's magazine also preached the moral necessity of helping those less fortunate (October 5 and 15, 1790; January 25, 1791), underscored the sacred duty of standing up to royal despotism (September 15, 1790), and pressed readers to organize vigilante groups (September 25, 1790). It is safe to assume that for these last two injunctions, the readers he had in mind were male, not female.
40. *Journal de la Mode et du Goût*, March 15, April 25, and May 15, 1790. On the pillorying of Marie-Antoinette, see, for example, Joan B. Landes, *Visualizing the Nation: Gender, Representation, and Revolution in Eighteenth-Century France* (Cornell University Press, 2001); Vivian Cameron, "Political Exposures: Sexuality and Caricature in the French Revolution," in *Eroticism and the Body Politic*, ed. Lynn Hunt (Johns Hopkins University Press, 1991), 90–107; Dena Goodman, ed. *Marie-Antoinette: Writings on the Body of a Queen* (Routledge, 2003); and John Hardman, *Marie Antoinette: The Making of a French Queen* (Yale University Press, 2019).
41. The new magazine's title masked this objective; so did much of its content. Along with light leisure reading, book reviews, and historical anecdotes, it offered only two hand-colored fashion plates, substituting for the third a black-and-white score sheet for a song, which was far less costly.
42. *Journal de la Mode et du Goût*, October 5, 1791, 1.
43. Richard Sennett, *The Fall of Public Man* (Knopf, 1977), 184.
44. *Journal de la Mode et du Goût*, September 25, 1791, 5. This quote may have been first published in the English press. In any case, in *Journal de la Mode et du Goût*, gender boundaries for the second sex were far less

restrictive than in other revolutionary writings. Le Brun appears to encourage women moving in on men's sartorial privileges. See, for example, *Journal de la Mode et du Goût*, March 5, 1790, 18. Yet the idea that this might be a sign that women could in fact become more like men in *other* ways appears unimaginable to him. Nevertheless, women did take action to claim their own freedom. See "Chaumette, Speech at City Hall Denouncing Women's Political Activism (November 17, 1793)," in *LIBERTY, EQUALITY, FRATERNITY: EXPLORING THE FRENCH REVOLUTION*, accessed August 23, 2021, https://revolution.chnm.org/d/489.

45. *Journal de la Mode et du Goût*, July 15, 1790, 4–5.
46. *Journal de la Mode et du Goût*, July 15, 1790, 4–5.
47. For other examples, see *Journal de la Mode et du Goût*, March 15, April 25, and May 15, 1790.
48. *Journal de la Mode et du Goût*, September 15, 1791, 4.
49. *Journal de la Mode et du Goût*, September 15, 1791, 4.
50. *Journal de la Mode et du Goût*, June 15, 1790, 1–2. See also February 5, 1792, 1–2.
51. Anonymous, *Instruction chrétienne sur les dangers du luxe* (Paris, 1725), 17. The catalogue of the Bibliothèque Nationale de France identifies the author as Maugras, a Doctrinarian priest.
52. *Journal de la Mode et du Goût*, October 5, 1790, 1–2. On this point, Le Brun's views were out of line with most revolutionary writers and artists, who believed patriotic women should be covered up. The clear exception was when a female figure appeared as an allegory of the republic, in which case a half-naked female body was common. See the classic study by Maurice Agulhon, *Marianne au combat: L'imagerie et la symbolique républicaines de 1789 à 1880* (Flammarion, 1979).
53. On the meaning of this turn away from exhibitionism to "transparency" for French men during the Revolution, see Hunt, *Politics, Culture, and Class*, 52–86.
54. *Journal de la Mode et du Goût*, January 25, 1791, 1.
55. *Journal de la Mode et du Goût*, March 15, 1790, 1–2.
56. *Journal de la Mode et du Goût*, March 5, 1790, 23. This quote and others recall other times of fierce political backlash.
57. In 1791, revolutionary writer and journalist Louis-Marie Prudhomme spelled out the party line on gender: "the tumult of [military] camps, the storms of public places, the agitations of the tribunals are not at all

suitable for the second sex. . . . A woman is only comfortable, is only in her place, in her family or in her household." "On the Influence of the Revolution on Women," in *The French Revolution and Human Rights: A Brief Documentary History*, trans. and ed. Lynn Hunt (Bedford/St. Martin's, 1996), 129–31.

58. *Journal de la Mode et du Goût*, December 5, 1790, 3–4. On men's hairstyles, see October 5, 1790, 2–3.
59. *Journal de la mode et du Goût*, November 15, 1790, 1. For all *Journal's* praise of patriotic simplicity, when the exceptions are indexed to powerful and "manly" institutions such as the army or National Guard, ornamentation of the most expensive and elaborate kind not only gets a pass, it gets praise, just as it had in *Magasin des Modes Nouvelles*. See, for example, the description of the engraving of a National Guard *chasseur* in *Journal's* April 25, 1790 issue, 1–2.
60. *Journal de la Mode et du Goût*, May 5, 1790, 4.
61. Black was also fashionable for "entrenched" aristocrats, male and female both, who wore it to show that far from celebrating the Revolution, they were mourning the fall of the monarchy. *Journal de la Mode et du Goût*, April 15, 1790, 1. On the history of black attire and masculinity, see John Harvey, *Men in Black* (Reaktion Books, 1995).
62. John Moore, *A View of the Causes and Progress of the French Revolution* (London, 1795), 1:150. Quoted in Maxwell, *Patriots Against Fashion*, 101.
63. *Journal de la Mode et du Goût*, March 5, 1790, 9 (article), 3 (description). This was presumably a paid advertisement. The fourth page of the June 5, 1790 issue identifies Sieur de Baran-Jubin, 27–28, arcades du Palais-Royal as the source of these municipal sashes, along with other plain and patterned fabrics and a variety of "high-quality" accessories (vests, shawls, belts, etc.).
64. La Mésangère's signature does not appear along with those of others from the school at La Flèche. See Annemarie Kleinert, *Le "Journal des dames et des modes" ou La Conquête de l'Europe féminine (1797–1839)* (Jan Thorbecke, 2001), 60–61. Yet La Mésangère was later made director of the boarding school, which could only have occurred if he had signed the oath of loyalty to the state. For more on the oath, see Jack Censer and Lynn Hunt, *Liberty, Equality, Fraternity: Exploring the French Revolution* (Penn State University Press, 2002), 61; Jean de Viguerie, *Une œuvre d'éducation sous l'Ancien Régime: Les Pères de la doctrine chrétienne en France et en Italie, 1592–1792 (Éditions de la nouvelle aurore, 1976),* 630;

and Timothy Tackett, *Religion, Revolution, and Regional Culture: The Ecclesiastical Oath of 1791* (Princeton University Press, 1986), 11–12, 47–48.

65. On the question of celibacy and citizenship from 1720 through the Napoleonic Era, see E. Claire Cage, *Unnatural Frenchmen: The Politics of Priestly Celibacy and Marriage, 1720–1815* (University of Virginia Press, 2015), 29–60.
66. *Journal de la Mode et du Goût*, June 5, 1790, 6. On the author, see J. Fleury, "Charles-Albert Demoustier," in *Encyclopédie du XIXe siècle: Répertoire universel des sciences des lettres et des arts*, 3rd ed., 25 vols. (Paris, 1872), 7:775. On these and other rumors versus the facts, see Cage, *Unnatural Frenchmen*, 29–60.
67. *Journal de la Mode et du Goût*, June 5, 1790, 6.
68. *Journal de la Mode et du Goût*, June 5, 1790, 6.
69. Annemarie Kleinert, "La Révolution et le premier journal illustré en France (1785–1793), *Dix-Huitième siècle*" 21, 304. For the details on these political reversals, see Kleinert's close reading of the periodical in "La Révolution" and "La Naissance d'une presse de mode à la veille de la Révolution et l'essor du genre au XIXème siècle," in *Le Journalisme d'Ancien Régime*, ed. Pierre Rétat (Presses Universitaires de Lyon, 1982), 189–97. Suellen Diaconoff calls the magazine a "political chameleon." "Gender Ideology and Politics in *Le Cabinet des Modes*," in *Les Femmes et la Révolution française* (Presses Universitaires du Mirail, 1990), 2:357.
70. See *Dictionnaire des Journalistes*.
71. *Journal de la Mode et du Goût*, October 25, 1790, 4.
72. *The Cambridge History of Christianity, Vol. 7: Enlightenment, Reawakening and Revolution 1660–1815*, ed. Stewart J. Brown and Timothy Tackett (Cambridge University Press, 2006), 539–41.
73. Cage, *Unnatural Frenchmen*, 84.
74. For statistics about compliance, see Cage, *Unnatural Frenchmen*, 82. For a breakdown of clerical marriages by percentage by period, see "Married Priests in France, 1789–1815," https://ageofrevolutions.com/2017/07/31/married-priests-in-france-1789-1815/. In brief, there were three "waves" of marriages: Between 1791 and 1793, priests had the option to marry and 8 percent did; between 1793 and 1794, priests were forced to marry and almost 70 percent did; from 1795 to 1815, priests had the option to marry and 22 percent did. On their motivations, see John McManners, *The French Revolution and the Church* (Harper & Row, 1969): 111–17 and Cage, *Unnatural Frenchmen*, 92–129. While the anticlerical laws passed

by the Constituent Assembly in 1791 insisted on heterosexuality to such an extent that they disallowed religious chastity, other parts of the 1791 Penal Code were surprising liberal: France became the first country to decriminalize sodomy, which had been a capital crime. To understand the history, mystery, and significance of this milestone ruling, see Bryant T. Ragan, "Same Sex Sexual Relations and the French Revolution: The Decriminalization of Sodomy in 1791," in *Everyday Politics and Culture in Revolutionary France: Essays in Honor of Lynn Hunt*, ed. Suzanne Desan, Bryant T. Ragan, and Victoria Thompson (Liverpool University Press, 2024), 123–44.

75. Gueniffey, *Bonaparte*, 103.
76. See Gueniffey, *Bonaparte*, 105.
77. Gueniffey, *Bonaparte*, 106.
78. A year later, menacing crowds pillaged and sacked the Bonapartes' home, and his family was banished. They fled to Toulon on the southern coast of France in June 1793.
79. Gueniffey, *Bonaparte*, 105. The war against foreign powers ready to invade France to teach the revolutionaries a lesson and bring the king back to power began two months later in late April.
80. Trichet, *Le Costume du clergé*, 167.
81. Besnard, *Un Prêtre en révolution: Souvenirs d'un nonagénaire*, ed. Martine Taroni (Presses Universitaires de Rennes, 2011), 328. By contrast, nuns faced a somewhat different dilemma. Le Brun approved the fact that they were now forced to wear attire that *revealed* rather than hid the shape of their female body. The dress, unlike a religious habit, also announced their social class and wealth. See the March 25, 1790 issue of *Journal*, which features a fashion engraving of one such scantily clad former nun, liberated from the convent and "newly returned to society."
82. The National Convention repeated this edict on April 3, 1793. Lynn Hunt, "Freedom of Dress in Revolutionary France," in *From the Royal to the Republican Body: Incorporating the Political in Seventeenth- and Eighteenth-Century France*, ed. Sara E. Melzer and Kathryn Norberg (University of California Press, 1998), 225.
83. Emmanuel de Las Casas, *Mémorial de Saint-Hélène,* 4 vols, ed. A. Fugier (Garnier, 1961), 1:101. Quoted in Gueniffey, *Bonaparte*, 108.
84. In November 1791, the Legislative Assembly had declared refractory priests—those who had not taken the oath—suspect.

85. Hunt, "Freedom of Dress," 241. See also Peter McPhee, *Robespierre: A Revolutionary Life* (Yale University Press, 2012), 62, 160 and Aileen Ribeiro, *Fashion in the French Revolution* (Holmes & Meier, 1988), 70.
86. Hunt, "Freedom of Dress," 241.
87. Five months later, in September, deputies of the National Convention decreed that all presses would be requisitioned by the government. Carla Hesse, *Publishing and Cultural Politics in Revolutionary Paris, 1789–1810* (University of California Press, 1991). In 1794, Le Brun's magazine became the *Almanach des modes françaises et anglaises*. See Annemarie Kleinert, *Die frühen Modejournale in Frankreich: Studien zur Literatur der Mode von den Anfängen bis 1848* (E. Schmidt, 1980), 46–48. Le Brun later went on to become a librettist and dramatist and took up politics.
88. For the span of the first eight years across all three fashion periodicals, *Cabinet des Modes*, *Magasin des Modes Nouvelles*, and *Journal de la Mode et du Goût*, the total was 332 images of women to seventy-nine of men, a ratio of four to one. Kleinert, *Die frühen Modejournale*, 72. The lopsided increase was almost entirely due to the last years of the latter magazine.
89. For one example of a man from La Flèche with extreme anti-republican views, see Charles Boucher, *La Flèche sous la Révolution: 1789–1805: Mémoires inédits du chirurgien Charles Boucher, publication intégrale et critique par Alain de Dieuleveult* (A. de Dieleuveult, 1982).
90. Cage, *Unnatural Frenchmen*, 89.
91. Censer and Hunt, *Liberty, Equality, Fraternity*, 103.
92. Jules Clère, *Histoire de l'Ecole de la Flèche, depuis sa fondation par Henri IV jusqu'à sa réorganisation en Prytanée impérial militaire* (Eug. Jourdain, 1853), 235.
93. Clère, *Histoire de l'Ecole de la Flèche*, 235.
94. Quoted in Roland Houlier, "Pierre-Antoine Lebouc de La Mésangère, 1761–1831, prêtre, écrivain et . . . journaliste de mode," in *Académie des sciences, belles-lettres et arts d'Angers. Mémoires* X (1988), 307. No source is given.
95. In Clère's and Houlier's accounts, La Mésangère appears as a former clerical father forced to abandon his sons. In fact, abandonment went two ways. The man who had to close the school had long been a "son" of the Church, which had "abandoned" him insofar as it was no more. Houlier further sentimentalizes La Mésangère's paternal function and saintlike disposition, claiming without citing a source that, in April 1793, when the revolutionary government was unable to pay board for the

students and salaries for the teachers, La Mésangère came through "by dipping into his own money." No other biographer or historian makes this claim. However, after his death, a great many of his contemporaries spoke of their gratitude for his great generosity. See chapter 6.

96. Kleinert writes that La Mésangère's letters often noted, "I refuse to ask my father for anything." "On 25 October 1804, angered that his father continued to favor his sister, La Mésangère wrote to [a friend from Baugé], 'Circumstances have distanced me from my father to such an extent that nothing I do pleases him.' Even after his father's death, he cared little about his father's properties, often writing to his childhood friend, a lawyer who managed the estate, that he wanted to 'hear nothing more about these annoyances.'" Archives Municipales de Baugé. Cited in Kleinert, *La Conquête*, 63. La Mésangère's mother died in 1800.
97. In 1795 and 1796, guerilla warfare led by the Chouans would again put up especially fierce resistance to the republic. See Honoré de Balzac's 1829 novel, *Les Chouans* (1829).
98. Clère, *Histoire de l'Ecole de La Flèche*, 245.
99. Bernard Beaupère, *Histoire du Prytanée national militaire* (Charles-Lavauzelle, 1985), 18.
100. Beaupère, *Histoire du Prytanée national militaire*, 18.

4. MAKEOVERS: MEN, REGIMES, MAGAZINES

1. Pierre La Mésangère, "Paris. Séjour de," in *Le Voyageur à Paris: Tableau pittoresque et moral de cette capitale*, 3 vols. (Paris, 1797), 2:162.
2. One twentieth-century author imagines the moment as more dramatic: "soon after arriving" in Paris, La Mésangère "learned that he had just been denounced as an aristocrat. It was only by leading a very discreet life that he could escape being detected." The article cites no sources. Roland Houlier, "Pierre-Antoine Lebouc de La Mésangère, 1761–1831, prêtre, écrivain et journaliste de mode," *Académie des sciences, belles-lettres et arts d'Angers: Mémoires* (Académie d'Angers, 1989), 10:307.
3. *Gazette nationale ou le Moniteur universel*, no. 39 (9 Brumaire an ii/ October 30, 1793). The rationale for the latter provision was not explained. As for women who snuck into the army disguised as men, the punishment was already encoded in army regulations. See Gretchen van Slyke,

"Women at War: Skirting the Issue in the French Revolution," *L'Esprit Créateur* 37, no. 1 (1997): 33–43.

4. J. M. Roberts, *French Revolution Documents*, vol. 1 (Basil Blackwell, 1966), 489. English translation: https://revolution.chnm.org/items/show/426.
5. Yet before and after this legislation, many dictated the clothing of others: husbands had some control over what their wives wore, both parents would dictate what the children wore, and men set the terms of dress in the army, schools, guilds, etc. It was a predominantly male prerogative. See Lynn Hunt, "Freedom of Dress in Revolutionary France," in *From the Royal to the Republican Body: Incorporating the Political in Seventeenth- and Eighteenth-Century France*, ed. Sara E. Melzer and Kathryn Norberg (University of California Press, 1998), 227; and Jennifer Heuer, "Hats on for the Nation! Women, Citizens, Soldiers, and the 'Sign of the French,'" *French History* 16, no. 1 (2002): 28–52.
6. Houlier, "La Mésangère," 307.
7. Later, La Mésangère "started to offer some Latin lessons," although it "gave him only enough to support a very modest lifestyle." Houlier, "La Mésangère," 307. If this was so, those same indicators would have been assets for parents who hired him in this role, and he would have had to dress up to look the part.
8. Patrice Gueniffey, *Bonaparte: 1769–1802* (Harvard University Press, 2015), 145.
9. Gueniffey, *Bonaparte*, 147.
10. Gueniffey, *Bonaparte*, 147.
11. He was about 5'6", average for this period. See Gueniffey, *Bonaparte*, 823n52.
12. Laure Junot, Duchesse d'Abrantès, *Mémoires de Madame la duchesse d'Abrantès, ou Souvenirs historiques sur Napoléon: la Révolution, le Directoire, le Consulat, l'Empire et la Restauration*, 10 vols. (Ladvocat, 1831–1835), 1:254.
13. Gueniffey, *Bonaparte*, 150.
14. Gueniffey, *Bonaparte*, 162–77.
15. See Gueniffey, *Bonaparte*, 153–59.
16. See Gueniffey, *Bonaparte*, 181.
17. For a superb account and analysis of this female revolution, see Anne Higonnet, *Liberty Equality Fashion: The Women Who Styled the French Revolution* (W. W. Norton, 2024). For insights into the sumptuary laws meant to keep the races apart in Martinique where Josephine grew up, see 3–11.

18. Gueniffey, *Bonaparte*, 178.
19. D. M. G. Sutherland, *The French Revolution and Empire: The Quest for a Civic Order* (Blackwell, 2003): 258.
20. Lynn Hunt and Jack Censer, *The French Revolution and Napoleon: Crucible of the Modern World*, 2nd ed. (Bloomsbury, 2017), 145; and Gueniffey, *Bonaparte*, 178.
21. Gueniffey, *Bonaparte*, 182.
22. Aileen Ribeiro, *Fashion in the French Revolution* (Homes & Meier, 1988), 133.
23. *Voyageur à Paris* was an exception. The augmented edition, published in 1797, remained anonymous.
24. Annemarie Kleinert, *Le "Journal des dames et des modes" ou La Conquête de l'Europe féminine (1797–1839)* (Jan Thorbecke, 2001), 62. See also Claude Viel, "Fourcroy et les lycées," *Revue d'Histoire de la Pharmacie* 10, no. 369 (2011): 13–30.
25. Lynn Hunt, *Politics, Culture and Class in the French Revolution* (University of California Press, 1984), 84. How much money would it have taken for La Mésangère to look once again like an educated man from the lower nobility? Writing in the political newspaper *Correspondance politique des départements et de Paris* on April 29, 1794 (10 floréal, an II), a journalist claimed that one could be republican and dapper without spending a fortune. Quoted in Ribeiro, *Fashion in the French Revolution*, 70.
26. *Correspondance politique*, April 29, 1794.
27. Ewa Lajer-Burcharth, *Necklines: The Art of Jacques-Louis David after the Terror* (Yale University Press, 1999), 2.
28. See Lajer-Burcharth, *Necklines*; and Higonnet, *Liberty Equality Fashion.*
29. Lajer-Burcharth, *Necklines*, 188.
30. There is some ambiguity in the caption as well. It is not clear who says "Ils le plaisantent," ["they joke around with him" or "they mock him"]. Is it presumed to be an outsider, the artist perhaps, looking at the scene? Perhaps the joke is on the men in the café who have eyes only for others who look just like themselves. If so, we the viewers are outsiders and voyeurs.
31. E. Claire Cage, "The Sartorial Self: Neoclassical Fashion and Gender Identity in France, 1797–1804," *Eighteenth-Century Studies* 42, no. 2 (Winter 2009): 193–215.
32. During this four-year period, news about the latest fashions occasionally appeared in the daily papers in France, but no engravings did. To see

illustrations and get the details about the latest styles, French readers would have had to subscribe to English or German magazines. Kleinert, *Le "Journal des Dames et des Modes,"* 14.

33. Unlike his business associate, La Mésangère, Sellèque appears to have been inclined toward radical Jacobinism. For a short time, in Chartres, before the National Convention decree of 1793 prohibited Jacobins from meeting, Sellèque was the secretary of one such club. For more on Sellèque's biography, see Kleinert, *Le "Journal des Dames et des Modes,"* 329, and passim.
34. See Kleinert, *Le "Journal des Dames et des Modes,"* 17, 329.
35. See Nina Rattner Gelbart, *Feminine and Opposition Journalism in Old Regime France: Le Journal des Dames* (University of California Press, 1987). See also Kleinert, *Le "Journal des Dames et des Modes,"* 12. While the original *Journal des Dames* had between three hundred and one thousand subscribers, Sellèque and La Mésangère considered one thousand their minimum target. Kleinert, *La Conquête*, 13.
36. In 1786, Italy started publishing *Giornale delle dame e delle mode di Francia* [Ladies' French Fashion Journal], but it was a clear imitation of *Cabinet des Modes*, and, five months later in 1787, it chose a more gender-neutral title. See Kleinert, *Le "Journal des Dames et des Modes,"* 32.
37. For a fuller list, see Kleinert, *Le "Journal des Dames et des Modes,"* 21, 34.
38. Leora Auslander, "The Gendering of Consumer Practices in Nineteenth-Century France," in *The Sex of Things: Essays on Gender and Consumption*, ed. Victoria de Grazia and Ellen Furlough (University of California Press, 1996), 80–81.
39. Kleinert, *Le "Journal des Dames et des Modes,"* 34–35. In the fourth issue, a brief, unattributed plug for La Mésangère's still anonymous *Voyageur à Paris* appeared. Some miscellaneous articles in the early years were signed "La M.," but this combination was fairly common, so it was not necessarily referring to La Mésangère who, in any case, would not be listed as a member of the magazine staff for twenty-one months. Nor did the feminine "La" in "La M." signal either a female writer or impersonation: Preceded neither by a "Mme" [Madame] or "Mlle [Mademoiselle]," readers would assume the author was male. I refer to the editorial voice during this period as Sellèque's because when La Mésangère took over in mid-July 1799 and after Sellèque's death on the first day of 1800, the magazine editor's tone, style, affect, attitude, and content were markedly different from his predecessor's.

40. *Journal des Dames et des Modes*, March 20, 1797, 4. The entire first issue is reproduced in Kleinert, *Le "Journal des Dames et des Modes,"* 373–80.
41. *Journal des Dames et des Modes*, March 20, 1797, 5. For an excellent compendium of information on the magazine, see Siobhán McIlvanney, "*Le Journal des Dames et des Modes* (1797–1839): A Pioneering Presence in the Early French Women's Press," in *The Francophone Women's Magazine: Inside and Outside of France* (University Press of the South, 2010), 3–21. See also Siobhán McIlvanney, *Figurations of the Feminine in the Early French Women's Press, 1758–1848* (Liverpool University Press, 2019).
42. Kleinert, *Le "Journal des Dames et des Modes,"* 20.
43. Women who made a significant number of literary contributions to the magazine in the early years include Caroline Wuiet (1766–1834) and Constance de Salm-Dyck née Pipelet, but the majority were male. Kleinert, *Le "Journal des Dames et des Modes,"* 51. On Salm-Dyck, see Elizabeth Colwill, "Epistolary Passions: Friendship and the Literary Public of Constance de Salm, 1767–1845)," *Journal of Women's History* 12, no. 3 (2000): 39–68.
44. Between 1799 and 1802, Albertine Clément, also known by her married name Clément-Hémery (1778–1855), who had edited several small political journals and was a frequent contributor of miscellaneous prose and poetry to the magazine, became part owner. On August 17, 1799, she took over La Mésangère's previous responsibilities: running the periodical's operation, managing mailings, subscriptions, and complaints. However, her gender did not land her the "feminine" part of the job. Fashion and the fashion engravings remained La Mésangère's domain. See Kleinert, *Le "Journal des Dames et des Modes,"* 336–37, and passim.
45. *Journal des Dames et des Modes*, October 27, 1797. Quoted in Kleinert, *Le "Journal des Dames et des Modes,"* 21.
46. Kleinert, *Le "Journal des Dames et des Modes,"* 20–21.
47. Kleinert, *Le "Journal des Dames et des Modes,"* 13, 21, 29.
48. Kleinert, *Le "Journal des Dames et des Modes,"* 19, 32.
49. Throughout this period, fashion editors in England and Germany counterfeited entire issues and lifted passages and engravings from French fashion magazines. The success of *Journal des Dames* made it a favorite target. Kleinert, *Le "Journal des Dames et des Modes,"* 35–49.
50. See Kleinert, *Le "Journal des Dames et des Modes,"* 31–32. Technically, the addition of the words "et des modes" [and fashion] was supposed to be an indication that *Journal des Dames* had taken over *Journal des Modes et Nouveautés.*

51. Madeline Spieler, *Empire and Underworld: Captivity in French Guiana* (Harvard University Press, 2012), 18. Deportation was the newly favored "humane" way of ridding the nation of its enemies without spilling blood on French streets.
52. Jeremy Popkin, *Revolutionary News: The Press in France, 1789–1799* (Duke University Press, 1990), 173–74. See also Hugh Gough, *The Newspaper Press in the French Revolution* (Dorsey Press, 1988).
53. Kleinert, *Le "Journal des Dames et des Modes,"* 49–50.
54. Kleinert, *Le "Journal des Dames et des Modes,"* 33.
55. Kleinert, *La Conquête*, 35, 316.
56. See Kleinert, *Le "Journal des Dames et des Modes,"* 17n12.
57. *Le Mois*, an vii, no. 7 (October 2, 1799), 3.
58. *Le Mois*, an vii, no. 7 (October 2, 1799), 1–2.
59. Some twentieth-century scholars claim that Caroline Wuïet was a coeditor, but Kleinert disputes the attribution. *Le "Journal des Dames et des Modes,"* 300, 322.
60. On *La Correspondance des Dames*, *L'Arlequin*, *Le Mois*, and *La Mouche*, see Kleinert, *Le "Journal des Dames et des Modes,"* passim. See also Annemarie Kleinert, "La Naissance d'une presse de mode à la veille de la révolution et l'essor du genre au XIXe siècle," in *Le Journalisme d'ancien régime: Questions et propositions, Table Ronde CNRS*, June 12–13, 1981 (Presses Universitaires de Lyon, 1982), 189–97.
61. *Journal des Dames et des Modes*, May 19, 1797.
62. The Egyptian expedition was distinctive for its ambitious scope and "the project's twofold pretention of making science operate under the aegis of war and of associating the growth of knowledge with territorial conquest." Marie-Noëlle Bourguet, "Science and Memory: The Stakes of the Expedition to Egypt (1798–1801)," in *Taking Liberties: Problems of a New Order from the French Revolution to Napoleon*, ed. Howard G. Brown and Judith A. Miller (Manchester University Press, 2002), 93. See also Darcy Grimaldo Grigsby, *Colossal: Engineering the Suez Canal, Statue of Liberty, Eiffel Tower, and Panama Canal* (Periscope, 2012), Chapter One.
63. *Journal des Dames et des Modes*, May 3, 1798, 2.
64. *Journal des Dames et des Modes*, May 3, 1798, 2.
65. Kleinert *La Conquête*, 50–51.
66. *Journal des Dames et des Modes*, July 8, 1799. Quoted in Kleinert, *Le "Journal des Dames et des Modes,"* 51.
67. Kleinert, *Le "Journal des Dames et des Modes,"* 52.

68. Gueniffey, *Bonaparte*, 600. They represented two contradictory ends of a broad political spectrum that was typical of this period. One of the men, who served as Bonaparte's second-in-command in the Consulate, was Jean-Jacques-Régis de Cambacérès, a government official who was also a jurist and businessman. Considered by many a man of the Revolution, he always regretted having voted for the king's death. He dressed, writes the historian Gueniffey, "as people dressed around 1775," when Louis XVI reigned, "covered with lace and baubles of all kinds." He was also known to have intimate relations and sexual liaisons with men, a point that Bonaparte took in stride. Gueniffey asserts that Bonaparte had no moral scruples on this count, "provided that no scandal erupted." *Bonaparte*, 601–3. The other was Charles-François Lebrun (no relationship to the revolutionary fashion editor Le Brun), a monarchist who believed that parliamentary interference prevented the monarchy from carrying out "indispensable reforms" yet defended the Third Estate and could not stand his fellow noblemen. Gueniffey, *Bonaparte*, 601.
69. *Correspondance de Napoléon 1er*, no. 4422 (to the French, December 15, 1799), 6:25. Cited in Gueniffey, *Bonaparte*, 617, 907n1.
70. Gueniffey, *Bonaparte*, 617, 904n14.
71. Gueniffey, *Bonaparte*, 582.
72. Albert Vandal, *L'Avénèment de Bonaparte* (Plon-Nourrit, 1912), 2:150–51. Quoted in Gueniffey, *Bonaparte*, 616, 907n74.
73. From the memoirs of Josephine's page, Marco de Saint-Hilaire, *Les Petits appartements des Tuileries, mémoires du page Victor Joseph de . . .*, which was reviewed in *Journal des Dames et des Modes* (April 20, 1831). Quoted in Kleinert, *La Conquête*, 87–88.
74. See Gueniffey, *Bonaparte*, 589.
75. The December 21, 1799 issue of *Journal des Dames et des Modes* noted that Hayden's "The Creation of the World," which was playing that night, was *le must* of the season and ticket prices were sky high. In the following issue, someone from the magazine who claims to have been there reports that three of the magazine's engravings were inspired by costumes from "this brilliant gala." *Journal des Dames et des Modes*, December 31, 1800. No mention is made of the assassination attempt. Kleinert, *Le "Journal des Dames et des Modes,"* 53.
76. Kleinert, *Le "Journal des Dames et des Modes,"* 53–57.
77. On these peacock stances in contrast with La Mésangère's Invisible Man, see Margaret Waller, "Trouble in Argus City: Peacocking,

Invisibility, and Masculinity," *Romanic Review* 107, no. 1–4 (2017), 28–29. Neither of these Argus stances—a presumably disembodied, objective voice nor outsized self-aggrandizement and display—were viable options for women. See Waller, "Disembodiment as a Masquerade: Fashion Journalists and Other 'Realist' Observers in Directory Paris," *Esprit Créateur* 37, no. 1 (Spring 1997): 44–54, and Waller, "Realism and Its Others: Reading Bodies in Balzac's *Le Père Goriot* and Girardin's *La Canne de M. de Balzac*," in *Approaches to Teaching Balzac's* Old Goriot, ed. Michal Ginsburg (MLA, 2001), 98–108.

78. Yet he expanded the range of subjects on which he might comment well beyond fashion.
79. These detached observers resembled not only previous Invisible Men in the fashion press but also the *flâneur* whom La Mésangère had described in his *Voyageur à Paris*. One exception to the disembodied male persona in *Journal des Dames et des Modes* was the theater and art critic, "Le Voltigeur" [the Acrobat], who occasionally mentions having to do his toilette and remarks on what paintings moved him, but these do not go far toward embodying him or making him visible to the reader.
80. Nonetheless, beginning in the 1810s, righteous moral lessons and policing increasingly took up more space. See Siobhán McIlvanney, "*Le Journal des Dames et des Modes* (1797–1839)," 3, 7.
81. La Mésangère had a close friendship with the widowed female concierge of his apartment building. Whether theirs was an amorous relation, no evidence survives. In any case, they never married. See Kleinert, *Le "Journal des Dames et des Modes,"* 181.
82. *Journal des Dames et des Modes*, June 29, 1804, 447.
83. See "Compère," in *Dictionnaire de l'Académie Française*, Huitième Édition (The ARTFL Project, 1932–), https://artflsrv04.uchicago.edu/philologic4.7/publicdicos/navigate/18/6474.
84. *Journal des Dames et des Modes*, December 31, 1814, 573.
85. *Journal des Dames et des Modes*, December 31, 1814, 573.
86. Quoted in Kleinert, *Le "Journal des Dames et des Modes,"* 49.
87. Quoted in Kleinert, *Le "Journal des Dames et des Modes,"* 57.
88. See Kleinert, *Le "Journal des Dames et des Modes,"* 90.
89. For specific examples, see Kleinert, *Le "Journal des Dames et des Modes,"* 89–91.
90. Raymond Gaudriault, *La gravure de mode féminine en France* (Éditions de l'Amateur, 1983), 147. According to Kleinert, *Journal des Dames et des*

Modes's success and survival was due in part to the "quasi-official protection" Napoleon gave the magazine. Kleinert, *Le "Journal des Dames et des Modes,"* 85.

91. Kleinert, *Le "Journal des Dames et des Modes,"* 66. Some earlier historians claim that his periodical was not that popular. See Paul Cornu, "Essai bibliographique sur les recueils de mode au XVIIIe siècle et au début du XIXe siècle," in *Documents pour l'histoire de costume de Louis XV à Louis XVIII*, 3 volumes, ed. G. Schefer (Goupil, 1911), 1:26; and Evelyne Sullerot, *Histoire de la presse féminine en France des origines à 1848* (A. Colin, 1966), 87–114. Kleinert's more recent and thorough research proves the contrary. See *Le "Journal des Dames et des Modes,"* 57.

5. THE EMPERORS' TRIUMPH AND DISGRACE

1. For the classic history of the Haitian revolution, see C. L. R. James, *The Black Jacobins: Toussaint Louverture and the San Domingo Revolution* (Vintage, 1989).
2. Even when the Bourbon monarchy restored its throne after Napoleon's final defeat at Waterloo in 1815, the question of political legitimacy, which had been raised by the Revolution, lasted long after. See Sheryl Kroen, *Politics and Theater: The Crisis of Legitimacy in Restoration France, 1815–1830* (University of California Press, 2000).
3. Louis Vivien de Saint-Martin, *Histoire Générale de la Révolution Française, de l'Empire, de la Restauration, de la Monarchie de 1830, jusqu'à 1841*, 4 vols. (1842), 4:270. Porterfield quotes Damas Honard, *Napoléon: Ses opinions et jugements* (1838) in Todd Porterfield and Susan Siegfried, *Staging Empire: Napoleon, Ingres, and David* (Pennsylvania State University Press, 2006), 124. This is Porterfield's translation.
4. Quoted in Henri Gaubert, *Le Sacre de Napoléon Ier* (Flammarion, 1964), 1:46.
5. Gaubert, *Le Sacre*, 1:46. Gaubert claims that Napoleon made this remark to the Senate, but that does not appear to be true, and he cites no source.
6. On the traditional ceremony, see Richard A. Jackson, *Vive le roi! A History of the French Coronation from Charles V to Charles X* (University of North Carolina Press, 1984), esp. 19–20.
7. On privacy as a right the French royalty never had, see Jean-Claude Bologne, *Histoire de la pudeur* (Olivier Orban, 1986).

8. Susan Siegfried, "Ingres' *Napoleon I on his Imperial Throne*," in Porterfield and Siegfried, *Staging Empire*, 50.
9. On the coronation of the previous monarch, Louis XVI, see John McManners, *Church and Society in Eighteenth-Century France*, 2 vols. (Clarendon, 1998), 7–28. See also Siegfried, "Ingres' *Napoleon I*," 50.
10. During the crackdown on priests' attire in the seventeenth century, bishops too had felt it necessary to regulate clerical undergarments.
11. *Livre du sacre*, quoted in Madeleine Delpierre, "Une révolution en trois temps," in *Modes & révolutions, 1780–1804* (Paris-Musées, 1989), 36. The *Livre du sacre*, begun in 1804 and revised in 1805, was not published until 1815. In this official, laudatory volume complete with fine engravings, each detail might be said to reinforce the gravitas of the occasion. Although readers did not find the description of the coronation attire in La Mésangère's magazine, the two texts' plodding, connect-the-dots breakdown of a particular style bear a striking resemblance: nothing but the facts was presumably the best evidence of accuracy.
12. About this relationship and the ways the painting naturalizes Napoleon's power and obscures his illegitimacy, see Todd Porterfield, "David's *Sacre*" in Porterfield and Siegfried, *Staging Empire*, 122–35.
13. Louis Constant Wairy, *Recollections of the Private Life of Napoleon*, 3 vols., trans. Walter Clark (1895), 1:299. This was also his choice of attire on Sundays, and for ceremonies when he did not put on formal state dress.
14. Raoul Brunon, "Uniforms of the Napoleonic Era," in *The Age of Napoleon: Costume from Revolution to Empire, 1789–1815*, ed. Katell le Bourhis (The Metropolitan Museum of Art, 1989), 180.
15. Although David enjoyed Napoleon's favor, the emperor railed against the artist's 1806 portrait of him in full regalia as a swaggering new conqueror rather than a sovereign who had always worn this mantle of authority. For a comparison of the portraits, see Philippe Bordes and Alain Pougetoux, "Les Portraits de Napoléon en habits impériaux par Jacques-Louis David," *Gazette des Beaux-Arts* 125 (July–August 1983): 21–34.
16. Michel Foucault, *Discipline and Punish: The Birth of the Prison*, trans. Alan Sheridan (Vintage, 1995), 217.
17. Norman Bryson, "Géricault and Masculinity," in *Visual Culture: Images and Interpretation*, ed. Norman Bryson, Michael Ann Holly, and Keith Moxey (Wesleyan University Press, 1994), 242.

18. On the painting's totalizing ambitions, see Norman Bryson, *Tradition and Desire: From David to Delacroix* (Cambridge University Press, 1984), 110–13. On the role of whiteness, the detail, and display in Ingres's work in general, see Adrian Rifkin, *Ingres, Then and Now* (Routledge, 2000). On the subtle *un*doing of gender and its associated binaries in Ingres, which both complements and complicates my reading of the painting, see Carol Ockman, *Ingres's Eroticized Bodies: Retracing the Serpentine Line* (Yale University Press, 1995). Ingres's highly captivating portrait of a handsome young friend from 1805 and its subtle psychic alignment and distance from homoeroticism is, we might say, this painting's obverse. See Andrew Shelton, "Ingres, Painter of Men," *Art History* 44, no. 1 (2021): 16–51.
19. Siegfried, "Ingres' *Napoleon I*," 92. For a magisterial analysis of the painting and reactions to it, see 3–114; Susan Siegfried, "Reinventing Relics and Napoleon's Regal Body," in *The Eighteenth-Century Body: Art, History, Literature, Medicine*, ed. Angelica Goodden (Peter Lang, 2002), 157–80 and "The Politics of Criticism at the Salon of 1806: Ingres' *Napoleon Enthroned*," in *Proceedings of the Consortium on Revolutionary Europe*, vol. 2 (University of Georgia Press, 1980), 69–81. See also Delpierre, "Une révolution en trois temps," 11–40.
20. See Ockman, *Ingres's Eroticized Bodies*, 102–9.
21. See Siegfried, "Ingres' *Napoleon I*," 100–101. Emphasis added; As Siegfried notes, Ingres's excessive and intense investment in "the surface of Napoleon (face, costume, regalia, furniture, whatever showed) . . . reveals an anxiety over the possibility of making them signify as sacred" after the desacralization that had taken place during the Revolution. Siegfried, "Reinventing Relics," 177.
22. On the complex question of male and female nudity during and immediately after the French Revolution, see, for example, Vivian Cameron, "Political Exposures: Sexuality and Caricature in the French Revolution," in *Eroticism and the Body Politic*, ed. Lynn Hunt (Johns Hopkins University Press, 1991), 90–107; Elizabeth Colwill, "Pass As a Woman, Act Like a Man: Marie-Antoinette as Tribade in the Pornography of the French Revolution," in *Homosexuality in Modern France*, ed. Jeffrey Merrick and Bryant T. Ragan Jr. (Oxford University Press, 1996), 80–101; Thomas Crow, *Emulation: Making Artists for Revolutionary France* (Yale University Press, 1995); Darcy Grimaldo Grigsby, *Extremities: Painting Empire in Post-Revolutionary France* (Yale University Press, 2002) and

"Nudity *à la grecque* in 1799," *Art Bulletin* 80, no. 2 (June 1998): 311–35; Lynn Hunt, "Pornography and the French Revolution," in *The Invention of Pornography: Obscenity and the Origins of Modernity, 1500–1800*, ed. Lynn Hunt (Zone Books, 1993), 301–39; Ewa Lajer-Burcharth, *Necklines: The Art of Jacques-Louis David After the Terror* (Yale University Press, 1999); Joan B. Landes, "Representing the Body Politic: The Paradox of Gender in the Graphic Politics of the French Revolution," in *Rebel Daughters: Women and the French Revolution*, ed. Sara E. Melzer and Leslie W. Rabine (Oxford University Press, 1992), 15–37; and Abigail Solomon-Godeau, *Male Trouble: A Crisis in Representation* (Thames and Hudson, 1997), 177–225.

23. See John Ashton, *English Caricature and Satire of Napoleon I*, 2 vols. (1884).
24. See also the 1805 English caricature by James Gillray in which a diminutive Napoleon, carrying a wildly oversized hat, is reduced to a sideline voyeur position, watching through a gauze scrim as his wife Josephine and Madame Tallien dance in the nude for a leering Barrès. Reproduced in Jérémie Benoit, *L'anti-Napoléon: Caricatures et satires du Consulat à l'Empire* (Réunion des Musées Nationaux, 1996).
25. The dark-skinned, short man holding Josephine's train is presumably a reference to Raza Roustam (1781–1845), a Mameluke whom Napoleon chose as his personal bodyguard. Although Roustam did wear his "Oriental" costume to the coronation, he was very large and would have towered over Josephine. On the Mamelukes and their role in Napoleon's empire, see Darcy Grimaldo Grigsby, "Mamelukes in Paris: Fashionable Trophies of Failed Napoleonic Conquest," *UC Berkeley New Faculty Lecture Series* 5 (1996). On Cruikshank caricatures of Napoleon, see John Wardroper, *The Caricatures of George Cruikshank* (Godine, 1977).
26. Chandra Mukerji, *Territorial Ambitions and the Gardens of Versailles* (Cambridge University Press, 1997), 275.
27. The one notable exception to the revival of Old Regime dress was the wig, which some still wore, but now required of many of the higher-level court servants, it was associated with servitude.
28. Philippe Séguy, "Costume in the Age of Napoleon," in *The Age of Napoleon: Costume from Revolution to Empire, 1789–1815*, ed. Katell le Bourhis (The Metropolitan Museum of Art, 1989), 94–95.
29. Séguy, "Costume in the Age of Napoleon," 112. On the tension between the democratic and totalitarian potential of uniforms during this period,

see Lynn Hunt, *Politics, Culture and Class in the French Revolution* (University of California Press, 1984), 233.

30. During this period, especially for the less privileged, newly privileged (Napoleonic aristocrats), and newly disenfranchised (Bourbon nobility), the perceived distance between oneself and an ego ideal that cannot be attained played a key role in the formation of masculine subjectivity. On the crisis for men and their representation in art and literature in the aftermath of the French Revolution, see Norman Bryson, *Tradition and Desire: From David to Delacroix* (Cambridge University Press, 1987); Grigsby, *Extremities*; Solomon-Godeau, *Male Trouble*; and Margaret Waller, *The Male Malady: Fictions of Impotence in the French Romantic Novel* (Rutgers University Press, 1993).
31. Séguy, "Costume in the Age of Napoleon," 51.
32. *Mémoires de Mademoiselle Avrillion*, quoted in Séguy, *Histoire des modes sous l'Empire* (Tallandier, 1988), 141.
33. *Journal des Dames et des Modes* sometimes featured women's court costumes in its engravings. See, for example, Annemarie Kleinert, *Le "Journal des dames et des modes," ou La Conquête de l'Europe féminine (1797–1839)* (Jan Thorbecke, 2001), 94, figure 3.2.
34. See Naomi Schor, "The Scandal of Realism," in *A New History of French Literature*, ed. Denis Hollier (Harvard University Press, 1994), 656–60.
35. Claire Élisabeth Jeanne Gravier de Vergennes de Rémusat, *Mémoires de Madame de Rémusat, 1802–1808*, 3 vols. (C. Lévy, 1906), 1:112. She alleges that, in his opinion, "in a well-organized society, we [women], like certain insects, would be killed as soon as we had performed our duty by giving birth" (1:113).
36. Rémusat, *Mémoires*, 2:372. Other misogynist barbs attributed to Napoleon are cited in le Baron Marc de Villiers, *Histoire des Clubs de femmes et des légions d'amazones* (Plon, 1910), 280–81 and Laure Junot, duchesse d'Abrantès, *Mémoires de Madame la Duchesse d'Abrantès* (Garnier, 1893), 195–96.
37. In contrast to the anachronistic Napoleonic court styles for men, which made them look like apparitions from the Old Regime, the Napoleon-approved look for female courtiers during the Empire consisted of highly conservative versions of the revolution in dress that Mesdames Bonaparte, Tallien, and Récamier had instigated during Thermidor and the Directory, stripping away the intimations of sexual and personal freedom this look had represented and helped enact. See Anne

Higonnet, *Liberty Equality Fashion: The Women Who Styled the French Revolution* (W. W. Norton, 2024).

38. See Fiona Ffoulkes, "'Quality Always Distinguishes Itself': Louis Hippolyte LeRoy and the Luxury Clothing Industry in Early Nineteenth-Century Paris," in *Consumers and Luxury: Consumer Culture in Europe, 1650–1850*, ed. Maxine Berg and Helen Clifford (Manchester University Press, 1999), 183–205.
39. Séguy, "Costume in the Age of Napoleon," 97. Napoleon tolerated La Mésangère and his *Journal des Dames et des Modes*, but the man and his magazine did not have anything like the threateningly high profile and star power of Le Roy whose business made him the "ladies' man" of the female members of the French court. La Mésangère appears to have had no such personal appeal for his readers; nor was it one of his editorial personae.
40. Brunon, "Uniforms of the Napoleonic Era," 179, 184–85.
41. Brunon, "Uniforms of the Napoleonic Era," 181, 179.
42. Brunon, "Uniforms of the Napoleonic Era," 181.
43. Brunon, "Uniforms of the Napoleonic Era," 179.
44. Brunon, "Uniforms of the Napoleonic Era," 179.
45. Bryson, "Géricault," 339. See also Jean Pozzi, "Costumes historiques et pouvoir napoléonien," *Revue d'histoire diplomatique* 72, no. 2 (1959): 168.
46. Quoted in Frédéric Lacaille, "Carle Vernet et le règlement de 1812 sur l'uniforme de l'armée impériale," in *Uniformes napoléoniens* (Musée de l'Armée, Bibliothèque de l'Image, 2001), 5. By this logic, women who dressed up would always be frivolous and ornamental whereas military men, even in the most eye-popping uniforms—military, or, presumably, courtly—were, by definition, the embodiment of superior manliness.
47. Bardin, 1812, quoted in "French Infantry of the Napoleonic Wars," http://napoleonistyka.atspace.com/French_infantry.html.
48. Lacaille, "Carle Vernet et le règlement de 1812," 5 . See also Rafe Blaufarb, "The Social Contours of Meritocracy in the Napoleonic Officer Corps," in *Taking Liberties: Problems of a New Order from the French Revolution to Napoleon*, ed. Howard G. Brown and Judith A. Miller (Manchester University Press, 2002), 126–46.
49. Brunon, "Uniforms of the Napoleonic Era," 184.
50. Quoted in Brunon, "Uniforms of the Napoleonic Era," 183.
51. Philip Mansel, "Monarchy, Uniform and the Rise of the Frac 1760–1830," *Past & Present* 96 (1982): 103–32, https://www-jstor-org.ccl.idm.oclc.org/stable/650512.

52. See Siegfried, "Reinventing Relics," 157, 176.
53. Brunon, "Uniforms of the Napoleonic Era," 181.
54. Delpierre, "Une révolution," 38.
55. Kleinert, *Le "Journal des Dames et des Modes,"* 483. For a complete bibliography of La Mésangère's publications and information about them, see Kleinert, *La Conquête*, 330–32.
56. Annemarie Kleinert, "Un Prêtre fléchois devenu auteur, éditeur et journaliste: Pierre La Mésangère (1761–1831)," *Cahier Fléchois* 19 (1998): 40–41.
57. Kleinert, *Le "Journal des Dames et des Modes,"* 110.
58. Raymond Gaudriault, *La Gravure de mode féminine en France* (Editions de l'Amateur, 1983), 147; and Kleinert, *La Conquête*, 152, 167.
59. See Annemarie Kleinert, "Les Débuts de Gavarni, Peintre des mœurs et des modes parisiennes," *Gazette des Beaux-Arts* (November 1999), 215 and *Le "Journal des Dames et des Modes,"* 177–80.
60. The Goncourt brothers, redacted Gavarni's personal journal and published it after his death as *Gavarni, l'homme et l'œuvre* (1879), 61. It is impossible to say which, if any, of the comments attributed to Gavarni are direct quotes.
61. *Journal des Dames et des Modes*, May 15, 1804, 373.
62. Edmond and Jules de Goncourt, *Gavarni, l'homme et l'œuvre*, 61.
63. November 5, 1819, fashion plate description.
64. Ian Kelly, *Beau Brummell: The Ultimate Man of Style* (Free Press, 2006), 6.
65. Kelly, *Beau Brummell*, 6.
66. He was, however, commonly chided for being a "traitor" to his sex. For example, La Mésangère's fashion magazine was called "the delight of the ladies" but "the despair of their husbands" (84) who were the ones stuck with the bill for all "those hats, those dresses, those cashmeres, those flowers, those plumes so elegantly depicted in the engravings."Journaliste émérité, pseud. *Biographie indiscrète des publicistes . . .* (1826), 84–85.
67. See Kleinert, *La Conquête*, passim. On the differences between male- and female-edited "women's magazines" during this period, see *Masculin/féminin et presse au XIXe siècle*, ed. Christine Planté & Marie-Ève Thérenty (Presses Universitaires de Lyon, 2022), particularly Catherine Nesci, "Enseignement de la féminité et apprentissage de la connaissance dans les journaux féminins (1730–1830)," 39–58; Caroline Fayolle, "Résistances féministes dans la presse au tournant du XIX siècle," 59–76; and Marie-Ève Thérenty, "Le 'plafond de verre' des femmes journalistes du

XIXe siècle," in *Masculin/féminin et presse au XIXe siècle*, 337–54 . See also Cheryl Morgan, "Unfashionable Feminism? Designing Women Writers in the *Journal des Femmes* (1832–1836)," in *Making the News: Modernity and the Mass Press in Nineteenth-Century France*, ed. Dean de la Motte and Jeannene Przyblyski (University of Massachusetts Press, 1999), 207–32.

68. For a list of the places Balzac mentions La Mésangère in his work, see Kleinert, "Un Prêtre fléchois," 44n42.
69. Although Gavarni's generation adopted the epithet "dandy," it represented the opposite of the subtle elegance of the first dandy, the Englishman Beau Brummell (1778–1840) in the 1810s. On this phenomenon and its relationship to celebrity culture, see Rhonda K. Garelick, *Rising Star: Dandyism, Gender, and Performance in Fin-de-siècle Culture* (Princeton University Press, 1999).
70. Gavarni too made the male dressing gown a "kind of spectacle" of elite belonging at home. See Lise Schreier, "Portrait de l'artiste en robe de chambre, 1830–1870," *Romance Studies* 28, no. 4 (November 2010): 283. Also see Kleinert, *Le "Journal des Dames et des Modes,"* 146–47. There being no fashion magazine exclusively for men during this time, dandies consulted La Mésangère's journal. In 1834, after La Mésangère's death, Dufougerais, the new editor of *Journal des Dames et des Modes*, explicitly took on this responsibility.
71. For more on writers as dandies during this period, see Schreier, "Portrait de l'artiste," 279–95.
72. Janin signed his "M. La Mésengère" article later, including it in his several volume *Histoire de la littérature dramatique,* a collection of his writings on literature, drama, and politics in his *Histoire de la littérature dramatique*, 6 vols. (Michel Lévy Frères, 1854, [Slatkine Reprints, 1970]), 3:55.
73. Janin, "M. La Mésengère," 320. Janin also calls La Mésangère's expensive accessories— "a gold-handled cane, a diamond ring, stockings threaded with a contrasting color, and two watches"—absurd, and superannuated excess.
74. Kleinert, *Le "Journal des Dames et des Modes,"* 164; Janin, "M. La Mésengère," 323.
75. Janin, "M. La Mésengère," 324.
76. Janin, "M. La Mésengère," 325.
77. Janin, "M. La Mésengère," 322–23. A *cabinet* was a place for work, study, conversation, dressing, or bodily functions.

78. Janin, "M. La Mésengère," 324.
79. Janin, "M. La Mésengère," 325.
80. In Janin's long tirade, one passing comment suggests in a comic, roundabout way that La Mésangère might have done something potentially illegal (gambling) and indecent (frequenting low-life districts, possibly for sexual activity). But, to my mind, this allusion feels like a one-off and is too arcane to decode with certainty two centuries later. For a different view, see Kleinert, *Le "Journal des Dames et des Modes,"* 322.
81. Kleinert, *Le "Journal des Dames et des Modes."*
82. Kleinert, *Le "Journal des Dames et des Modes,"* 168–69, 342–43, 348–49, and passim.
83. Kleinert, *Le "Journal des Dames et des Modes,"* 168. See also 170, 172, 178, and "Les Débuts de Gavarni," 218.
84. Kleinert, "Un Prêtre fléchois," 43; Kleinert, *Le "Journal des Dames et des Modes,"* 179–80.
85. While Napoleon had personally held those ideals, he used them only to guide himself.
86. For excellent insights into the cultural and literary history of this period and the role that gender often played, see Sandy Petrey, *In the Court of the Pear King: French Culture and the Rise of Realism* (Cornell University Press, 2005).
87. Kleinert, "Un Prêtre fléchois," 45.
88. Kleinert, *La Conquête*, 180. For a list of those who attended the funeral, see Kleinert, "Un Prêtre fléchois," 45–46.
89. See Kleinert, *Le "Journal des dames et des modes,"* passim.
90. Among others at his funeral were "the poor, widows, and orphans who had benefited from his generosity and seventeen people to whom he had lent a total of 15,400 francs, a considerable sum at the time." Ferdinand Hoefer, "La Mésangère" in *Nouvelle Biographie générale*, 46 vols. (1866), 29:199–200; Kleinert, "Un Prêtre fléchois," 45–46.

6. AFTERLIVES

1. His books, periodicals, and series of engravings grew out of a similar passion for accrual and categorization, albeit for the purposes of public dissemination rather than private ownership. He amassed different kinds of information—texts, facts, images, and ideas—and brought

them all together, as in *Journal des Dames et des Modes*. Additionally, he would devote an entire volume or several to a particular category, as he did in *Paris Traveler* and *Dictionary of French Proverbs*.

2. Annemarie Kleinert, "Un Prêtre fléchois devenu auteur, éditeur et journaliste: Pierre La Mésangère (1761–1831)," *Cahier Fléchois* 19 (1998): 49.
3. Annemarie Kleinert, *Le "Journal des dames et des modes" ou La Conquête de l'Europe féminine (1797–1839)* (Jan Thorbecke, 2001), 186.
4. Kleinert, *Le "Journal des Dames et des Modes,"* 64.
5. Kleinert, *Le "Journal des Dames et des Modes,"* 83.
6. Kleinert, *Le "Journal des Dames et des Modes,"* 186 and "Un Prêtre," 39, 49–50. For the full inventory of that art and other precious objects, see *Catalogue du cabinet de feu M. La Mésangère* (1831). See also Kleinert, *Le "Journal des Dames et des Modes,"* 71, 82, 164, 186, 190.
7. Kleinert, "Un Prêtre," 45–46.
8. Leora Auslander, "The Gendering of Consumer Practices in Nineteenth-Century France," in *The Sex of Things: Essays on Gender and Consumption*, ed. Victoria de Grazia and Ellen Furlough (University of California Press, 1996), 80–81, 85.
9. Kleinert, "Un Prêtre," 48.
10. If de Montrol had heard, as one contemporary (Abbé Fayolle) is quoted as saying, that La Mésangère was a man with a deep passion not just for antiquities and other valuables but also for clothing, de Montrol might not have let La Mésangère pass muster so easily. Closing ranks by omitting eccentricities was a common form of denial and closeting. See below.
11. François Mongin de Montrol, "M. La Mésangère," *Mémoires et dissertations sur les Antiquités nationales et étrangères, publié par la Société Royale des Antiquaires de France* 10 (1834): xlvii.
12. Janin's 1830 article did not mention the nobiliary particle.
13. Anonymous, *Journal des Dames et des Modes*, November 15, 1834 (reprinted February 20, 1836). Quoted in Kleinert, *Le "Journal des Dames et des Modes,"* 1.
14. For a summary of the problems with the notions of two spheres—public and private, masculine and feminine, see Auslander, "The Gendering of Consumer Practices," 83 and n. 18.
15. De Montrol, "M. La Mésangère," xlviii.
16. He did make light of it in his 1830 article.

17. Janin wrote four pages on La Mésangère as part of his assessment of the literature, drama, and politics of 1831 and published it in a collection of his other published and unpublished writing. *Histoire de la littérature dramatique*, 6 vols. (1854), 3:57.
18. For other theories of "queer time" that might be relevant to further work on La Mésangère, see Emma Katherine Atwood, "Fashionably Late: Queer Temporality and the Restoration Fop," *Comparative Drama* 47, no. 1 (Spring 2013): 86: "By saying that the Restoration fop queers time, and not gender, I mean to define the fop in a new way, distinct from definitions that champion his gender play, his flamboyance, his ego, his Frenchification, or his role as a comic figure. I argue instead that the Restoration fop can be more comprehensively defined by his queer engagement with time and especially what I call his fashionable lateness." See also the very useful review of theories of queer time by Maria Pramaggiore and Páraic Kerrigan, "Queer Media Temporalities—Editorial," *Alphaville: Journal of Film and Screen Media* 16 (Winter 2018): 1–8.
19. Jacob Aplaca, personal communication.
20. Janin, *Histoire de la littérature dramatique*, 3:57.
21. Janin, *Histoire de la littérature dramatique*, 3:55. This point is well taken but exaggerated. La Mésangère did escape some censorship but not all (see chapter 4).
22. Janin, *Histoire de la littérature dramatique*, 3:55.
23. Janin, *Histoire de la littérature dramatique*, 3:55, 57.
24. By that time, the Empire having ended, feathers were almost entirely for the "fair sex."
25. Janin, *Histoire de la littérature dramatique*, 3:57.
26. Janin, *Histoire de la littérature dramatique*, 3:55.
27. In the earliest, 1847 version of Fayolle's comments, the quote continues in a footnote as if it were incidental, but this information is, if anything, more personal and, in its final line, more shocking than anything else said in the entire article.
28. Michaud jeune, in Louis-Gabriel Michaud, "La Mésangère," in *Biographie universelle, ancienne et moderne*, 1st ed., 84 vols. (1842), 70 (Supplément: 89).
29. Michaud, "La Mésangère," 70:89.
30. Fayolle's comments are also quoted in a later biographical entry, in Ferdinand Hoefer, *Nouvelle Biographie Générale*, 46 vols. (1859), 29:199–200.

31. Michaud, "La Mésangère," 70:89; Hoefer, "La Mésangère," 29:199–200. The Hoefer article is signed "P. L—y," a standard way of setting up a contributor's quasi-anonymity in reference books at the time.
32. François-Joseph-Marie Fayolle, quoted in Michaud, "La Mésangère," 70:89.
33. Fayolle, quoted in Michaud, "La Mésangère," 70:89.
34. Fayolle, quoted in Michaud, "La Mésangère," 70:89.
35. When he was a Doctrinarian priest, he was allowed no more than ten pairs. The idea of two thousand pairs of shoes still flabbergasts. In the 1980s, Imelda Marcos, the wife of the president of the Philippines and a world-famous shopaholic, left behind half that many (1,060), including "one pair, fitted with batteries, that sparkles in the dark" when she and her husband fled after being driven out of office in 1986. "Imeldarabilia: A Final Count," *TIME*, February 23, 1987. On the other hand, those running Marie-Antoinette's household are said to have "ordered . . . four new pairs of shoes each week," at least in part so they could "help themselves to those items for which she no longer had a need." This would mean approximately 2,000 pairs of shoes per year. Caroline Weber, *The Queen of Fashion: What Marie-Antoinette Wore to the Revolution* (Picador, 2007), 118.
36. Later biographical dictionaries do not, however, tend to put the last five sentences in a footnote as the original 1842 and the later 1859 version did. The entire passage is together.
37. Some notable, if slight variations: In 1859, an anonymous article in a regional periodical about Anjou quotes the Fayolle information without question or context. Almost entirely hagiographic, it describes La Mésangère as a devoted teacher, victim of the Revolution, poet, philosopher, and benefactor, and a great conversationalist with a prodigious memory. For most of these remarks, no original sources are cited. *Bulletin historique et monumental de l'Anjou* (1859), 129–33. In 1875, La Mésangère's "closet" got some play in the United States with the publication of an English translation of a French book by Augustin Challamel (1818–1894) published in 1862. It paraphrases without attribution Fayolle's claims and makes no remark about the astonishing numbers alleged except to conclude that La Mésangère's attire was "above criticism." *History of Fashion in France or the Dress of Women from the Greco-Roman Period to the Present Time* (1875), 10. Fairly blatant plagiarism was not unusual. Once a contemporary or historical figure was taken seriously by one biographical

reference book, very similar entries appeared in others. If they changed at all, it was only slightly.

38. Fayolle states that there were ninety snuffboxes, but the inventory from the public auction counted only sixty of them fit for sale on that occasion.
39. Michaud, "La Mésangère," 70:89.
40. Kleinert, *Le "Journal des Dames et des Modes,"* 71.
41. Kleinert, *Le "Journal des Dames et des Modes,"* 71.
42. To judge by the thousands of Napoleon souvenirs listed on Etsy every day, this pattern holds true. He is rarely represented in his coronation finery.
43. For the latter look, typical of images of the last phase of his life in exile on Saint Helena, he is often pictured at home staring out over the sea to nothingness, reading a book, gazing at a fire in the fireplace.
44. Today, the silhouette alone sells everything from chocolate to liqueur to movies. For Alan Taylor's *The Emperor's New Clothes* (2001) and Ridley Scott's *Napoleon* (2023), almost every publicity photo pictures Napoleon in his bicorn—only a very few of him in his laurel crown—as if a modern audience could not recognize him otherwise, further confirming the bicorn as Napoleon's brand.
45. The British Museum website identifies the scenes differently: "the royalist insurrection of 13 Vendémiaire (with, in the background, a view of Toulon, left, and a star rising over Paris, right), the Consulate, the Empire (with a building resembling the Panthéon in the background), the battle of Austerlitz (the hat resting on laurels, and eagle flying through an open sky), the battle of Wagram, the battle of Moscow (with the burning city in the distance), the battle of Waterloo (a falling star over the battlefield, a discarded eagle on the ground, a lightning bolt tearing through the sky), and the exile on Saint-Helena (with a flag flying over Saint-Helena in the background)," https://www.britishmuseum.org/collection/object/P_2013-7061-1?selectedImageId=1613747944. The engraving gives the images the following tags: Vendémiaire, Consulate, Empire, Austerlitz, Wagram, Moscow, Waterloo, Saint Helena. For details and a discussion of alternate identifications of the somewhat ambiguous scenes and an interpretation of the image as that of a "tragic hero" made for another Bonapartist friend, see Peter Hicks, "Painting by Steuben [The Life of Napoleon in Eight Hats]," *Napoleon.org* (Fondation Napoléon, 2017),

https://www.napoleon.org/en/history-of-the-two-empires/paintings/the-eight-ages-of-napoleon-i-or-the-life-of-napoleon-in-eight-hats/.

46. Tamar Garb's analysis of modern bourgeois masculinity later in the century stresses similar attributes: "decency, effort, sobriety and self-control," *Bodies of Modernity: Figure and Flesh in Fin-de-Siècle France* (Thames and Hudson, 1998), 35.
47. See, for example, *Journal des Dames et des Modes*, March 5, 1806.
48. On Napoleon's hats, see Colombe Samoyault-Verlet, "The Emperor's Wardrobe," in *The Age of Napoleon: Costume from Revolution to Empire, 1789–1815*, ed. Katell le Bourhis (Metropolitan Museum of Art, 1989), 207.
49. Raoul Brunon, "Uniforms of the Napoleonic Era," in *The Age of Napoleon: Costume from Revolution to Empire, 1789–1815*, 181.
50. Samoyault-Verlet, "The Emperor's Wardrobe," 207.
51. Hannah L. Lippard, personal communication.

BIBLIOGRAPHY

Abrantès, Laure Junot, duchesse d.' *Mémoires de Madame la Duchesse d'Abrantès: Souvenirs historiques sur Napoléon, la Révolution, le Directoire, le Consulat, l'Empire et la Restauration.* 10 vols. 1893.

Agulhon, Maurice. *Marianne au combat: L'imagerie et la symbolique républicaines de 1789 à 1880.* Flammarion, 1979.

Airiau, Paul. "Le Prêtre catholique: masculin, neutre, autre? Des débuts du XIXe siècle au milieu du XXe siècle." In *Hommes et masculinités de 1789 à nos jours*, ed. Régis Revenin, 191–207. Autrement, 2007.

Amann, Elizabeth. *Dandyism in the Age of Revolution: The Art of the Cut.* University of Chicago Press, 2015.

Archives Château Réquista. September 13, 1763. Quoted in Jean de Viguerie. *Une œuvre d'éducation sous l'Ancien Régime: Les Pères de la doctrine chrétienne en France et en Italie: 1592–1792.* Éditions de la Nouvelle Aurore, 1976.

Ariès, Philippe. *Centuries of Childhood: A Social History of Family Life.* Trans. Robert Baldick. Vintage, 1962.

Arizzoli-Clémentel, Pierre. "Joseph Cardinal Fesch and the Liturgical Vestments of Lyon." In *The Age of Napoleon: Costume from Revolution to Empire, 1789–1815*, ed. Katell le Bourhis, 135–48. The Metropolitan Museum of Art, 1989.

Ashton, John. *English Caricature and Satire on Napoleon I.* 2 vols. 1884.

Aston, Nigel. *Christianity and Revolutionary Europe, 1750–1830*. Cambridge University Press, 2002.

Atwood, Emma Katherine. "Fashionably Late: Queer Temporality and the Restoration Fop." *Comparative Drama* 47, no. 1 (Spring 2013): 85–111.

Auslander, Leora. "The Gendering of Consumer Practices in Nineteenth-Century France." In *The Sex of Things: Essays on Gender and Consumption*, ed. Victoria de Grazia and Ellen Furlough, 79–112. University of California Press, 1996.

Avrillion, Marie-Jeanne-Pierrette. *Mémoires de Mademoiselle Avrillion, première femme de chambre de l'impératrice, sur la vie privée de Joséphine, sa famille et sa cour.* 2 vols. 1833. Quoted in Philippe Séguy. *Histoire des modes sous l'Empire*. Tallandier, 1988.

Baker, Keith Michael. "Condorcet." In *A Critical Dictionary of the French Revolution*, ed. François Furet and Mona Ozouf, 204–13. Belknap Press, 1989.

Bartel, Paul. *La Jeunesse inédite de Napoléon d'après de nombreux documents*. Amiot-Dumont, 1954.

Balzac, Honoré de. *Les Chouans*. 1829.

Bardin, Etienne Alexandre. "Cocarde." In *Dictionnaire de l'armée de terre, ou Recherches historiques sur l'art et les usages militaires des anciens et des modernes*, 17 vols. 1843.

Beaupère, Bernard. *Histoire du Prytanée national militaire*. Charles-Lavauzelle, 1985.

Bell, David. *The First Total War: Napoleon's Europe and the Birth of Warfare as We Know It*. Houghton Mifflin, 2007.

Bell, David. "The Unbearable Lightness of Being French: Law, Republicanism and National Identity at the End of the Old Regime." *American Historical Review* 106, no. 4 (October 2001): 1215–35, doi:10.2307/2692946.

Bendjebbar, André. *La Vie quotidienne en Anjou au XVIIIe siècle*. Hachette, 1983.

Benhamou, Reed. "Fashion in the *Mercure*: From Human Foible to Female Failing." *Eighteenth-Century Studies* 31, no. 1 (Fall 1997): 27–43, https://www-jstor-org.ccl.idm.oclc.org/stable/30053643.

Benoit, Jérémie. *L'Anti-Napoléon: Caricatures et satires du Consulat à l'Empire*. Réunion des Musées Nationaux, 1996.

Berg, Maxine, and Elizabeth Eger, eds. *Luxury in the Eighteenth Century*. Palgrave Macmillan, 2007.

Besnard, François-Yves. *Un Prêtre en révolution: Souvenirs d'un nonagénaire.* Ed. Martine Taroni. Presses Universitaires de Rennes, 2011.

Bingham, Captain D. A. *A Selection from the Letters and Despatches of the First Napoleon with Explanatory Notes*, vol. 1 (1884).

Hanne Blank. *Straight: The Surprisingly Short History of Heterosexuality.* Beacon Press, 2012.

Blaufarb, Rafe. "The Social Contours of Meritocracy in the Napoleonic Officer Corps." In *Taking Liberties: Problems of a New Order from the French Revolution to Napoleon*, ed. Howard G. Brown and Judith A. Miller, 126–46. Manchester University Press, 2002.

Blum, André. "La Caricature politique en France sous le Consulat et l'Empire." *Revue des Etudes Napoléoniennes* 13 (January–June 1918): 296–312, https://gallica.bnf.fr/ark:/12148/bpt6k154892.

Bobker, Danielle. *The Closet: The Eighteenth-Century Architecture of Intimacy.* Princeton University Press, 2020.

Bois, Benjamin. *La Vie scolaire et les créations intellectuelles en Anjou pendant la Révolution, 1789–1799.* Félix Alcan, 1929. Quoted in André Bendjebbar. *La Vie quotidienne en Anjou au XVIIIe siècle.* Hachette, 1983.

Bologne, Jean-Claude. *Histoire de la pudeur.* Olivier Orban, 1986.

Bonaparte, Napoléon. *Correspondance générale.* Vol. 1, *Les Apprentissages, 1784–1797.* Ed. Thierry Lentz. Fayard, 2004.

Bonaparte, Napoléon. *Correspondance générale.* No. 31, 1789. Quoted in Patrice Gueniffey. *Bonaparte: 1769–1802.* Trans. Steven Rendall. Harvard University Press, 2015.

Bonaparte, Napoléon. *A Selection from the Letters and Despatches of the First Napoleon with Explanatory Notes.* 3 vols. Ed. D. A. Bingham. 1884.

Bordes, Philippe. *Jacques-Louis David: Empire to Exile.* Yale University Press, 2005.

Bordes, Philippe, and Alain Pougetoux. "Les Portraits de Napoléon en habits impériaux par Jacques-Louis David." *Gazette des Beaux-Arts* 102 (July–August 1983): 21–34.

Boucher, Charles. *La Flèche sous la Révolution, 1789–1805: Mémoires inédits du chirurgien Charles Boucher; publication intégrale et critique par Alain de Dieuleveult.* A. de Dieuleveult, 1982.

Bourguet, Marie-Noëlle. "Science and Memory: The Stakes of the Expedition to Egypt (1798–1801)." In *Taking Liberties: Problems of a New Order from the French Revolution to Napoleon*, ed. Howard G. Brown and Judith A. Miller, 92–109. Manchester University Press, 2002.

Bourke, Joanna. "The Great Male Renunciation: Men's Dress Reform in Inter-war Britain," *Journal of Design History* 9, no. 1 (1996): 983–1008.

Breward, Christopher. *The Hidden Consumer: Masculinities, Fashion, and City Life, 1860–1914*. Manchester University Press, 1999.

Bruna, Denis, ed. *Fashioning the Body: An Intimate History of the Silhouette*. Yale University Press, 2015.

Brunon, Raoul. "Uniforms of the Napoleonic Era." In *The Age of Napoleon: Costume from Revolution to Empire, 1789–1815*, ed. Katell le Bourhis, 179–202. The Metropolitan Museum of Art, 1989.

Bryson, Norman. "Géricault and 'Masculinity.'" In *Visual Culture: Images and Interpretations*, ed. Norman Bryson, Michael Ann Holly, and Keith Moxey, 228–59. Wesleyan University Press, 1994.

Bryson, Norman. *Tradition and Desire: From David to Delacroix*. Cambridge University Press, 1984.

Bulletin Historique et Monumental de l'Anjou (1859–1860), 6:120–33.

Buringh, Eltjo, and Jan Luiten Van Zanden. "Charting the 'Rise of the West': Manuscripts and Printed Books in Europe, a Long-Term Perspective from the Sixth through Eighteenth Centuries." *The Journal of Economic History* 69 no 2 (2009): 409–45.

Butler, Judith. "Critically Queer," *GLQ: A Journal of Lesbian and Gay Studies* 1, no. 1 (1993): 17–32.

Butler, Judith. "Sex and Gender in Simone de Beauvoir's *Second Sex*," *Yale French Studies* 72 (1986): 35–49.

Cady, Joseph. "The 'Masculine Love' of the 'Princes of Sodom' 'Practising the Art of Ganymede' at Henri III's Court: The Homosexuality of Henri III and His *Mignons* in Pierre de L'Estoile's *Mémoires-Journaux*." In *Desire and Discipline: Sex and Sexuality in the Premodern West*, ed. Jacqueline Murray and Konrad Eisenbichler, 123–54. University of Toronto Press, 1996.

Cage, E. Claire. "The Sartorial Self: Neoclassical Fashion and Gender Identity in France, 1797–1804." *Eighteenth-Century Studies* 42, no 2 (Winter 2009): 193–215.

Cage, E. Claire. *Unnatural Frenchmen: The Politics of Priestly Celibacy and Marriage, 1720–1815*. University of Virginia Press, 2015.

Cameron, Vivian. "Political Exposures: Sexuality and Caricature in the French Revolution." In *Eroticism and the Body Politic*, ed. Lynn Hunt, 90–107. Johns Hopkins University Press, 1991.

Caron, Auguste. *Toilette des dames, ou Encyclopédie de la beauté*. Paris, 1806.

Carrington, Dorothy. *Napoleon and His Parents: On the Threshold of History.* Dutton, 1990.

Cauvin, Thomas. *La Flèche et ses environs.* Res Universis, 1990.

Censer, Jack R., and Lynn Hunt, *Liberty, Equality, Fraternity: Exploring the French Revolution.* Penn State University Press, 2002.

C. H., "Characteristic Traits of Bonaparte in His Youth and a Refutation of Diverse Anecdotes Published on this Subject," 1797.

Challamel, Augustin. *History of Fashion in France, or the Dress of Women from the Greco-Roman Period to the Present Time.* Scribner, 1882.

Chapin, Chloe. " 'His Ghost Walks Among Us Still': Troubling the Sartorial Legacy of Beau Brummell." *Fashion Theory* 29, no. 1 (2025): 75–101. https://doi.org/10.1080/1362704X.2024.2437839.

Chapin, Chloe. "Masculine Renunciation or Rejection of the Feminine?: Revisiting J. C. Flügel's *Psychology of Clothes.*" *Fashion Theory* 26, no. 7 (2021): 983–1008.

Chuquet, Arthur. *La Jeunesse de Napoléon.* 3 vols. Paris, 1897–1899.

Clerc, Catherine. *La Caricature contre Napoléon.* Promodis, 1985.

Clère, Jules. *Histoire de l'Ecole de la Flèche, depuis sa fondation par Henri IV jusqu'à sa réorganisation en Prytanée impérial militaire.* Eug. Jourdain, 1853.

Clifford, Dale L. "Can the Uniform Make the Citizen? Paris, 1789–1791." *Eighteenth-Century Studies* 34, no. 3 (Spring 2001). https://www.jstor.org/stable/30053984.

Colley, Linda. *Britons: Forging the Nation, 1707–1787.* Yale University Press, 1992.

Colwill, Elizabeth. "Epistolary Passions: Friendship and the Literary Public of Constance de Salm, 1767–1845." *Journal of Women's History* 12, no. 3 (2000): 39–68.

Colwill, Elizabeth. "Pass as a Woman, Act Like a Man: Marie-Antoinette as Tribade in the Pornography of the French Revolution." In *Homosexuality in Modern France*, ed. Jeffrey Merrick and Bryant T. Ragan Jr., 54–79. Oxford University Press, 1996.

Cornu, Paul. "Essai bibliographique sur les recueils de mode au XVIIIe siècle et au début du XIXe siècle." In *Documents pour l'histoire de costume de Louis XV à Louis XVIII.* 3 vols., ed. G. Schefer, 1:24–31. Goupil, 1911.

Crawford, Katherine B. "Love, Sodomy, and Scandal: Controlling the Sexual Reputation of Henry III." *Journal of the History of Sexuality* 12, no. 4 (October 2003): 513–42.

Cronin, Vincent. *Napoleon Bonaparte: An Intimate Biography.* Morrow, 1972.

Crow, Thomas. *Emulation: Making Artists for Revolutionary France.* Yale University Press, 1995.

Darnton, Robert. *The Literary Underground of the Old Regime.* Harvard University Press, 1982.

Davidson, Denise Z. "Imagining the Readers of the *Journal des dames et des modes.*" Unpublished paper presented at the interdisciplinary workshop More than Fashion: The *Journal des dames et des modes (1797–1839).* University of Michigan, Ann Arbor, April 2009.

Delpierre, Madeleine. "Une révolution en trois temps." In *Modes & révolutions, 1780–1804*, 11–40. Paris-Musées, 1989.

Diaconoff, Suellen. "Gender Ideology and Politics in *Le Cabinet des Modes.*" In *Les Femmes et la Révolution française.* Presses Universitaires du Mirail, 1990.

Edwards, Lydia. *How to Read a Suit: A Guide to Changing Men's Fashion from the 17th to the 20th Century.* Bloomsbury, 2020.

Fayolle, Caroline. "Résistances féministes dans la presse au tournant du XIX siècle." In *Féminin/Masculin dans la presse du XIX siècle*, ed. Christine Planté and Marie-Eve Thérenty, 59–76. Presses Universitaires de Lyon, 2022.

Ferguson, Gary. *Queer (Re)Readings in the French Renaissance: Homosexuality, Gender, Culture.* Ashgate, 2008.

Ffoulkes, Fiona. "'Quality Always Distinguished Itself': Louis Hippolyte LeRoy and the Luxury Clothing Industry in Early Nineteenth-Century Paris." In *Consumers and Luxury: Consumer Culture in Europe, 1650–1850*, ed. Maxine Berg and Helen Clifford, 183–207. Manchester University Press, 1999.

Fillin-Yeh, Susan. *Dandies: Fashion and Finesse in Art and Culture.* New York University Press, 2001.

Fleury, J. "Charles-Albert Demoustier." In *Encyclopédie du XIXe siècle: Répertoire universel des sciences des lettres et des arts.* 3rd ed. 25 vols. Paris, 1872, 7:775.

Flügel, John Carl. *The Psychology of Clothes.* Hogarth Press, 1930.

Foucault, Michel. *Discipline and Punish: The Birth of the Prison.* Trans. Alan Sheridan. Vintage, 1979.

Foucault, Michel. *The History of Sexuality.* Vol 1. Trans. Robert Hurley. Random House, 1978.

Garb, Tamar. *Bodies of Modernity: Figure and Flesh in Fin-de-Siècle France.* Thames & Hudson, 1998.

Garelick, Rhonda K. *Rising Star: Dandyism, Gender, and Performance in the Fin de Siècle*. Princeton University Press, 1999.

Gelbart, Nina Rattner. *Feminine and Opposition Journalism in Old Regime France: Le Journal des Dames*. University of California Press, 1987.

Gaubert, Henri. *Le Sacre de Napoléon Ier*. Flammarion, 1964.

Gaudemet, Jean. "Préface." In *Le Costume du clergé: ses origines et son évolution en France d'après les règlements de l'église*. Editions du Cerf, 1986.

Gaudriault, Raymond. *La Gravure de mode féminine en France*. Editions de l'Amateur, 1983.

Gazette française, November 17, 1796. Quoted in Richard Wrigley. *The Politics of Appearances: Representations of Dress in Revolutionary France*. Berg, 2002.

Gillispie, Charles. *Science and Polity in France: The End of the Old Regime*. Princeton University Press, 1980.

Ginsberg, Madeleine. "Fashion Plates." In *Encyclopedia of Clothing and Fashion*, ed. Valerie Steele, 65–67. Vol. 2. Charles Scribner's Sons, 2005.

Glasson, Ernest. "Les Origines du costume de la magistrature." *Nouvelle Revue historique de droit français et étranger* 8 (1884): 109-37.

Goncourt, Edmond de, and Jules de Goncourt. *Gavarni, l'homme et l'œuvre*. 1879.

Godechot, Jacques. *The Taking of the Bastille, July 14th, 1789*. Trans. Jean Stewart. Scribner's, 1970.

Godlewski, Guy. "La Vie quotidienne de Napoléon à Brienne." *Revue du Souvenir Napoléonien* 265 (August 1972): 4–10, https://www.napoleon.org/histoire-des-2-empires/articles/la-vie-quotidienne-de-napoleon-a-brienne/.

Goodman, Dena. *Marie-Antoinette: Writings on the Body of a Queen*. Routledge, 2003.

Gough, Hugh. *The Newspaper Press in the French Revolution*. Dorsey Press, 1988.

Granger, Sylvie. "Terpsichore au collège: La danse dans l'enseignement jésuite." In *La Flèche: Quatre siècles d'éducation sous le regard de l'Etat*. Prytanée National Militaire, 2006.

Grigsby, Darcy Grimaldo. *Colossal: Engineering the Suez Canal, Statue of Liberty, Eiffel Tower, and Panama Canal*. Periscope, 2012.

Grigsby, Darcy Grimaldo. *Extremities: Painting Empire in Post-Revolutionary France*. Yale University Press, 2002.

Grigsby, Darcy Grimaldo. "Mamelukes in Paris: Fashionable Trophies of Failed Napoleonic Conquest." *UC Berkeley New Faculty Lecture Series* 5 (1996).

Grigsby, Darcy Grimaldo. "Nudity à la grecque in 1799." *Art Bulletin* 80, no. 2 (June 1998): 311–35. doi:10.2307/3051235.

Gueniffey, Patrice. *Bonaparte: 1769–1802*. Trans. Steven Rendall. Harvard University Press, 2015.

Halperin, David M. *One Hundred Years of Homosexuality and Other Essays on Greek Love*. Routledge, 1990.

Hardman, John. *Marie Antoinette: The Making of a French Queen*. Yale University Press, 2019.

Harvey, John. *Men in Black*. Reaktion Books, 1995.

Haudrère, Philippe. "Le Cadre de la vie quotidienne des nobles à Angers au XVIIIe siècle." *Annales de Bretagne et des pays de l'Ouest* 106, no. 3 (1999): 93–104. doi:10.3406/abpo.1999.4044.

Herold, J. Christopher. *The Age of Napoleon*. American Heritage, 1963.

Hesse, Carla. *Publishing and Cultural Politics in Revolutionary Paris, 1789–1810*. University of California Press, 1991.

Heuer, Jennifer. "Hats on for the Nation! Women, Citizens, Soldiers, and the 'Sign of the French.'" *French History* 16, no. 1 (2002): 28–52.

Hicks, Peter. "Painting by Steuben [The Life of Napoleon in Eight Hats]." *Napoleon.org* (Fondation Napoléon, 2017). https://www.napoleon.org/en/history-of-the-two-empires/paintings/the-eight-ages-of-napoleon-i-or-the-life-of-napoleon-in-eight-hats/.

Higonnet, Anne. *Liberty Equality Fashion: The Women Who Styled the French Revolution*. W.W. Norton, 2024.

Hoefer, Ferdinand. "La Mésangère." In *Nouvelle Biographie Générale*. 46 vols. (1866), 29:199–200.

Houlier, Roland. "Pierre-Antoine Lebouc de La Mésangère, 1761–1831, prêtre, écrivain et journaliste de mode." In *Supplément aux Bulletins des Années 1987–1988*, 305–17. Vol. 10 of *Académie des sciences, belles-lettres et arts d'Angers: Mémoires*. Académie d'Angers, 1989.

Houtin, Albert. *Une vie de prêtre: Mon expérience, 1867–1912*. F. Rieder, 1926.

Hunt, Lynn. "Freedom of Dress in Revolutionary France." In *From the Royal to the Republican Body: Incorporating the Political in Seventeenth- and Eighteenth-Century France*. Ed. Sara E. Melzer and Kathryn Norberg. University of California Press, 1998.

Hunt, Lynn. "Pornography and the French Revolution." In *The Invention of Pornography: Obscenity and the Origins of Modernity, 1500–1800*, ed. Lynn Hunt, 301–40. Zone Books, 1993.

Hunt, Lynn. *Politics, Culture and Class in the French Revolution.* University of California Press, 1984.

Hunt, Lynn, and Jack R. Censer. *The French Revolution and Napoleon: Crucible of the Modern World.* 2nd ed. Bloomsbury, 2017.

"Imeldarabilia: A Final Count." *TIME*, February 23, 1987.

Jackson, Richard A. *Vive le roi! A History of the French Coronation from Charles V to Charles X.* University of North Carolina Press, 1984.

Jagose, Annamarie. *Orgasmology.* Duke University Press, 2012,

James, C. L. R. *The Black Jacobins: Toussaint Louverture and the San Domingo Revolution.* Vintage, 1989.

Janin, Jules. "La Mésengère." In *Histoire de la littérature dramatique.* Michel Lévy Frères, 1854. Slatkine Reprints, 1970, 3:54–58.

Johnson, Paul Christopher, Pamela E. Klassen, and Winnifred Fallers Sullivan. *Ekklesia: Three Inquiries in Church and State.* University of Chicago Press, 2018.

Jones, Jennifer. "Repackaging Rousseau: Femininity and Fashion in Old Regime France." *French Historical Studies* 18, no. 4 (1994): 939–67.

Jones, Jennifer. *Sexing la Mode: Gender, Fashion and Commercial Culture in Old Regime France.* Berg, 2004.

Journal des Dames et des Modes, préface du deuxième tome, 1838. Quoted in Annemarie Kleinert. *Le "Journal des dames et des modes" ou La Conquête de l'Europe féminine (1797–1839).* Jan Thorbecke, 2001.

Journaliste émérite [pseud.]. *Biographie indiscrète des publicistes, feuillistes, libellistes, journalistes, libraires, furets de coulisses, et autres du 19e siècle.* 1826.

Julia, Dominique. "L'éducation des ecclésiastiques aux XVIIe et XVIIIe siècles." In *Problèmes de l'histoire de l'éducation: Actes des séminaires organisés par l'École française de Rome et l'Università di Roma—la Sapienza (janvier–mai 1985).* Collection de l'École Française de Rome 104. Publications de l'École Française de Rome, 1988.

Kaplan, Steven L. *La Fin des corporations.* Trans. Béatrice Vierne. Fayard, 2001.

Kates, Gary. *Monsieur d'Eon Is a Woman: A Tale of Political Intrigue and Sexual Masquerade.* John Hopkins University Press, 2001.

Katz, Jonathan Ned. *The Invention of Heterosexuality.* University of Chicago Press, 2007.

Kelly, Ian. *Beau Brummell: The Ultimate Man of Style*. Free Press, 2006.

Kleinert, Annemarie. "Les Débuts de Gavarni, Peintre des mœurs et des modes parisiennes." *Gazette des Beaux-Arts* 141, no. 1570 (November 1999): 213.

Kleinert, Annemarie. *Die frühen Modejournale in Frankreich: Studien zur Literatur der Mode von den Anfängen bis 1848*. E. Schmidt, 1980.

Kleinert, Annemarie. *Le "Journal des dames et des modes" ou La Conquête de l'Europe féminine (1797–1839)*. Jan Thorbecke, 2001.

Kleinert, Annemarie. "La Naissance d'une presse de mode à la veille de la Révolution et l'essor du genre au XIXème siècle." In *Le Journalisme d'Ancien Régime*, ed. Pierre Rétat, 189–97. Presses Universitaires de Lyon, 1982.

Kleinert, Annemarie. "Un Prêtre fléchois devenu auteur, éditeur et journaliste: Pierre La Mésangère (1761–1831)." *Cahier Fléchois* 19 (1998): 28–53. https://annekleinert.de/documents/articles/pub13/pub13.pdf.

Kroen, Sheryl. *Politics and Theater: The Crisis of Legitimacy in Restoration France, 1815–1830*. University of California Press, 2000.

Kuchta, David. *The Three-Piece Suit and Modern Masculinity: England, 1550–1850*. University of California Press, 2002.

Kwass, Michael. "Big Hair: A Wig History of Consumption in Eighteenth-Century France." *The American Historical Review* 111, no. 3 (June 2006): 630–59. doi:10.1086/ahr.111.3.631.

Lacaille, Frédéric. "Carle Vernet et le règlement de 1812 sur l'uniforme de l'armée impériale." In *Uniformes napoléoniens*, ed. Carle Vernet, 5–9. Musée de l'Armée, 2001.

La Flèche: Quatre siècles d'éducation sous le regard de l'État. Prytanée National Militaire, 2006.

Lajer-Burcharth, Ewa. "The *Muscadins* and the *Merveilleuses*: Body and Fashion in Public Space under the Directory, 1795–1799." In *Repression and Expression: Literary and Social Coding in Nineteenth-Century France*, ed. Carrol F. Coates, 137–46. Peter Lang, 1996.

Lajer-Burcharth, Ewa. *Necklines: The Art of Jacques-Louis David after the Terror*. Yale University Press, 1999.

La Mésangère, Pierre de. *Galerie française de femmes célèbres par leurs talents, leur rang ou leur beauté* [. . .]. 1827.

La Mésangère, Pierre de. *Le Voyageur à Paris: Tableau pittoresque et moral de cette capitale*. 3 vols. 1797.

La Motte, Antoine Houdar de. *Fables nouvelles*. 1719.

Landes, Joan B. "Representing the Body Politic: The Paradox of Gender in the Graphic Politics of the French Revolution." In *Rebel Daughters: Women and the French Revolution*, ed. Sara E. Melzer and Leslie W. Rabine, 15–37. Oxford University Press, 1992.

Landes, Joan B. *Women and the Public Sphere in the Age of the French Revolution*. Cornell University Press, 1988.

Landes, Joan B. *Visualizing the Nation: Gender, Representation, and Revolution in Eighteenth-Century France*. Cornell University Press, 2001.

La Revellière-Lépeaux, Louis-Marie de. *Mémoires de Larevellière-Lépeaux: Membre du Directoire exécutif de la République française et de l'Institut national*. 3 vols. Paris, 1895.

Larrey, Baron Hippolyte. "Souvenirs dictés par Madame Mère." In *Madame mère (Napoleonis mater), Essai historique*. 2 vols. Vol. 2. 1892.

Lemaire, Joseph. *Le Dentiste des dames*. 1812.

Lentz, Thierry. "Introduction: Les apprentissages de Bonaparte." In *Correspondance générale de Napoléon Bonaparte*. 15 vols., ed. Fondation Napoléon, 1:19–37. Editions Fayard, 2004.

Le Roux, Nicolas. *La Faveur du roi: Mignons et courtisans au temps des derniers Valois*. Champ Vallon, 2001.

L'Éstoile, Pierre de. *Mémoires-Journaux*. Ed. Pierre-Gustave Brunet, Aimé Champollion-Figeac, Eugène Halphen et al. 12 vols. Paris, 1875–1896. Quoted in Katherine B. Crawford. "Love, Sodomy, and Scandal: Controlling the Sexual Reputation of Henry III." *Journal of the History of Sexuality* 12, no. 4 (October 2003): 524.

Lentz, Thierry et al. eds. *Le Mémorial de Sainte-Hélène: Le manuscrit original retrouvé*. Perrin, 2017.

Lhommede, Agathe. "Lebrun-Tossa." In *Dictionnaire des journalistes (1600–1789)*. IHRIM UMR 5317/MSH-LSE USR 2005 (2019). https://dictionnaire-journalistes.gazettes18e.fr/journaliste/476-jean-brun-dit-lebrun-tossa.

Lipovetsky, Gilles. *The Empire of Fashion: Dressing Modern Democracy*. Trans. Catherine Porter. Princeton University Press, 1994.

Love, Heather. *Feeling Backward: Loss and the Politics of Queer History*. Harvard University Press, 2007.

MacArthur, Elizabeth J. "Embodying the Public Sphere: Censorship and the Reading Subject in Beaumarchais's 'Mariage de Figaro.'" *Representations* 61 (Winter 1998): 57–77.

Maillard, Jacques. *L'Oratoire à Angers aux XVIIe et XVIIIe siècles*. Klinksieck, 1975.

Mann, Bonnie, and Martina Ferrari, eds. *On ne naît pas femme: on le devient: The Life of a Sentence*. Oxford University Press, 2017.

Mansel, Philip. "Monarchy, Uniform and the Rise of the Frac 1760–1830." *Past & Present* 96 (1982): 103–32. https://www-jstor-org.ccl.idm.oclc.org/stable/650512.

Marchant de Burbure, François-Roger-Fidèle. *Essais historiques sur la ville et le collège de La Flèche*. Pavie, 1803.

Martin, Brian. *Napoleonic Friendship: Military Fraternity, Intimacy, and Sexuality in Nineteenth-Century France*. University of New Hampshire Press, 2011.

Martin, David Marshall. *Ecclesiastical Dress and Vestments of the Roman Catholic Church from the Eleventh Century to the Present: A Handbook of Patterns, Construction, and Vesting Procedures for Use in the Theatre*. University Microfilms International, 1983.

Martin, Morag. *Selling Beauty: Cosmetics, Commerce, and French Society, 1750–1830*. Johns Hopkins University Press, 2009.

Maugras, Jean-François. *Instruction chrétienne sur les dangers du luxe*. 1725.

Maxwell, Alexander. *Patriots Against Fashion: Clothing and Nationalism in Europe's Age of Revolutions*. Palgrave Macmillan, 2014.

McCabe, Ina Baghdiantz. *A History of Global Consumption: 1500–1800*. Routledge, 2015.

McIlvanney, Siobhán. "*Le Journal des Dames et des Modes* (1797–1839): A Pioneering Presence in the Early French Women's Press." In *The Francophone Women's Magazine: Inside and Outside of France*, ed. Annabelle Cone and Dawn Marley, 3–21. University Press of the South, 2010.

McIlvanney, Siobhán. *Figurations of the Feminine in the Early French Women's Press, 1758–1848*. Liverpool University Press, 2019.

McKever, Rosalind, and Claire Wilcox, eds. *Fashioning Masculinities: The Art of Menswear*. With Marta Fraceschini. V&A Publishing, 2022.

McManners, John. *Church and Society in Eighteenth-Century France*. 2 vols. Clarendon, 1998.

McManners, John. *French Ecclesiastical Society Under the Ancien Régime: A Study of Angers in the Eighteenth Century*. Manchester University Press, 1960.

McManners, John. "Religious Vocation." In *Church and Society in Eighteenth-Century France*. 2 vols. Clarendon Press, 1998.

McManners, John. *The French Revolution and the Church*. Harper & Row, 1969.

McNeil, Peter. "Conspicuous Waist: Queer Dress in the "Long Eighteenth Century." In *A Queer History of Fashion: From the Closet to the Catwalk*, ed. Valerie Steele, 71–107. Yale University Press, 2013.

McPhee, Peter. *Robespierre: A Revolutionary Life*. Yale University Press, 2012.

Mellor, Alec. *Histoire de l'anticléricalisme français*. Mame, 1966.

Merrick, Jeffrey, and Bryant T. Ragan Jr., eds. *Homosexuality in Early Modern France: A Documentary Collection*. Oxford University Press, 2001.

Merrick, Jeffrey. *Sodomy in Eighteenth-Century France*. Cambridge Scholars Publishing, 2020.

Michaud jeune. "La Mésangère." In Louis-Gabriel Michaud, *Biographie universelle, ancienne et moderne*. 1st ed. 84 vols. (1842), 70. Supplément: 89.

Miller, Monica L. *Slaves to Fashion: Black Dandyism and the Styling of Black Diasporic Identity*. Duke University Press, 2009.

Modes & révolutions, 1780–1804. Paris-Musées, 1989.

Moers, Ellen. *The Dandy: Brummell to Beerbohm*. University of Nebraska Press, 1978.

Montrol, François Mongin de. "La Mésangère." In *Mémoires et dissertations sur les antiquités*. Vol. 10, xliv–xlviii. Société Royale des Antiquaires de France, 1836.

Moore, John. *A View of the Causes and Progress of the French Revolution*. London, 1795. Quoted in Alexander Maxwell. *Patriots Against Fashion: Clothing and Nationalism in Europe's Age of Revolutions*. Palgrave Macmillan, 2014, 101.

Morgan, Cheryl. "Unfashionable Feminism? Designing Women Writers in the *Journal des Femmes* (1832–1836)." In *Making the News: Modernity and the Mass Press in Nineteenth-Century France*, ed. Dean de la Motte and Jeannene Przyblyski, 207–32. University of Massachusetts Press, 1999.

Mukerji, Chandra. *Territorial Ambitions and the Gardens of Versailles*. Cambridge University Press, 1997.

Muñoz, José. *Disidentifications: Queers of Color and the Performance of Politics*. University of Minnesota Press, 1999.

Nesci, Catherine. "Enseignement de la féminité et apprentissage de la connaissance dans les journaux féminins (1730–1830)." In *Féminin/Masculin dans la presse du XIX siècle*, ed. Christine Planté and Marie-Eve Thérenty, 39–58. Presses Universitaires De Lyon, 2022.

Nye, Robert A. *Masculinity and Male Codes of Honor in France*. Oxford University Press, 1993.

Ockman, Carol. *Ingres's Eroticized Bodies: Retracing the Serpentine Line.* Yale University Press, 1995.

O'Connor, Adrian. *In Pursuit of Politics: Education and Revolution in Eighteenth-Century France.* Manchester University Press, 2017.

"On the Influence of the Revolution on Women." In *The French Revolution and Human Rights: A Brief Documentary History.* Ed. and trans. Lynn Hunt. Bedford/St. Martin's, 1996.

Outram, Dorinda. *The Body and the French Revolution: Sex, Class and Political Culture.* Yale University Press, 1989.

Pardailhé-Galabrun, Annik. *La Naissance de l'intime: 3.000 foyers parisiens, XVII–XVIII siècles.* Presses Universitaires de France, 1988

Pellegrin, Nicole. *Les Vêtements de la liberté: Abécédaire des pratiques vestimentaires françaises de 1780 à 1800.* Éditions Alinéa, 1989.

Petrey, Sandy. *In the Court of the Pear King: French Culture and the Rise of Realism.* Cornell University Press, 2005.

Pichichero, Christy. *The Military Enlightenment: War and Culture in the French Empire from Louis XIV to Napoleon.* Cornell University Press, 2017.

Plongeron, Bernard. *La Vie quotidienne du clergé français au XVIIIe siècle.* Hachette, 1974.

Pollock, Linda A. *Forgotten Children: Parent-Child Relations from 1500 to 1900.* Cambridge University Press, 1983.

Popkin, Jeremy. *Revolutionary News: The Press in France, 1789–1799.* Duke University Press, 1990.

Potron, Daniel. *Le Prytanée militaire de La Flèche à travers la carte postale.* Coconnier, 1981.

Porterfield, Todd, and Susan Siegfried. *Staging Empire: Napoleon, Ingres, and David.* Pennsylvania State University Press, 2006.

Pozzi, Jean. "Costumes historiques et pouvoir Napoléonien." *Revue d'Histoire Diplomatique* 72, no. 2 (1959): 162–71.

Pramaggiore, Maria, and Páraic Kerrigan. "Queer Media Temporalities: Editorial." *Alphaville: Journal of Film and Screen Media* 16 (Winter 2018): 1–8.

Prévost, Antoine François, abbé. *Manon Lescaut.* 1731.

Prudhomme, Louis-Marie. "On the Influence of the Revolution on Women." In *The French Revolution and Human Rights: A Brief Documentary History.* Ed. and trans. Lynn Hunt. Bedford/St. Martin's, 1996.

Purdy, Daniel L. *The Rise of Fashion: A Reader.* University of Minnesota Press, 2004.

Purdy, Daniel L. *The Tyranny of Elegance: Consumer Cosmopolitanism in the Era of Goethe.* Johns Hopkins University Press, 1998.

Ragan, Bryant T., Jr. "Same Sex Sexual Relations and the French Revolution: The Decriminalization of Sodomy in 1791." In *Everyday Politics and Culture in Revolutionary France: Essays in Honor of Lynn Hunt*, ed. Suzanne Desan, Bryant T. Ragan, and Victoria Thompson, 123–44. Liverpool University Press, 2024,

Ragan, Bryant T., Jr., and Jeffrey Merrick. *Eighteenth-Century Homosexuality in Global Perspective.* Special issue of *Historical Reflections* 33, no. 1 (Spring 2007).

Ragan, Bryant T., Jr., and Jeffrey Merrick. *Homosexuality in Early Modern France: A Documentary Collection.* Oxford University Press, 2001.

Rambuss, Richard. *Closet Devotions.* University of North Carolina Press, 1998.

Reddy, William M. *The Invisible Code: Honor and Sentiment in Post-Revolutionary France, 1814–1848.* University of California Press, 1997.

Rémusat, Claire Élisabeth Jeanne Gravier de Vergennes de. *Mémoires de Madame de Rémusat, 1802–1808.* 3 vols. Calmann-Lévy, 1906.

Réveille, Jean. "Anticlericalism in France." *The American Journal of Theology* 9, no. 4 (October 1905): 605–20. doi:10.1086/478564.

Revenin, Régis, ed. *Hommes et masculinités de 1789 à nos jours.* Éditions Autrement, 2007.

Ribeiro, Aileen. *Dress in Eighteenth-Century Europe, 1715–1789.* Holmes & Meier, 1984.

Ribeiro, Aileen. *Fashion in the French Revolution.* Homes & Meier, 1988.

Richardson, Frank M. *Napoleon: Bisexual Emperor.* Horizon Press, 1972.

Rifkin, Adrian. *Ingres Then, and Now.* Routledge, 2000.

Roberts, Andrew. *Napoleon: A Life.* Penguin, 2014.

Rudeen, Christopher M., and Elizabeth Lunbeck. "The Analyst's New Clothes: Reading J. C. Flügel into *Fashioning Masculinities.* On *Fashioning Masculinities: The Art of Menswear*, Victoria and Albert Museum." *Psychoanalysis and History* 25, no. 1 (2023): 122–27.

Ruppert, Jacques, Renée Davray-Piekolek, Madeleine Delpierre, and Pascale Gorguet-Ballesteros. *Le Costume français.* Flammarion, 1996.

Saint-Martin, Louis Vivien de. *Histoire Générale de la Révolution Française, de l'Empire, de la Restauration, de la Monarchie de 1830, jusqu'à 1841.* 4 vols. (1842).

Saint-Ursin, P. J. Marie de. *L'Ami des femmes, ou Lettres d'un médecin, concernant l'influence de l'habillement des femmes sur leurs mœurs et leur santé* [. . .]. 1805.

Samoyault-Verlet, Colombe. "The Emperor's Wardrobe." In *The Age of Napoleon: Costume from Revolution to Empire, 1789–1815*, ed. Katell Le Bourhis, 203–16. The Metropolitan Museum of Art, 1989.

Schom, Alan. *Napoleon Bonaparte*. HarperCollins, 1997.

Schor, Naomi. *Reading in Detail: Aesthetics and the Feminine*. Methuen, 1987.

Schor, Naomi. "The Scandal of Realism." In *A New History of French Literature*, ed. Denis Hollier, 656–60. Harvard University Press, 1994.

Schreier, Lise. "Portrait de l'artiste en robe de chambre, 1830–1870." *Romance Studies* 28, no. 4 (November 2010): 279–95. doi:10.1179/174581510X12817121842218.

Séguy, Philippe. "Costume in the Age of Napoleon." In *The Age of Napoleon: Costume from Revolution to Empire, 1789–1815*, ed. Katell Le Bourhis, 23–118. The Metropolitan Museum of Art, 1989.

Sennett, Richard. *The Fall of Public Man*. Knopf, 1977.

Sibalis, Michael. "The Regulation of Male Homosexuality in Revolutionary and Napoleonic France, 1789–1815." In *Homosexuality in Modern France*, ed. Jeffrey Merrick and Bryant T. Ragan, 80–101. Oxford University Press, 1996.

Sibalis, Michael. "Une subculture d'efféminés. L'homosexualité masculine sous Napoléon Ier." In *Hommes et masculinités de 1789 à nos jours, contributions à l'histoire du genre et de la sexualité en France*, ed. Régis Revenin, 75–95. Autrement, 2007.

Andrew Shelton. "Ingres, Painter of Men." *Art History* 44, no. 1 (2021): 16–51.

Siegfried, Susan. "The Politics of Criticism at the Salon of 1806: Ingres' *Napoleon Enthroned*." In *Proceedings of the Consortium on Revolutionary Europe*, 69–81. Vol. 2. University of Georgia Press, 1980.

Siegfried, Susan. "Reinventing Relics and Napoleon's Regal Body." In *The Eighteenth-Century Body: Art, History, Literature, Medicine*, ed. Angelica Goodden, 157–80. Peter Lang, 2002.

Silverman, Kaja. "Fragments of a Fashionable Discourse." In *Studies in Entertainment: Critical Approaches to Mass Culture*, ed. Tania Modleski, 130–52. Indiana University Press, 1986.

Simon, Marie. *La Mode enfantine*. Editions du Chêne, 1999.

Solomon-Godeau, Abigail. *Male Trouble: A Crisis in Representation*. Thames and Hudson, 1997.

Somerville, Siobhan B. "Queer." In *Keywords for American Studies* and *Keywords for Gender and Sexuality Studies*. New York University Press, 2021.

Spang, Rebecca L. "The Frivolous French: 'Liberty of Pleasure' and the End of Luxury." In *Taking Liberties: Problems of a New Order from the French Revolution to Napoleon*, ed. Howard G. Brown and Judith A. Miller, 110–25. Manchester University Press, 2002.

Spieler, Madeleine. *Empire and Underworld: Captivity in French Guiana*. Harvard University Press, 2012.

Stanton, Domna C. *The Aristocrat as Art: A Study of the* Honnête Homme *and the Dandy in Seventeenth- and Nineteenth-Century Fiction*. Columbia University Press, 1980.

Steele, Valerie. "A Queer History of Fashion: From the Closet to the Catwalk." In *A Queer History of Fashion: From the Closet to the Catwalk*. Ed. Valerie Steele. Yale University Press, 2013.

Steele, Valerie. *The Corset: A Cultural History*. Yale University Press, 2001.

Sullerot, Evelyne. *Histoire de la presse féminine en France des origines à 1848*. A. Colin, 1966.

Sutherland, D. M. G. *The French Revolution and Empire: The Quest for a Civic Order*. Blackwell, 2003.

Tackett, Timothy. *The Coming of the Terror in the French Revolution*. Harvard University Press, 2015.

Tackett, Timothy. *Religion, Revolution, and Regional Culture: The Ecclesiastical Oath of 1791*. Princeton University Press, 1986.

Taylor, Alan, dir. *The Emperor's New Clothes*. Paramount Pictures, 2001.

Taylor, Joan E. *What Did Jesus Look Like?* Bloomsbury, 2018.

The Cambridge History of Christianity, Vol. 7: Enlightenment, Reawakening and Revolution 1660–1815. Ed. Stewart J. Brown and Timothy Tackett. Cambridge University Press, 2006.

Thérenty, Marie-Ève. "Le 'plafond de verre' des femmes journalistes du XIXe siècle." In *Féminin/Masculin dans la presse du XIX siècle*, ed. Christine Planté and Marie-Ève Thérenty, 337–54. Presses Universitaires De Lyon, 2022.

Trichet, Louis. *Le Costume du clergé: Ses origines et son évolution en France, d'après les règlements de l'Église*. Editions du Cerf, 1986.

Trumbach, Randolph. *Sex and the Gender Revolution, Vol 1: Heterosexuality and the Third Gender in Enlightenment London*. University of Chicago Press, 1998.

Urbach, Henry. "Closets, Clothes, Disclosure." *Assemblage* (1996): 62–73.

Van Slyke, Gretchen. "Women at War: Skirting the Issue in the French Revolution." *L'Esprit Créateur* 37, no. 1 (Spring 1997): 33–43. https://www-jstor-org.ccl.idm.oclc.org/stable/26288117.

Vandal, Albert. *L'Avénèment de Bonaparte.* Vol. 2. Plon-Nourrit, 1912.

Viel, Claude. "Fourcroy et les lycées." *Revue d'Histoire de la Pharmacie* 369 (2011): 13–30.

Viguerie, Jean de. *L'Institution des enfants: L'Éducation en France XVIe–XVIIIe siècle.* Calmann-Lévy, 1978.

Viguerie, Jean de. *Une œuvre d'éducation sous l'Ancien Régime: Les Pères de la doctrine chrétienne en France et en Italie: 1592–1792.* Éditions de la Nouvelle Aurore, 1976.

Villiers du Terrage, Baron Marc de. *Histoire des clubs de femmes et des légions d'amazones: 1793–1848–1871.* Plon-Nourrit, 1910.

Vivien de Saint-Martin, Louis. *Histoire générale de la Révolution française, de l'Empire, de la Restauration, de la Monarchie de 1830, jusques et compris 1841.* 4 vols. 1842.

Voltaire, François Marie Arouet de. "Philosophical Dictionary." In *Homosexuality in Early Modern France: A Documentary Collection*, ed. Jeffrey Merrick and Bryant T. Ragan Jr., 156–59. Oxford University Press, 2001.

Wairy, Louis Constant. *Recollections of the Private Life of Napoleon.* 3 vols. Trans. Walter Clark. Merriam, 1895.

Waller, Margaret. "Disembodiment as a Masquerade: Fashion Journalists and Other 'Realist' Observers in Directory Paris," *Esprit Créateur* 37, no. 1 (Spring 1997): 44–54.

Waller, Margaret. *The Male Malady: Fictions of Impotence in the French Romantic Novel.* Rutgers University Press, 1993.

Waller, Margaret. "Realism and Its Others: Reading Bodies in Balzac's *Le Père Goriot* and Girardin's *La Canne de M. de Balzac.*" In *Approaches to Teaching Balzac's* Old Goriot, ed. Michal Ginsburg, 98–108. MLA, 2001.

Waller, Margaret. "Trouble in Argus City: Peacocking, Invisibility, and Masculinity." *Romanic Review* 107, no. 1–4 (2016): 25–46. http://ccl.idm.oclc.org/login?url=https://search-proquest-com.ccl.idm.oclc.org/docview/1953806892?accountid=10141.

Wardroper, John. *The Caricatures of George Cruikshank.* Gordon Fraser Gallery, 1977.

Weber, Caroline. *Queen of Fashion: What Marie Antoinette Wore to the Revolution.* Henry Holt, 2006.

Wilde, Oscar. "The House Beautiful." In Kevin O'Brien, *Oscar Wilde in Canada: An Apostle for the Arts.* Toronto, 1982.

Wrigley, Richard. *The Politics of Appearances: Representations of Dress in Revolutionary France.* Berg, 2002.

INDEX

Page locators in *italics* indicate figures.

INDEX

Les Huit époques de Napoléon [The Eight Ages of Napoleon] (von Steuben), 242–46, 301n45
Limonas, Father, 33–34, 45–46, 62, 124
lions. See dandies (*lions, fashionables,* and *la Jeune France*)
Livre du Sacre (coronation commemorative volume), 181, 290n11
Louis-Philippe I, 221–22
Louis XIV, 16, 63; portraits of, 186, 191–92
Louis XV, 52
Louis XVI, 52, 63, 74, 177, 178, 190, 273n8, 287n68, 290n9; body partially naked during coronation, 179; Carlo Buonaparte as representative to court of, 27; demands for removal of, 125; Estates General meeting, 86–87; execution of, 126, 267; and guilds, 75–77; loyal subjects identified by clothing, 93, 95; veto of radical measures, 124
Louis XVIII, 207
Love, Heather, 233
lower nobility, 3–4, 10–11, 14, 22
Lucet, Jean-Jacques, 157–59
Lycée des Arts, 145–46

Magasin des Modes Nouvelles Françaises et Anglaises, 82–88, 153–54, 271n93, 275n39; anti-luxury attitude, 83–84; changes in after Revolution, 97–102, 274n19; comic anecdotes in, 87–88; cosmopolitanism of, 82–85; final issue of, 106; French chauvinism in, 85–86; pronouns for editors used in, 98, 101, 271n97; on quasi-military attire, 101–3, *103*; and Revolution, 89, 97
male attire: bourgeois, 28, 51, 117, 146–47; columnar/phallic look, 60, 113, 117, 123, 212–14, *213*; exhibitionism in, 113, 117, 147, 191–93, 199–201, *200*, 203; in first half of nineteenth century, 117–18; leg coverings required, 21–22, 23, 36, 100; modern, xvi, xx; for revolutionary mayors, 115–18; superiority displayed through, 3, 6, 22–23, 29, 62, 197–203, *200*, 211–14, *213*, 294n46; three-piece suit, 252n5. *See also* clerical attire; military attire; teaching priests
Male Malady, The (Waller), xix
Marat, Jean-Paul, 160
Marie-Antoinette, 125, 126, 177, 190
markets, less restrictive, 75–77
marriage: marriage market, 75, 167; required of clergy, 121–22, 172, 278n84; unhappy, theme of, 172
The Marriage of Figaro (Beaumarchais), 15, 255n20
masculinity: clothing required for legibility, 17; to "become" a man, 32, 63, 68; as form of renunciation, 199; Great Display of Ostentation, 250; multiple meanings of, 244–45; *le mal du siècle*, xix; observation as privilege of, 84–85, 168;

Printed and bound by CPI Group (UK) Ltd, Croydon, CR0 4YY

03/08/2026

14934635-0001